INDIA AND HUNGARY:
PERSPECTIVES ON THE CHANGING WORLD ORDER

India and Hungary: Perspectives on the Changing World Order

Edited by
NIRMALA JOSHI
Professor Jawaharlal Nehru University

SAMSKRITI

SAṀSKRITI
C-9020 Vasant Kunj, New Delhi-110070

ISBN 81-87374-04-7
9 788187 874041

Typeset and printed by Reprographics India, New Delhi.
Published by M. Sengupta for Saṁskṛiti, New Delhi.

Contents

III

Economic Reforms in India & Hungary

Note on Editor and Contributors

Prof. Nirmala Joshi is presently the Director of the Russian and Central Asian Area Studies Programme in the Centre for Russian, Central Asian and East European Studies, School of International Studies, Jawaharlal Nehru University, New Delhi. She has contributed several articles to scholarly journals and is the author of *Foundation of Indo-Soviet Relations: A Study of Non-official Attitudes and Contacts* 1917-47.

Prof. Andras Balogh is the former Ambasador of the Republic of Hungary to India. He was also the Director-General of the Hungarian Institute of International Affairs, Budapest. Hungary.

Prof. V.P. Dutt is the former Pro Vice-Chancellor of the Delhi University and a member of the Rajya Sabha, Prof. Dutt an expert on Chinese affairs has writen extensively on Indian foreign policy. His latest book on India's *Foreign Policy in a Changing World* was published in 1999.

Dr. O.N. Mehrotra is a Senior Fellow at the Institute of Defence Studies and Analyses has been a keen observer and commentator on Russian and East European affairs. He is a regular ontributor to newspapers and scholarly journals.

Prof. H.S. Chopra is an expert on European Affairs. Prof. Chopra taught at the Centre for American and West European Studies, School of International Studies, Jawaharlal Nehru Univeresity, New Delhi. He has written several books and has contributed to scholarly journals. Among his several publications include the folowing books edited by him; *SAARC 2000 and Beyond* (1995) *India and the*

European Union: Into the Twenty First Century (1998) *Nationality, Identity and Regional Co-operation: Experiences of European Integration and South Asian Perception* (1999).

Mr. Sasvari Szilard a member of the Hungarian Parliament, he is the President of the Culture and Media Committee of the Parliament. He is also the Vice-President of the Faction of Fidez Hungarian Civic Party.

Dr. Shashikant Jha is an Associate Professor at the Centre for Russian, Central Asian and East European Studies, School of International Studies, Jawaharlal Nehru University, New Delhi. He has specialised in the study of government and political processes of East and Central European countries. Besides contributing to scholarly journals he has edited *Ethnicity and Nation Building in Eastern Europe* and is the co editor of *Reform, Conflict and change in the CIS and Eastern Europe*. He has travelled extensively in Eastern Europe and Russia.

Prof. Shams-ud-Din is presently the Chairman of the Centre for Russian, Central Asian and East European Studies, School of International Studies, Jawaharlal Nehru University, New Delhi. He has authored two books; *Secularization of Politics in the USSR : A Case study of Soviet Cultural Policy in Uzbekistan.* (1980) and *Soviet-Afghanistan Relations* (1985) He has edited the following books; *Perestroika and Nationality Question in the USSR* (1990), *Perspectives on the Emerging World Order* (1996), and *Nationalism in Russia and Central Asian Republics* (1999).

Dr. Sandor Suranyi is a Professor inthe Department of World Economy at the Budapest University of Economic Sciences, Budapest.

Dr. Gulshan Sachdeva is a Ph.D in Economic Science from the Hungarian Academy of Sciences, Budapest. At present he is an Assistant Professor at the Centre for Russian, Central Asian and East European Studies, School of International Studies, Jawahrlal Nehru University, New Delhi, where he teaches post-Socialist economic transformation in Russia and Eastern Europe. He has written many articles in international journals and writes regularly in newspaper on current economic issues.

Dr. Rama Sampath Kumar presently working as an Assistant Professor in the Centre for Central Europian Studies, University of Mumbai, Mumbai. She has contributed research papers to several professional journals and has participated in national as well as international seminars.

Dr. Alokesh Barua is an Associate Professor at the International Trade and Development Division of the School of International Studies, Jawaharlal Nehru University, New Delhi. He teaches International Trade Theory and Environmental and Resource Economics. He has published numerous papers on the subject in national and international journals. He has edited a book on *Global Order: Recent Changes and Responses* and is one of the Co-editors of *Indian Economy in Transition: Environmental and Development Issues.*

Dr. Arun Kumar is an Associate Professor at the Centre for Economic Studies and Planning, School of Social Sciences, Jawaharlal Nehru University, New Delhi. He has been known for having coordinated the work of producing Alternative Budgets for 1993-94 and 1994-95. He has worked on the Report on the Black Economy in India which was submitted to the Government of India in 1995. He has written extensively in various books, journals etc. His recent publication is *The Black Economy in India* published by Penguin India.

Preface

The end of cold war represented a turning point in the previously existed world order. It marked the end of the broadly bipolar structure which the international system had assumed since the late 1940's. Important changes also took place at the level of nation state with the disintegration of the USSR, Czechoslovakia and Yugoslavia. Further, more than 400 million people in about thirty countries of the former Soviet bloc are also witnessing transformation of their economic systems. In the last one decade, almost all of them have experienced serious problems in transforming their economies from centrally planned economies to market economies. These include output and consumption decline, inflationary pressures, privatisation deadlocks and unemployment. Many countries also faced increasing social and political tensions in their societies.

These developments have coincided with major events in the development of globalisation. The concepts of global governance, global production, global markets, global threats, global communications, global issues are widely used by politicians, investors, scholars, and journalists. Introduction of World Wide Web and fibre-optic cable link have further accelerated this process. All this has affected structure of global politics, roles and functions of nation states as well as multilateral organisations. With these new developments, the world has become a fundamentally different place.

These developments have also undermined the earlier dominance of theories: world politics viz., realism, liberalism, world system theory. In the contemporary international relations theory, many new approaches are being developed to best explain the world politics in the era of globalisation. Another major concern of scholars is to understand the effects of end of cold war on international security. Many issues like environment, human rights, gender issues, nuclear proliferation, nationalism and poverty and hunger have become important issues of international politics.

Although environmental problems are not new, they have emerged as a major focus in the last two three decades in the international politics. These include industrialisation and rapid population growth which have largely increased the scale and over exploitation of natural resources. Similarly human rights are a good example of the processes of globalisation. Although challenged by many critics, the idea that human rights --- political, social and economic, should be internationally protected, is emerging very strongly in the international system.

Interestingly along with globalisation, nationalism which was seen as a thing of the past, has also resurfaced in many parts of the world. Some consider it as a product of globalisation, while others as a reaction to globalisation. Whatever the cause, the 1980's and 1990's have seen a resurgence of nationalsim in many countries.

It is being observed that in the new global order, apart from relations among states, many non-state actors are also becoming more important. These include multinational corporations, non-governmental organisations and terrorist groups, to name a few. Further, a major concern for international relations is to understand international political economy in a globalized world. Today the international political system based on territorial states is being overtaken by an economic system based on world markets and production. The issues of trade, finance and investment are fundamentally different in a globalized economy. The boundaries between politics and economics as well as national and international are increasingly becoming less noticeable. Due to high levels of interdependence national economies are becoming sensitive, and even vulnerable to changes at the global level.

Interestingly, the era of globalisation has also witnessed renewed interest in regionalism all over the world. A number of governments have begun to explore and participate in regional groupings of various kind. Every important country in the Americas, Asia, Africa and Europe today is member of one or more regional groupings. About 55 to 60 per cent of world trade now occurs within such trading blocs. And increasing number of policy makers and scholars seems to believe that these arrangements provide more than traditional gains from trade. It is also argued that trade between neighbouring countries raises trust between them and reduces the likelihood of conflict.

To understand these very issues a round table conference of Indian and Hungarian scholars was organised by the Centre for Russian, Central Asian and East European Studies, School of Interntaional Studies, Jawaharlal Nehru University on 17-18 November 1998 at Delhi. Despite vast differences in the size and levels of development, it was interesting to note that scholars and policy makers in both the countries are dealing with many common issues. These include economic liberalisation of their economies, adjusting to emerging economic regimes established by the World Bank, the International Monetary Fund and World Trade Organisation and altering their foreign policies to the new global order.

Hungary has a rich tradition of Indology. Despite being a small country in the middle of Europe, it always attracted attention of Indian scholars. Even during socialist times, the Hungarian socialist project used to be the most innovative in Eastern Europe. A serious attempt was made in this country to create market socialism especially since the New Economic Mechanism of 1968. While the Hungarian project was not problem free, it was incomparably superior model to that of centrally planned command economy.

The post-socialist economic transformation is also relatively smooth in the country. This is because it was able to introduce many institutional reforms in the past. In addition, it had relatively better macroeconomic situation on the eve of change by virtue of its early start.

The Hungarian transformation has coincided with the economic reforms in India. Despite differences in economic structures many issues were found to be common during discussions. These issues include sustainable growth, fiscal policy reforms, industrial restructuring, issues related to foreign investment, privatisation and public sector reforms.

Perspectives from Hungarian scholars on changing world politics is also useful. Being geographically located in the middle of Europe, their perspectives could enrich our understanding of European developments as well as on changing international politics.

The book is divided into three sections: (1) changing world order (2) experiences with democracy (3) economic reforms in India and Hungary. The present book is also organised on the same lines. We hope that issues discussed in the book will help scholars as well as policy makers in both the countries to understand each other better. This may help in strengthening Indo-Hugarian relations in the fields of polities, commerce and culture. The conference was made possible by the generous support extended to us by the University Grants Commission. We are grateful to them for their valuable assistance. We are thankful to the Indian Council of Cultural Relations and the Indian Council of Social Science Research for their cooperation and support. Our thanks to the Hungarian Embassy for their support. We must acknowledge our appreciation and thanks to the Hungarian scholars who presented papers and participated in the deliberations of the Conference. We also place on record our appreciation and thanks to the Indian participants, especially to those who took the trouble of contributing papers. Finally, a word of thanks to my colleagues, the staff and the students of the Centre who worked tirelessly for the conference.

New Delhi **Nirmala Joshi**
December 1999

I
Changing World Order

1

Trends in the International Political System on the Eve of the New Millennium

ANDRÁS BALOGH*

The year 2000 invokes a great many expectations as to its being a decisive turning point in many respects. Although in the field of international politics no such turning point is expected, it could be a good occasion to set up a prognosis for the next 10 to 15 years. In this study we would like to look at the main trends in international politics, by examining the main factors of the developments in order to foretell the most possible options.

We will do so being aware that:

- in the fields that follow processes other than the ones discussed also exist, but since they are as yet not so relevant or dominant, we cannot take them into consideration --- they are listed in the Epilogue;
- there may be events, where entirely different conclusions may be drawn;
- our attitude is traditional, therefore, we do not discuss non-state or non-governmental actors.

Our basic assumptions are the following:

1 The US will not aim at dominance, but will keep its hegemonic role.
2. The European Union will be stabilised, but can only expect restricted deepening and expansion.
3. Cooperation between North America and Western Europe will be the axis of world politics.

*András Balogh: Former Hungarian Ambassador to India.

4. The US and the European Union will (be able to) cooperate with Japan.
5. Russia will keep its western orientation.
6. China will develop rapidly, but will have to take difficult decisions.
7. Central Europe will remain weightless.
8. The periphery will not disappear.

These assumptions show that we reject widely held alternative world view whereby:

1. The commitment or capability of the US to play a global role is decreased;
2. Other centres of the same weight the US has come into existence (EU, Germany, Japan, China);
3. The Atlantic Alliance loses its role or dissolves eventually;
4. Russia becomes a superpower again, or, to the contrary, becomes absolutely weightless and dissolves into its most basic elements;
5. An Asian power concentration is formed with the participation of China, Russia, India, Iran or others;
6. An American-Chinese bipolar system is formed on the pattern of the American-Soviet system of the second half of the 20th century;
7. The conflicts between civilisations lead to major global wars;
8. History ends.

Going back to the starting of our analysis we do not believe that the so-called western values are becoming exclusive in the near future. We are convinced that a period follows, in which great powers will neither rise or fall. Only an international political forecast/prognosis --- however much uncertainties and contradictions it may include --- can be the right basis to start from when drawing the main lines/outlines of the Hungarian foreign policy doctrine. This is the aim of the second part of the present study.

1. The US does not aim at dominance, but will keep its hegemonic role

Following the end of the Cold War foreign policy debates most frequently centred on the future development of the international political scene, if a new political system comes into being, led and dominated by the only superpower, the United States or the pre-World War II multipolar situation returns, with several, relatively equal powers dominating and directing international foreign policy.

From the very beginning the dominant view has been that with the disappearance of the Soviet Union, the United States remains the only (and lonely) superpower and for a long time the Pax Americana will rule. This view was clearly supported by the rapid operation by the coalition led by the US to terminate the aggression against Kuwait, as well as the successful American intervention in Bosnia and Kosovo.

The holders of an opposing view, those who reject the reality of a unipolar system, argue that the United States, despite its enormous resources, cannot face the global challenges of the present and especially of the future alone, yet it cannot rely on the unanimous and long-lasting support of either the international community or the American society. The US can play a decisive role within a cooperative system only. They argue that after the collapse of the bipolar system and with the unification of Germany, Europe has regained its initiative capability and the progress of European integration may result in the formation of a new power centre comparable to the US. In addition, the US not only has to establish relations with a European power of a potentially larger economy on an equal basis, but will have to face competition in other parts of the world as well, first of all in the extremely fast growing South East Asia, with Japan, the second largest economy of the world and China with the largest population.

The disputes on the new international order are matched with debates on the concepts of the philosophy of history (Fukuyama, Huntington) and on the nature of capitalism, questioning its capacity of operation (George Soros). It is also a widely held opinion that the United States passed its zenith in the 1970's, when its long period of stagnation started (Wallerstein).

We argue, however, that for the time being it is only the United States which possesses all the important properties of a great power, i.e. a huge economic potential, a system of political institutions, a defence capacity and an ideology, which entitle it to claim a global role. From among the major powers it is only the United States that can build lasting and organic contacts to any other power centre. Only the United States is capable of deciding which alliance it wishes to join. All the potential rivals of the United States have disappeared by the end of the century. By potential rivals we mean states that are capable of empire building. Irrespective of victory or defeat, all the empires of Western Europe stopped being entities suitable for a global role. The same is valid for Japan. Since the disintegration of the Soviet Union, Russia has fought for the maintenance of its territorial integrity, to stop the trend toward pauperisation and to avoid overall chaos. In the foreseeable future China will not become an equal partner in international relations.

What is to be expected from the US side in the years to come? Presumably, both the concept of isolation and its vehement refusal will be debated. A great part of the American society apparently does not share the political vision of the elite, is not aware of the importance of the American economic, financial, political and military role, and many directly oppose it. Therefore, it may be presumed that populist antagonists of an active American foreign policy will also appear. At the same time the US has been so caught in the web of all aspects of globalisation, that an introversive turn could only be taken upon a dramatic internal economic and political crisis. It is highly likely that the US intends and is able to establish an organic and long-lasting relationship of alliances covering all the important spheres of foreign policy and economy with the most significant factors of world policy, among them the European Union. In the case of the EU besides an intensive economic relationship American military presence in the long run may also be presumed. The various economic cooperative formations (e.g. G7 turned G8) or the system of multilateral (and in the case of Japan bilateral) defence treaties (NATO) provides a workable framework of international relationship in the long run. This may be completed by an American effort to establish a partnership with Russia, though this American-Russian relationship is likely to be burdened with disturbances of operation and relapses. These American ambitions may only be diverted by a serious internal crisis in Russia or a fundamental change in Russia's orientation. The US considers it useful to continue certain elements of the old United States-Soviet Union relationship not only for disarmament purposes, but rather for the maintenance of a global equilibrium. Partnership with Russia may also help strengthen and stabilise the positions of the pro-western forces within Russia, and increases the capability for manoeuvering the US against Western Europe and Japan. As regards China, it is not yet decided if in the long run the policy of containment of China will be similar to the American foreign policy towards the Soviet Union in the 50's and 60's, or if a partnership similar to the one with the present Russia will come into the foreground. It seems that uncertainties in this regard are rooted partly in the contrasting interests of leading American groups, and partly in the difference in their evaluation of the Chinese situation. In the long-term, policies aiming at containment, isolation and dissolution of the administrative unity of China and at a wider cooperation with China, which, however, will lack meaningful military dimensions, will most probably be present simultaneously in the American foreign policy. The US, whether it likes it or not, is interested in the maintenance of a dynamic status quo, therefore, even if hesitatingly and sometimes with a bad conscience, it will undertake the role of the global policeman.

Our final conclusion is that the US has neither the ambition nor the capability to obtain and maintain the traditional dominant role in world politics. Instead, more emphasis will be put on considerations enforcing a hegemonic role for the US, which suits both the traditions and the internal social expectations of the US much better and which can be expected to be tolerated by the significant factors of the international scene.

2. *The European Union will be stabilised, but can only expect restricted deepening and expansion*

The dispute on the capability of the European integration to survive has now been settled. In the years of the disintegration of the Communist bloc and of the Soviet Union, many regarded the European integration process as a product of the bipolar system, as a response to the particular circumstances of the post-World War II period, when the former great powers of global relevance were forced to withdraw and had to defend their interests jointly against the Soviet expansion. No doubt the threat of Soviet aspirations may have had a role in the integration efforts, however, developments after 1990 proved that the European integration process is deeply rooted in the historical and cultural traditions, economic and political experiences of the Western European countries and, at the same time, correspond to the new realities of the world. Therefore, European integration continued after the disintegration of the bipolar system and the prospect of a new European federate state took shape.

The European Union has become one of the great economic power centres of the world with possibilities of further development both to deepen and to expand. However, despite the decisions set down in the Maastricht Treaty, the European Union is still only an economic giant whose political and military role is rather limited. The EU has not been able to establish either an effective common foreign and security policy nor a significant defence potential, but depends on the United States in these respects instead. This dependence can scarcely be expected to loosen in the foreseeable future. This one-sided situation results from the hesitation of the European integration between the concepts of the inter-state and the supra-national status. In certain fields, mainly in some significant spheres of the economy and finance, the practice of supra-nationality has grown well ahead; however, it has not been enough to promote the Union to surpass the priority of nation state decisions in other important fields. The EU consists of states of different size and weight having partly different views as to the degree of integration: some are not as much interested in giving up their sovereignty, they are rather making use of the institutional system of the EU for their own national interests. Regionalism, which is an important aspect of the Union's activities, may well promote supra-nationality, but may, to a certain extent, also block the Union's development into a united state entity.

Special attention is due to: there is no unified and strong European Union without a unified and strong Germany. But a strong Germany might invoke the suspicion of the weaker states, which may not be entirely reconciled to the past, that a strong Germany will not be subordinate to the Union, on the contrary, the Union might be subordinate to Germany.

The Union's potential to expand is different from that of any other power centre. Neither the US or Japan can full integrate formerly independent states. In principle, the European Union can expand over the whole of Europe, which means an enormous potential in population and economic resources, surpassing that of any other player in world politics. This, however, is a theoretical possibility only. If the goals formulated in the Maastricht Treaty are pursued and only states with similar economies and societies can be integrated, the process would cover a very limited number of states only. Switzerland and Norway, which from these points of view would have the best chance to join the Union, are staying out due to political reasons. On the other hand, the East and Central European countries, the Baltic states and the two Mediterranean island-states are ready and fairly compatible to join the EU, yet their accession faces certain obstacles. Therefore, further expansion eastward is not conceivable even in the middle term.

Protracted and selective extension, however, will raise several questions. The Union will have to face the contradictions of the relations to the states outside the Union. The new division of Europe, however, will not be the result of the slow, sometimes over-cautious policy of the EU, but rather of huge differences which already exist and which will for the foreseeable future make any significant extension impossible.

On the basis of the above it may be presumed that the European Union will be able to preserve its results, but both its inner cohesion building and its territorial expansion will be slow and controversial. The establishment of a United States of Europe on the model of the US can hardly be expected in the next 10 to 15 years. Dependent on transatlantic links for a long time to come, the Union will proceed very slowly towards the common security and defence policy, and will have to face the pressure of Eastern European states outside the Union demanding economic and military defence against them on the one hand, while demanding efforts at a partnership with them on the other.

The European Union is going to depend on the transatlantic alliance in the long run. Process towards a common foreign, security and defence policy will be very slow, while the pressure from the eastern European states will be permanently great. Thus the Union will be a significant participant in world politics, but equal to the US and Japan in its economic power only, therefore its global political role will be secondary and complementary.

In its foreign relations a special emphasis will be laid on the cooperation with and in the Mediterranean region. Although the southern and eastern shore states will not become members of the Union in the foreseeable future, particular relations to the former colonies will be preserved. The dialogue with the Asian states will be reinforced, undoubtedly due to economic considerations. The stability of Russia and Eastern Europe and the economic relations to them are of a primary interest to the Union, but they will be subordinate to the transatlantic relations.

3. *The cooperation between North America and Western Europe will constitute the axis of the events of world politics*

The debate on the relationship of the US and the European Union has intensified. There are significant differences in concepts and perceptions, and conflicting interests in the fields of economy, commerce, security policy (e.g. on the role of NATO in Europe), culture, and the evaluation of such concrete issues as the Middle East or China. A difference of opinion was apparent in the various stages of the Balkan crisis as well. It must be noted, however, that in most cases no unified European (EU) opinion was formed and the opinions of the different EU member states regarding the trans-atlantic links have considerably diverged. Diverging standpoints have taken shape on the possible role of the Western European Union, its relations to NATO and to the European Union. As regards the different institutional reforms in the context of foreign policy, be it the United Nations Organisation or the World Trade

Organisation, different interests and emphases can be perceived.

In spite of the disagreement on different issues regarding commercial relations or the liberalisation of commerce, it must be noted that beside diverging interests, sometimes different values and different policies, there is a principal community of values and interests underlying the trans-atlantic alliance. The question is how much the trans-atlantic community will be able to preserve this close cooperation and the determination of joint actions. For the time being, trans-atlantic relations are of primary importance in the long-term strategy of both the US and the European Union, as well as of its member states. The importance of the trans-atlantic link is emphasised in any proposal regarding the independent European defence identity. Since no dramatic strengthening of either isolationism or a turn towards the Pacific Ocean can be expected in the US in the foreseeable future, one may assume that a United States, committed to an unavoidable global role but aiming at hegemony, will continue to rely on Western Europe for a number of reasons.

Common cultural heritage will remain a special link in spite of the fact that the population of European origin in the US is decreasing. The success of the mutually shared political and economic principles will serve as a firm basis for the trans-atlantic relations in the future, too. The most important factor of world economy and world trade may remain the close cooperation between North America and Western Europe. Both power centres are going to face the same challenges that they are facing now. In the past one of the external factors which ensured the homogeneity and cohesion of the Atlantic community was the peculiar structure and the ambitions of the Soviet Union. This cementing force, the Soviet Union as the main threat disappeared, but other challenges have taken its place, e.g. migration, terrorism, organised crime, the proliferation of weapons of mass destruction, etc. The threat these challenges pose will increase, which may strengthen the trans-atlantic cooperation. But the fact that it was not only the external threats that kept NATO together was clearly proved after the disintegration of the Warsaw Treaty Organisation, when NATO's vitality was shown beyond all expectations. NATO is and will be interested in preserving its defence cooperation, in spite of the profound reforms it has ventured on in the past years. There is a consensus between North America and the European allies that the defence identity and capability of NATO be preserved and there is no intention whatsoever to turn NATO into forum of political discussions only. The special axis between Washington and Brussels is under continuous development, but it will have a defining role in many spheres of world politics.

4. *The United States and the European Union will be able to cooperate with Japan*

In the past decades three power centres have emerged in the global economy: the United States, Western Europe and Japan. Japan, the world's second largest economy, under the pressure of the crises in East Asia during the past years, could not continue its dynamic growth, which resulted in the prompt substitution of the so far absolute admiration by prophecies of the collapse of the Japanese economic and financial system. However, according to evaluations considering factors with longer range effects, even though the spectacularly dynamic growth of Japan has stopped, the collapse of Japan or its becoming a second rate economic centre is out of question. At the same time, everything we said so far with regard to Western Europe, namely that it is not capable of developing all the attributes of a superpower, is especially valid for Japan, too, regardless of the depth and the duration of the crisis.

Japan has got a much smaller territory, population and economic potential than Western Europe, and, more importantly, it is unable to draw any important outsiders into its scope of influence. Similarly to Western Europe, it is unable to take on a global political role, and its defence force can only be strengthened within a limited scope. In the foreseeable future its dependence on the United States in foreign and security policy is much greater than that of Western Europe.

As regards the international relations of the so-called triad, our starting point is that in the long-term a Northern American-Western American-Japanese dominance will determine the world trade world economic relations, and on this basis a cooperative relation is foreseen in the most important fields of foreign and security policy.

Economic rivalry and significant conflicts of values can be expected among the three economic power centres in the future. This, in the case of Japan, however, may only have limited political dimensions. The cooperative relation, expected to continue to be dominant in the future, has got a firm basis i.e. the economic system and the political institutions are identical or are based on similar principles and all three power centres have their own tools to maintain the status quo, advantageous for all three. Their mutual interest in maintaining the present global political system in all probability will be sufficient to hold their diverging interests together. In the relationship among the three power centres the United States will play a central role, which means that a political situation in which a combined Western European-Japanese front is formed against the United States, can be ruled out for certain.

5. Russia will keep on orienting towards the West

Russia is invariably the weakest link in the international political system and is very likely to remain so. Russia is not a superpower any more and does not have the chance to become one again in the near future, but it is undoubtedly more than a "usual" regional power. The communist era was an experiment to modernise a backward country, which aimed at the separation from the global capitalist system dominated by the West. Consequently, its failure led to a wide spread acceptance of western values not only by the elite, but by significant segments of the society, too. It is no use discussing how much either the elite or the whole of the society comprehended the peculiarities of the western model, how much it could be adapted to Russian circumstances or what merits and faults the western politicians, who promoted Russian transition, had. What is essential, is, that decisive groups of the Russian elite today are interested in the adaptation of a western economic and political model and the maintenance of the relations to Western Europe and the United States.

Analysts are greatly disturbed by the fact that the efficient western model does not work in Russia, where the past ten years have brought about a disastrous economic relapse, social uncertainty and hopelessness. In principle there are several options for the future development of Russia, but as yet it is unclear which way it would go. The first option is that Russia returns to the policy of isolation, which would correspond not only to the practice of the communist era, but more or less to the Russian foreign policy preceding that, and which may be followed by an aggressive behaviour towards the outside world. Second, Russia may try to establish an alternative power centre as opposed to the transatlantic world or the American-EU-Japanese troika, which would lead to cooperation among Asian powers opposed to or rivals of the West. The third option is that Russia considers a partnership with the transatlantic community. As for the isolation, the extraordinary economic and social cataclysms of the past decade, the feeling of humiliation deeply felt by most of the Russian society and the frustration of the traditional elite may undoubtedly provide a basis for it. The second option, the so-called Asian connection does not seem to have any perspective not only because it lacks traditions in Moscow's politics, but also because of the reason why these traditions are missing; the relations among the possible partners, e.g. China, India, Iran, etc. all in controversy with the West, although to a different extent, make it impossible to form any meaningful and close cooperation. However much these states are united by their interests contrasting with the West, they are so different from each other that close cooperation among them in foreign and security issues is temporarily impossible. The third option, partnership with the west, seems to be the most realistic: western orientation has had strong traditions in Russia's foreign policy ever since the northern war. Russia has been a participant or a subject to each significant European foreign policy resolution for the past two centuries. The question is whether this option, which would be the most favourable for Moscow and the world, has a chance to survive.

In the past two hundred years Russia has been an organic part of Europe, an important participant in each power constellation. Theoretically, Russia could turn back to this situation. As compared to the period before World War I, however, there has been a qualitative change due to the intensive integration process in Western Europe, the multipolar character of Europe ceased to exist and Russia is not one of the equally powerful states any more as it was in the Napoleon wars or in the great power politics of the last century. Consequently, Russia's western orientation would mean the acceptance of a subordinate partnership. Thus, even the option apparently the most favourable for Russia cannot satisfy Russia's traditional great power ambitions, which obviously have not and will not disappear in the near future. This contradiction will survive for a long time, since Russia will not be able to utilise its otherwise rather good conditions in a rapid modernization process affecting all the spheres of the economy, society and politics. By Russia's good conditions we mean the abundant supplies of raw materials, enormous territory, large population, educated labour force, which provide significant resources for the maintenance of research and development and may serve as a basis for modernisation, in spite of their deterioration. These properties, however, can scarcely be organised into a system because of the slow pace, and even delay, of modernisation.

An additional difficulty is that beside the need to set up a new economic system and to establish a new political culture, Russia still has to go through the phases of nation building, long completed in other parts of the world, if it wants to play a significant role in the formation of international developments. Russia has never existed and operated in the present framework. It is searching for its identity, its borders are uncertain and the future of the relations between the centre and the regions is, as yet, unclear. Russia has not yet been able to settle its relations with the former Soviet republics. The notion of the empire has not yet been replaced by that of the nation state. The forthcoming period, therefore, will bring uncertainties that may determine the destiny of not only Russia, but of the world as well.

Russia has the foreign policy option of a western orientation, but almost certainly it will result in an unequal partnership. Nevertheless, Russia could cooperate with the different actors of the Atlantic community and with Japan, which would highly strengthen global security. The transatlantic community is willing to establish a cooperative relationship, as is indicated by several American and European initiatives. Partnership between NATO and Russia could serve as an important stimulator to help Russia take its due place in global security policy.

6. *China will develop rapidly, but will have to take difficult decisions*

China --- the Chinese development is usually considered unique, the essence of which is the combination of the traditional communist political structure and the successful market economy. This is considered not only a special, but also an irrational and uncertain way of development, since in the Chinese development organically not fitting, sometimes even contradicting elements play a role. We think, however, that this summary verdict is highly influenced by the ideological-political developments in Europe, and does not take into consideration the experiences of East Asia in the past 3-4 decades. East Asian experiences show that the exceptionally dynamic development of the private property based market economy has not been coupled with the pluralist democratic characteristics of the Western European and North American social-economic development anywhere in East Asia, on the contrary, without exception this way (of development) was characterised by a strong --- mostly authoritarian --- state power, or even an open dictatorial control, the limited implementation of human and minority rights, the elements of central control, the bank system under strong state control and protectionism. What is happening in China has very little to do with either the models following from the theory of Marxism or the known Soviet model. In China, neither the Communist Party not its ideology can be compared to the Russian "example", both have come to an independent life/both have become independent. While Marxist ideology today serves as the justification of the operation of the state and of the leading role of the party exclusively, the communist party itself is the organiser and protector of the dynamically developing capitalist economy, and, at the same time, the main guarantee of the maintenance of the unity and operability of the country. I.e. the modern Chinese state --- as regards its type and function --- cannot be compared to the Soviet or Eastern European model, but rather to the South Korean, Taiwan, Singapore and other East Asian little tigers.

It would be a mistake to consider China simply as a "big tiger" and to think that its perspective is exactly same as that of the little tigers, which are much more developed than China as regards their economic and social structures and political institutions. There are qualitative differences. The most important specifically Chinese characteristics are the incomparably huge size of the country and its population, the backwardness of its economy, which distinguishes China from its fast developing neighbours, and last, but not the least, the fact that there are no similar world economic and global political conditions given for China to maintain the rapid growth as for the East Asian little tigers. That is to say, China cannot count on the United States to overlook the anti democratic and protectionist deeds and to open the American markets, as the little tigers could, since the United States consider China not only a potential rival, but also a potential enemy. The United States does not feel the need to open its markets out of political considerations, to provide aid to China, to stabilise it and to provide a protective umbrella for it. Due to the differences we can safely state, that the fate of China is unique, in spite of the fact that it has started on a way similar from many points of view to that of the fast developing East Asian countries the analogies may give ideas, but cannot show the way.

The main/basic question of the years, or rather decades to come, with regard to China will be if the democratisation process and a profound transformation as its consequence is unavoidable/ inevitable. If this transformation can be performed in a relatively peaceful way? If the administrative unity of China remains. If China can become part of the global international political system by becoming a cooperative organic part of it.

The reasons are clear even today. It is evident that the whole of the Chinese society is not led by any uniform and modern social-political value system. At the moment on the basis of the rapid growth, it is the effort at the biggest possible consumption that has permeated the society. The deideologisation of the leading elite can be perceived, and in the future no coherent and efficient ideology can be expected to appear. It is no contradiction to say that the possibility cannot be excluded that a part of the leading elite --- relying on the dissatisfied groups of the society --- try to return to the classical socialist-Marxist orthodoxy, and even today there are signs of an approach to the ideological roots of the etatism of the past, i.e. of Confucianism, what's more, a certain spread of Christianity and Islam can also be perceived. There is an increasing possibility that a nationalism stronger than here-to-for is becoming more marked in the Chinese political thinking.

It can be forecast that both in the Chinese society and in the huge territory of China the differences are going to grow further, and on the basis of these differences the different interests of the different groups of society and the specific efforts of the different regions will be better articulated. It will be increasingly difficult for the leading groups to control the possible contradictions (expectable) in the Chinese society among the circumstances of an increasingly slower economic growth. The regional differences ever present in China will get a bigger emphasis in regions, where the non-Han character of the region is strong, first of all in Tibet and East Turkestan. Nevertheless, it can be assumed that in accordance with Chinese traditions regional differences will only be able to decentralise central power, but will not be able to seriously challenge the unity of the state. One should not forget that in China even in the politically most turbulent periods the different movements against the central rule did not step up in the name of/with the wish of separatism, but --- paradoxically --- they showed an interest in getting hold of the whole of the country and in reorganising it on a different basis.

For the world it is a very significant factor that China does not have globally relevant military forces now, nor is it going to have such in the near future. The growth of its military capability will be enough for China to remain a regional great power, and even to strengthen its regional positions, but in global politics China cannot be expected to play a globally defining role. No expansive Chinese politics can be expected outside China's own region, since any expansive desire would be nipped in its bud by the facts that

- China's relative backwardness will remain in the long-term,
- the space of the growth of the Chinese armed forces will lag behind the growth of the world's military forces, and
- there are no historic traditions of expansionist efforts.

In the next decades a united China with a much bigger economic strength than at present and with a huge scientific potential, can be expected. This China, however, will have to face very marked inner social tensions, which will be coupled with efforts at the democratisation of the society, the greater independence of the regions and the preservation of the national identity on the minorities' side. China will become an increasingly significant part of world economy and world trade, but will not be a power centre of a weight comparable to the United States or Western Europe.

7. *Central Europe will remain weightless*

In Europe there are two regions that may be considered as independent political and economic entities; the EU with the historically, culturally and economically related Western European states and Russia. East of the Union and west of Russia, however, there is a region, the so-called "Intermediate-Europe", the geographical extension of which is larger than that of the Union and the population than that of Russia. In the course of history invaders from the east and west have easily gained possession of this region, but none has been able to retain it. This region has never been ruled by one homogenous economic and political power, it is in itself more heterogeneous than either Western Europe or Russia.

The region is hopelessly in love with Western Europe, which does not return this affection. On the other hand, the states of the region are bound to each other, and especially to their neighbours, by mutual contempt, disgust and often hatred. This huge territory comprising Central and Eastern Europe, the Baltics and the Balkans, does not even have a single and common name to it. Names denoting a part of some parts of the region are historically changing, have peculiar overtones and are considered definitely pejorative. The peoples of the region perceive themselves as totally different from the others, while most of the historians make similar, stereotype statements about their nations:

- we have the oldest and most glorious history, which is denied and usurped by the neighbours;
- we defended the West against the Mongolians, the Turks, the Russians and others for centuries;
- the ideal borders of our country should encircle twice, thrice, ten times the territory we have today;
- we are essentially part of the West, not like our neighbours;
- it is a peculiar miracle in history that we survived in the sea of bloodthirsty conquerors and collaborating neighbours;
- it is useless studying the neighbours' history or learning their language.

The region of "Intermediate-Europe" will never be organised into a consistent economic or political unit, though its sub-regions, Central Europe, the Baltics or the Balkans show certain homogeneity, on the ground of which more or less lasting, but very fragile formations may come into existence. Even sub-regional cooperations can only be formed with significant limits and their role in world economy and international politics will be practically irrelevant. Central Europe and the Baltics have a good chance of becoming organic parts of the European Union and of the trans-atlantic cooperation. They have a chance to lead regional cooperations with a defined aim and for a defined period only in the framework of these integrations and international cooperations. It may be assumed that the cohesion of the Visegrad Group within the Union will be much small than that of the Scandinavian states. The Ukraine, Belarus and the Balkans will exist between the EU and Russia and it will depend on the temporary balance of power and the intentions of the two great economic and political entities whether they become buffer zones or fall into a sphere of influence. A gradually stabilising Russia may re-integrate Belarus, perhaps the Ukraine and may get strongholds in the Balkans.

In the short term, "Intermediate-Europe" will become increasingly differentiated, not only due to historical, cultural and economic reasons, but also due to the fact that some Central European states will be able to join the European Union, while others --- for the foreseeable future --- will not. These profound differences might turn the region into a scene of lasting conflicts, which may question the stability and territorial integrity of certain states in the region. The possibility of a continues pressure on the European and global balance of power and security owing to prolonged local conflicts cannot be entirely ruled out.

8. The periphery will not disappear

Following the turn of the millennium, no new trends can be expected in the so-called "periphery", a term used to denote states not belonging to either Western Europe, North America or Japan. Neither the "third world" or the "developing world" could be correctly used for ideological, political, economic or military reasons, and especially because the performance of many of the states falling in this category is much worse than a couple of decades ago and development in many of them is not sufficient even to project a real perspective of catching up. Economic and commercial data show that efforts at catching up have only been successful in East and South East Asia, though the possibility of a sustainable development has become uncertain there, too.

The second part of the 20th century has seen the remarkable success of the countries of the periphery, which broke the half-a-millennium-old tradition of European expansion, attained political independence in the decades following World War II, and then, making use of the Cold War, proclaimed their "third way" in economic, foreign and domestic policy issues. Due to their great number they exercised considerable influence in the international organisations. The United Nations was an especially important arena for them: the General Assembly was not able to pass a resolution against the group of the "developing states". The Non-Aligned Movement was another forum to express and formulate the common interests of the periphery.

The indisputable success cannot hide the fact that the position of the former colonies in world commerce and economy did not improve and the gap between the industrialised and non-industrialised states has increased. The gap, the social uneasiness, the collapse of the hope of anti-colonist struggles led to the lack of stability of the new states, while the controversial process of the search for national identity opened the way for superpower rivalry in the periphery states. From World War II to 1990, the two opponent military powers waged all their ` hot' wars in the periphery. While during the whole period of the Cold War there was no armed conflict between the two blocks, not a day passed in the periphery without a war. The countries of the periphery have started from different levels, as is clearly conspicuous when for example the medium-developed states of Central and South America are compared to those of the Sahel zone. These differences have not disappeared, but even countries which originally started from approximately the same level, such as the South Asian and South-East Asian states, have become different from the 70's onwards.

The bipolar system collapsed, but the South, as it is often called collectively, did not win. Instead, it lost the attention and interest of the northern states (huge areas have become relatively irrelevant with the exception of South Africa the whole of the African continent to the south from the Sahara) and the general degradation of the periphery was the result. The pheriphery has become the scene of unresolved issues of global relevance.

There has not been any coordinated action among the periphery states since 1990. They seem to be unable to present joint actions in the international organisations and to cooperate among themselves, partly due to the fact that a differentiation process has been taking place among them. The Non-Aligned Movement, while officially still existing, cannot claim much attention in the global diplomatic playing field. There is little chance that even the potential giants of the periphery could become globally relevant political or military powers in the near future. Natural and human resources of a state have a huge role in international political relations, if the state plays a strategic role or if it is capable of significant independent action owing to some special mineral, fuel or agricultural product. It is also important whether the state is capable of increasing its own military potential, as some states have done by acquiring weapons of mass destruction, and others may follow suit. The crucial question is if and how the periphery states can gain better positions to join the international division of labour. Since the chances of that are minor, the periphery is not supposed to become an independent global political and military player.

In principle, cooperation among these countries could improve their positions, yet it may be presumed that such cooperations would be present in political rhetoric only. This can easily be understood since even in a relatively low-intensity cooperation the states of the periphery could be united by the difference of interests against the colonising power or the developed states, the only exception being the lasting forms of cooperation of the oil producing countries. Therefore, in the near future more intensive cooperation of the periphery states cannot be expected, which does not exclude cultural, political or economic cooperation in certain regions, as some initiatives show in South America or the Mediterranean. Cultural and religious centres may also have a significant integrating power, and the efficiency of a Muslim or Buddhist cooperation might increase. These cooperations, however, are not linked. What is more, they may be absolutely repulsive (objectionable?) for other countries of the periphery. Efficient political and/or military cooperation against the West is not foreseen either, basically due to the traditional differences and hostile relations among the possible partner states of the periphery (e.g. Iraq and Iran, India and Pakistan, Somalia and Eritrea). Local conflicts, on the other hand, may be expected in the periphery, deriving mostly from inner social tensions, weakness and lack of modernisation and the conflicts of interests with the western world.

In spite of the trend of globalisation, it is not probable that the developed states of the world would want intensive relations on an equal basis with the states of the periphery. The centre will be still interested in avoiding the pressure of migration, in preventing the arms race, local wars and environmental pollution threatening the centre and joining these regions in the flow of world commerce by preserving the status quo intact. It can be assumed that the centre will reinforce its missionary activities, will enforce human rights, the spread of democratic norms and of open economy and society. As the West will face difficulties that surpass its economic and political might and as it will also have to solve its own problems, the West can hardly afford to give enough aid to forward these goals. There is a danger that the centre will follow its own interests under the pretext of enforcing human rights and democracy, while the authoritarian leading groups of the periphery will reject the introduction of basic democratic freedoms and institutions with reference to egoistic western interests.

The differentiation of the periphery may lead to uneven development. It is highly probable that democratic structures will be preserved in states with the tradition of a pluralist democracy, like India or Mexico. It is also likely that in some regions the gap dividing them from the developed world will become smaller and on the basis of the economic results modern democratic culture may take root. Yet, it must be noted that the acceptance of pluralist democracy and market economy does not necessarily mean identification with western interests.

In the years following the turn of the millennium, the periphery will remain the scene of inner and outer conflicts, and the conflicts of interests of some periphery states or regions with the centre will become permanent. The controversies in most cases will not lead to armed conflicts, but the centre-periphery relationship will be characterised by tensions and differences of perceptions.

Epilogue: some disturbing, but non-negligible possibilities not taken into account

Above we tried to summarise the most important trends, putting stress on factors which can be seen today and are likely to become dominant. Processes which seem to be of secondary relevance only, though undoubtedly present, have been disregarded on purpose. We are aware that intellectual currents, technical novelties, social and political concepts invisible today may appear, while there are several developments that are visible today, which, if realised, may undermine our concept of the world.

In what follows we would like to specify six of them, one of which alone would be enough to change our forecast entirely, and what is more, could change the course of history. We will not elaborate on them, since, on the one hand, we do not think that they are going to be realised, and on the other hand, even if they are realised, they might have unpredictable consequences and effects. Nevertheless, for the sake of further thinking and to demonstrate the unstable nature of the above, we are going to list them as follows:

1. There are several examples from history, from the ancient times of Europe or from the time of the Soviet Union, as well as from history outside Europe, when society loses faith in the system of values so far accepted, and does not have the resolve to carry on the work of its forerunners. In such situations tendencies that might seem irrational may gain momentum (local nationalism might destroy the European integration or the isolationists get the upper hand in the USA, etc).
2. We tend to forget that in the next 10-15 years demographic issues may have a disastrous effect not only on the periphery through an explosion in the population but, due precisely to the very low birth-rate coupled with a decrease in society's reproduction capacity and the increase in the ratio of the elderly, unprecedented difficulties may develop in Europe, Japan and the United States with an ageing and shrinking population. The "demographic time bomb" therefore may have a destructive effect on production, social security and political systems and may further increase the emigration pressure.
3. The polarisation of the global population may continue, and while in the developed northern societies there is a theoretical possibility for handling the differences within society, these may grow exponentially in some of the periphery societies, since meeting "basic needs", otherwise very difficult to

define, will continue to cause difficulties. In the context of polarisation, organised crime and terrorism may increasingly become a source of international threat.

4. With the further spread of globalisation, the divergence between the groups representing global interests and the groups unable to make use of the advantages of globalisation and representing national or other interests, may deepen. An even more dangerous source of threat would be if democratic institutions go on operating within a national framework in the first place, and the globalisation of production and science is not followed by the globalisation of democratic control.
5. Change in the environment and the danger of environmental deterioration cannot be assessed as yet. Environmental damages, including global warming, are very difficult to forecast. Several historic examples show, however, that in certain circumstances changes in the environment can be followed by a profound changes in societies and civilisations, or even by their extinction.
6. Finally, the possibility of a further spread and use of weapons of mass destruction, so far contained but not entirely eliminated, continues to exist --- again with unpredictable consequences.

2

The New World Order : An Indian Perspective

V. P. DUTT*

The old world order died with the demise of the Soviet Union and the overwhelmingly one-sided victory of the United States in the Gulf war, the two almost coinciding with each other. With great fanfare and fuss there was an attempt to put a world order in place by George Bush in 1990-91, but it became a casualty of the recession in the United States and subsequently the continuing and determined bid by the United States to perpetuate its own dominance. As the U.S. economy picked up by the mid-nineties, so did U.S. efforts to fashion a new world other under its hegemony.

There are elements and trends in the international situation that Washington is making a systematic effort to harden into the new order. The world is going through a transitional phase, that could last a long time, in which many contradictory elements coalesce and collide. It is this extreme contrariness of the international situation that has to be grasped in order to fully understand the present world. It is as yet early to predict the final shape of these contending trends.

But the most dominant characteristic of the international situation is the dominance of the United States over whatever world order there is at the movement. It is not only the only super power with global reach but has shown rare determination to make its will prevail.

Every security doctrine that the U.S. administrations --- from

* V.P. Dutt is former Pro-Vice-chancellor Delhi University and former Member of Parliament.

Bush to Clinton — have put forward in the nineties has some common features. Their primary objective is to maintain the hegemony of the United States over whatever political world order gets established. The phraseology employed to embody or cover up this fundamental aim could vary, but not the goal. A concomitant objective, or a natural corollary of these security doctrines was to ensure that Germany and Japan desisted from the temptation to cross the nuclear rubicon. The second principal objective was to prevent any other country from fabricating nuclear weapons and to secure the nuclear monopoly of the five nuclear powers and Washington's own nuclear supremacy. The third common feature was the understanding about the nature of the threat that the U.S. faced or could face. In addition to nuclear proliferation, it was either "instability" or "uncertainty" that Bush mentioned or ethnic conflicts that raged from the "Caucuses to Kashmir" in Bill Clinton's colourful phraseology, in other words local conflicts as well as misadventures by "rogue states".

The present world situation, to use the words of a retired Indian diplomat in another context, is pyramidal in form, with a single power at its apex. "This power, apart from its inherent strengths, — intellectual, technological, military, economy - is supported, militarily by its assertive leadership of an expanding NATO, economically by the G-7, and politically by the Security Council. The attempts of the US to engage or co-opt a China all too willing to be seated at the high table can be seen from this angle".

Below this powerful level are, in addition to its NATO allies, those countries with which the U.S. has special relations: Israel, Japan, Australia, South Korea (all under the U.S. nuclear umbrella). At the bottom of the pyramid are the non-nuclear states controlled most effectively by the NPT and its implementing mechanism, the IAEA".[1]

However, despite the core kernel of reality in this forbidding analysis, the U.S. is constrained by many factors that inhibit the use of the power as well as its reach. Chief among these is domestic opinion and the unwillingness of the people to get involved in

1. Arundhati Ghose in *Hindustan Times*, 8 November 1998.

conflicts that did not appear to have any vital bearing on U.S. national interests.

The U.S. intellectual establishment is divided broadly between two or three main trends. One section speaks unabashedly for the "benevolent empire" of the United States. Its core argument was summed up by Robert Kagan. A world without U.S. hegemony would be a bad world, a violent world and a world full of all kinds of terrors for USA and the Western countries. Taking the global deployment of the U.S. troops, "the sun never sets on them", and "logically, according the this line of thinking, American goals should include not just the protection of America and its citizens from any actions that militant Islamists might direct against U.S. interests but also the prevention of the rise of militant Islam itself: not just a suitable response to a hostile Russia, if one were to emerge, but to prevent the very revival of the Russian people and the State.[2]

There are others who have no hestitation in writing "In Praise of Cultural Imperialism"[3]. They believe that globalization has economic roots and political consequences, but that it has also brought into focus the power of culture in this global environment. Cultural hegemony is also the consequence of the market-place. "Language, religion, political and legal systems, and social customs are the legacies of victors and marketers and reflect the judgement of the marketplace of ideas throughout popular history". And so "Americans should not deny the fact that of all the nations in the world, theirs is the most just and the best model for the future".

It should be noted that while the American administration refrains from subscribing to the more extreme --- and crude --- forms of this assertion of American nationalism it pursues the core elements embodied in this framework.

There is yet another view within the foreign policy elite that would prefer a more cooperative and collective approach than the unilateralist pursuit of American hegemonism. It is convinced that

---

[2]See Robert Kagan, "The Benevolent Empire". *Foreign Policy*, (Washington) Summer 1998, pp. 24-34.

[3]David Rothkopf, "In Praise of Cultural imperialism", Ibid., Summer 1997, pp. 38-52.

the costs of such a unilateral pursuit would prove to be prohibitive. Take two Instances, Bosnia and the expansion of NATO. The burden of U.S. involvement in Bosnia was initially estimated at below $ 1.5 billion, but had surpassed $ 7 billion by April 1998 and was set to grow over the years. Similarly, NATO expansion would cost the American exchequer anywhere between $ 25-35 billion annually over the next 10 to 12 years.[4]

The cost in bloodshed of U.S. boys could also be unacceptably excessive if USA were to impose its will everywhere. Moreover, the pursuit of hegemony could have "a corrosive effect on the country's internal relations. It was pointed out that USA was developing into two societies. Those who reaped the benefits of globalism and those who "paid its price in terms of military service, endangered jobs and repressed wages, the former constituting just about 15 to 25 per cent of the population. The vast majority will no doubt be asked to pay the price of their country's policy of hegemony".[5]

This undoubtedly is a minority view, not shared by the U.S. administration, but where it scores is the unpopularity of involvement in areas and countries that might be only dimly perceived by the people in the United States as having a bearing on U.S. interests. The case of Somalia has been a chastening experience. The U.S. public may be supportive of the exercise of American hegemonism if it did not imply sending American boys to distant lands to fight and die for the sake of demonstrating American hegemony, but unless the establishment with the help of the media could build up a credible case and atmosphere for the use of American boys, it may not be so generously supportive. The U.S. administration successfully did so in the case of Iraq but not so successfully in the case of Somalia.

There were other countervailing factors too. In some senses the world was still unipolar, but in many other senses it was being increasingly pulled towards multipolarity. The politico-military and economic centres did not necessarily converge. The U.S. remained

[4]See for instance, Ted Carpenter and Barbara Conry, NATO Enlargement: Illusion and Reality, Cato Institute, Washington, 1998.

[5]Charles William Maynes, "The Perils of (and for) an Imperial America", *Foreign Policy*, Summer 1998, pp. 36-47.

a major economic centre, but no longer the sole dominant one. There were new economic centres both in Europe and Asia that could not be scoffed off. The emergence of Europe with Germany at its centre and with a certain Franco-German understanding that had long-term economic and political implications and was a significant development of the second half of the 20th century. The integration of Western Europe that came about with the coming into effect of the European treaty on the midnight of 31st December 1992 created a market of some 327 million people, and with Europe-12 enlarging into Europe-15, the market came to comprise 380 million people --- the largest market in the world. As one U.S. analyst put it, "Europe's 850 million people are the only 850 million people on the face of the globe that are both well-educated and start out not poor".[6]

Another gigantic step forward was taken with the introduction of a single European currency on 1 January 1999. It was the boldest step towards integration with 11 states with a population of 300 million people and accounting for one-fifth of the world's output, and stepping out of the stranglehold of history and adopting the euro as their common currency. The 11 "Euroland" countries, Germany, France, Italy, Spain, Belgium, the Netherlands, Luxemburg, Austria, Ireland and Finland had come together at a time when inflation was down to below 1 per cent and the gap between the highest and the lowest inflation among European countries had narrowed considerably.

The German Chancellor, Gerhard Schroder reflected the general optimism in Europe: "Our future begins on 1 January 1999: the euro is Europe's key to the 21st century. The era of solo national fiscal and economic policy is over". In an even more optimistic vein, Win Duisenberg, President of the new European central bank, commented: "The euro is far more than a medium of exchange .... It is part of the identity of a people. It reflects what they have in common now and in the future.[7]

At the very least --- and that was not a small matter --- the

---

[6]Lester Thurow, "Head to Head". Warner Brother, USA, 1993, p. 245.

[7]*The Guardian*, London, 1 January 1999, p. 1.

currency threatened the current sway of the dollar and had the potential of either replacing the dollar or offering an additional currency in the international market. In any case a powerful new currency had made its appearance on the economic horizon of the world. There was no question but that the establishment of a single currency was another strong link in the chain of events leading towards greater political integration with far-reaching consequences for relations both with USA and the rest of the world.

This relationship with USA, even if it could not be described as a love-hate relationship, certainly encompassed elements of exasperation and mutual indispensability. The U.S.-Europe relationship is a typical illustration of the duality, indeed the triplity, of the new international situation which this writer has been emphasizing. On the one side is "Euro-bashing" in the United States and deep skepticism in Europe about U.S. hegemonistic policies. On the other side is the continued dependence of Europe on U.S. military strength and even on U.S. political initiatives, like in Bosnia and Kosovo. Yet on a third side, so to say, is the lurking and often explicit U.S. fear of European integration and Europe's hankering for some kind of an independent role. These contradictory sentiments and trends would continue to characterize a somewhat ambivalent relationship between Europe and America.

As two transatlantic academics ruefully noted: "Just as European anti-Americanism damaged Western solidarity during the Cold War, so American Eurobashing threatens to unravel transatlantic cooperation in the post-Cold War era"[8].

The elite in the United States worries about the economic competition from a United Eruope. Yet American "economic triumphalism" looks at the foot-dragging slow-paced European economy with considerable disdain, heaping particular criticism upon the "burdens" that this European welfare systems impose upon the economy. The Americans are particularly critical of the German "social market". To the Europeans the German economy is a "standing rebuke" to the U.S. neoliberal critics. If they had

8. William Wallace and Jan Zcolonka, "Misunderstanding Europe", Foreign Affairs (New York), November-December 1998, p. 66.

been right, German economy would have imploded long ago[9]. In fact it is precisely this "social contract" that could be maintaining Germnay's social stability despite the economic buffets of the last decade. What seems to be happening is that the economic cycles of the two economies have not coincided. When the American economy was going through a recessionary phase, that of Europe was on the upswing. The European downswing came at a time when the U.S. economy was witnessing an uplifting. Since the uplifting has gone on for a number of years (9 to be precise), it has bred now optimism about a permanent about-turn and a new determination to retain U.S. hegemony over the international order.

But , as this writer has been pointing out the extreme contrariness of the international situation, these events or developments should not lead us to conclude that Europe and America are on a course of conflict and separation. But these are inhibiting factors to the establishment of a world-wide order ruled over by the United States.

Four countries, ıncluding U.K., preferred to stay out for the time being but it is only a question of time before they also join the Euroland. The political integration of the European Union is certainly much slower, as many member-countries remain jealously protective of their sovereignty. It might require many more years before genuine political integration is achieved, but the process is virtually irreversible, the "House of Eruope" is going to be among the most potent centuries in the world.

There are other significant developments in the offing. Although parts of Central Eruope are convulsed by ethnic conflicts, many countries of Eastern Europe, Hungary, the Czech Republic, Slovenia among them, are only a doorstep away from joining the European Union. They are also keen to be embraced by NATO. How all this will effect the balance of forces in Europe remains to be seen.

It would be wrong to ignore Russia as a factor and a force in world affairs and in a future world order. Even now Russia is a very significant military power It has the nuclear weapons and the capability to destroy the world. It is a large Eurasian landmass with

[9]Ibid.

immense resources, despite the dissolution of the Soviet Union. As Paul Kennedy has noted in his well-known book *The Rise and Fall of Big Powers,* Russia has risen, declined, and risen again many times in modern history, and even though Kennedy himself is somewhat sceptical about Russia's future as a big power (he was writing about the time of Soviet Union), but there is sufficient evidence in his own book about the potential of the landmass, whether it is called Soviet Union or Russia.

Presently, Russia is in deep economic trouble and political uncertainty, but its vast landmass and immense resources provide the essential ingredients of a great power, currently in trouble but destined to bounce back. Whether this happens in a cooperative climate or not, would depend partly on internal development but partly also on the policies of the NATO countries, especially those of the United States. Russia's own approach and attitude has seen a transformation twice.

Soon after the disintegration of the Soviet Union, Russia was possessed by American mania. America was the role model. Specially under Andrei Kozyrev as foreign minister, the foreign policy tilted heavily towards the West. Kozyrev's entire foreign policy thrust was based on the assumption that the interests of the new Russian state were identical with those of the West led by USA and that Russia's salvation lay in following the American route and also that the U.S. would in a way guide Russia into a democratic, developed, prosperous capitalist state. But realities soon dawned on the Russian people as well as significant sections of the elite that not all Russia's interests were on four square with those of the United States, that Washington had no magic mantra for Russia's economic problems, and that American purse strings were not so generously open as they had earlier imagined---there were harsh conditionalities even for aid from Washington-supported international financial institutions.

There is no denying Russia's current travails. The state controlled economy has given way to mafia-dominated economy or what is often described as anarchic-capitalist economy. The institutions of state have been so enfeebled that law and order cannot be effectively maintained. The shock therapy that was administered by advisors like Jeffrey Sacks and the IMF created more pain and suffering but failed to implant in Russia an American-type of free market economy. The social costs of the ill-conceived attempt at the shock therapy in the early years of Boris Yeltsin's Presidency were enormous. The Russian living standards dropped precipitously --- sometimes as much as 50 per cent. The Russians survived through the parallel economy and through recourse to their plot of land and by growing their own food.[10] What Russia saw was bogus privatization which brought affluence to a few and suffering to many.

Significantly, as Prof. John Gray of the London School of Economics has pointed out, "the average Russian privatized company still had over 40 per cent of its shares owned by its workers and over 10 per cent by the state. This pluralist pattern of ownership seems likely to persist. Russian capitalism will not evolve towards the Anglo-saxon model of shareholder ownership; it will be a pluralist system containing many owner-managed firms, as a Germany".[11] Russia enjoys many advantages that would support its capability to rise again. It is endowned with considerable material and human resources. It accounts for 10 per cent of the world's oil output and 30 per cent of its gas. Nearly 15 per cent of the world's non-ferrous metals production comes from Russia. Its abundance of natural resources combine with a highly educated population to provide it with an opportunity to come back as a major player in the international arena.

Nevertheless the current Russian decline comparably reduces its effectiveness in world politics. It would take many years before Russia returns as another central pole in the emerging world order. Whether this happens in a cooperative climate would depend on the policies of the NATO countries.

New economic deployments have marked the reemergence of Asia on the world scene. Chief among the new economic centres was Japan. It had the second largest GNP in the world and could outstrip the United States sometimes in the 21st century. It was the largest creditor nation as well as the largest donor nation. Japan was currently passing through a recession, a downturn that has been

---

[10]Robert Skidelsky, *The world After Communism*, Macmillan, London, 1995.

[11]John Gray *False Dawn: The Delusions of Global Capitalism*, Granta Books, London, p. 146.

agonizingly prolonged, and some of the shine of Japan's economic miracle has dimmed. But undoubtedly Japan would remain an important economic centre in the world. Japan was too powerful economically to be sidelined politically for too long.

Japan is in a peculier dilemma. It would like to play a greater and more independent role in world affairs but it cannot let go its security connection with the United States and consequently remains anchored to Washington which impacts on Japan's foreign policy. Japan's security anxieties have been heightened by North Korea's testing of ballistic missiles one of which fell into Japanese territory. U.S.-Japan security accord is partly aimed at North Korea and there are reports, which particularly worry China, that Taiwan might have been included in its ambit.

Japan occasionally chaffs at the constraints imposed on it by the fact of being a junior ally of the United States. Japan is a candidate for a permanent seat in the United Nations. It has taken part in some peace keeping operation of a non-combat nature. Its real problem is that there is not sufficient consensus within the country on what kind of larger role it should play in world affairs. Japanese nationalism is not a factor to be discounted. Again and again, ministers in the LDP government have had to resign for publicly casting doubt on whether Japan was really that guilty in the events preceding the Sino-Japanese war and leading into the Second World War, as well as for the sneering remarks of many high-level Japanese leaders regarding the U.S. society, the most recent case being that of Justice Minister Shozaburo Nakamura.[12] It was also quite instructive that while Japan offered South Korea a more handsome apology over World War II atrocities it could not being itself to do the same in regard to China when Chinese President Ziang Zemin visited Japan in November 1998[13].

The world order would partly hinge on the nature of the relationship between Japan and USA (as also between Japan and China). As in the case of the U.S.-Europe equation, Japan's relations with the U.S. too would hover between the abrasive and the cooperative.

[12]International Herald Tribune (Singapore), 6 and 7 January 1999.

[13]*Far Eastern Economic Review*, Hong Kong, 10 December 1998, p. 21.

The management of U.S.-Europe and U.S.-Japan relations would occupy an important place in the political and economic agenda of the 21st century. The options would not necessarily be limited to a rupture or a position of "vassalhood" (which is how Brezezinsky has described it). The European community is painfully aware of its continued dependence on the United States (look what happened when Europe tried to develop its own independent position towards Bosnia). A similar caution is evident in any independent position that Japan might otherwise like to evolve. Yet the elements of friction would also remain — embedded in this contradictory scenario.

Yet another critical factor is the rise of China both economically and strategically. China is perceived to be a rising economic power, but its steady accretion to its military strength is no less significant. A very sympathetic U.S. economist has put China's average growth rate between 1980-95 at 9.6 per cent (although he acknowledges a brief slowdown between 1989-91 when the economy grew at the rate of 5.4 per cent --- there is a similar downturn in 1998 as a consequence of the recession in East and South-east Asia). The size of the Chinese economy was estimated to be within the range of $2.0 to $3.2 trillion.[14] Whatever the range of figures to be accepted, the fast growth of the Chinese economy was undoubted.

China is already an important strategic factor in Asia and its military clout would only be increasing in the future. Over the last 15 years China has been increasing its spending on defence by an annual six per cent in real terms. It has been steadily modernizing its defence forces. It has territorial disputes with India, Japan and most countries of South-east Asia. It has given no evidence of surrendering any of its claims but has shown readiness to put them aside for the time being in the interests of economic growth.

Both China and Japan would increasingly become alternative centres of power in economic as well as military terms. Japan today has the third largest military budget in the world. It is constrained, however, to function under the aegis of the United States whose

---

[14]Greg Mastel, *The Rise of the Chinese Economy*, M.E. Sharpe. USA, 1997, pp. 9-14.

atomic shield is a central factor in the Japanese security scenario.[15] Although China faces no such constraints and over the very long run, it could be one of the challengers to American hegemony, it is instructive to note that in the short run, and currently, China does not challenge U.S. supremacy except in areas and on issues that impinge on its own vital national interests.

Not to be ignored either is the transforming scenario of the Asia Pacific region. Until at least the second half of the Nineties, it was among the fastest growing regions of the world. The "tiger economies" (South Korea, Hong Kong, Taiwan and Singapore), as well as the rapidly growing economies of Thailand, Malaysia, Indonesia, and Vietnam, altered the economic balance that had hitherto privileged in the world. Their political and military clout was limited but their accumulating economic strength was pushing the process of cooperation and integration that could be helpful in bridging political voids and trans-Pecific divergences.

Most of these countries suddenly received a rude economic shock with their economies tumbling down rather rapidly and precipitously. Their economic system appears somewhat jaded. However, the same Western analysts who were going to town about the rise of Asia may be writing the epitaph too soon. The economic difficulties are not insurmountable and the many strength of these economies should not be underestimated. In any case many of these countries are in the throes of both economic and political restructuring and some of them at least could rebound back strongly.

Taking Asia and the Asia Pacific region as a whole, clearly the relationship between Russia and China, China and Japan, Russia and India, China and India, Russia and Japan, and between all of them individually and severally with the United States would necessarily be critical determinants of the future world order. Of course the hegemony of the United States would persist beyond the 20th century, but even as it is, it is no longer all-pervasive, and its dominance will be further eroded over the next twenty years,

[15]Zalmay Khalilzad and Lan O. Lesser, *Sources of Conflict in the 21st Century*, Rand, 1998.

even though it remains power number one of this region and generally in the world.

This writer is not dilating upon the importance of West Central Asia to a world order because it is axiomatic and all-too-obvious. Oil and natural gas are precious resources; the last Gulf war was an eloquent testimony to that basic fact of international relations. West and Central Asia both have vast resources of oil and natural gas, and Central Asia is rich in many other minerals too. The correlation of forces, both domestic and external, ideological no less than materialistic would certainly be important factors in the shaping of a new world order.

One of the seminal new developments that is of unique importance in the new world order is the primacy of the economic struggle. It does not supplant military supremacy, nor does it drive away continuing political struggles, but its central importance is now well-established. Increasingly, countries of the world were giving primary attention to economic development to achieve new influence in the world. In any case, in the new situation, military strength was a chimera unless accompanied by economic strength.

The limitation and "delusions" of global capitalism, however, have become increasingly evident over the last three years. Patterned on the ill-perceived American model, global capitalism's universal prescription has been the dominance of unregulated free market. The World Bank, the IMF and other international leading agencies have presented a universal package regardless of situational differences, of limiting the budget deficit and "freeing" the market, From Mexico to Moscow from Bangkok to Jakarta, the same conditionalities are imposed.

The consequences in many cases have been social devastation, widespread unemployment, rising inequalities, and deep pain inflicted on society. The results have often been incommensurate with the costs. Ironically, in many countries, governments have been forced to step in and impose more restrictions and work towards a more regulated market. It is also not coincidental that in most cases those who introduced the unregulated (free) market did not stay in power even if they were seen to be succeeding.

The most instructive case has been that of Mrs. Thatcher, the "iron lady", who had to quit rather ignominiously, despite all the tom-toming of her successes in imposing a free market on England. Similarly, even if Reagan did not have to go the way of Thatcher, Reaganism met with the same fate. Even George Soros, who had been held by many Asian leaders as the villain of the economic troubles of Malaysia, Thailand and Indonesia, sees a bleak future for global capitalism of the American variety.

As Prof. John Gray of the London School of Economics has put it:

The free market cannot last in an age in which economic security for the majority of people is being reduced by the world economy. The regime of laissez-faire is bound to trigger counter-movements which reject its constraints. Such movements---whether populist and xenophobic, fundamentalist or neo-communist---can achieve few of their goals; but they can still rattle to pieces the brittle structures that support global laissez-faire. Must we accept that the world's economic life cannot be organized as a universal free market and that better forms of governance by global regulation are unachievable? Is a late modern anarchy our historical fate? ...

A reform of the world economy is needed that accepts a diversity of cultures, regimes and market economies as a permanent reality. A global free market belongs to a world in which western hegemony seemed assured.

So there were other lessons too in this new struggling "global order". The market ***mantra*** was not a magic cure for all the economic problems, nor did unbridled globalism provide a flying house for rapid economic growth. There was no single model of economic development that held good for every country. Each country had its own peculiar situation and problems and could not be fitted into a single straightjacket. Necessarily every country had to adjust to the phenomenon of the global market, but neither economism by itself without concomitant political restructuring and pluralism, nor the free market could do without social stability, a more equitable distribution of wealth and caring for a poor in many cases.[16]

India and the World Order

India has all along struggled against an inequitous world order. Right from the dawn of independence and since Jawaharlal Nehru's time, India has raised its voice against hegemony and for a more democratic structure in the world. In a way both Pokhran-I and II were challenges to an established order that had given rise to a new cartel of powers in the world, with one power in partial command. Without going into the rights and wrongs of the recent nuclear explosions (although other options often talked about are not very convincing), (and certainly India displayed very poor management of its international relations after the nuclear explosions), the agenda for India for a world order should be very clear. It must extensively extend its cooperation with other countries to struggle for total nuclear disarmament and a more democratic world order. The era of world cooperation is contending with the era of dominance and both will coexist for a long time. It would be the endeavor of India to join other countries, including those of our friends in East and Central Europe, in strengthening elements of cooperation and restricting the trends towards dominance.

---

[16]John Gray, n. 11, p. 20.

3

India in the Changing Strategic World Order

O. N. MEHROTRA*

The strategic world order began to change with the de-ideolization of Soviet foreign policy and elimination of intermediate-range nuclear weapons from the European theatre in the mid-1980s. As the political, economic, military and ideological barriers, which had descended across the continent of Europe in 1945, weakened and the Soviet capacity to pursue a global strategy began to decline as well as the dilemma of Soviet leadership on maintenance of an empire surfaced, the Soviet empire gradually collapsed in Eastern and Central Europe. It brought about the end of the Cold War and thus began a new strategic world order or disorder as many prefer to call it.

Unlike Asia, European strategic environment was changed dramatically. There had been systemic changes in Europe. The Soviet-led Warsaw Pact of its allies in Europe was dissolved but the United States-led North Atlantic Treaty Organisation (NATO) has gained more strength and is being expanded eastward in spite of Russian objection. Almost all European countries have decided to introduce free market economy and many of them are making frantic efforts to join the European Union (EU). At the same time they have adopted democratic political system and held free and fair elections. There have also been educational and social changes. In fact now it appears that hardly any ideological difference existed in Europe. Though Cold War era's flash points in Europe have

---

* Dr. Mehrotra is a Senior Fellow at the Institute for Defence Studies and Analyses, New Delhi.

vanished, yet some new flash points have emerged in the Balkans. However the main European security concerns have disappeared from the continent in the post-Cold War period.

But there is not much systemic change around India in the post-Cold War period. Unlike in Europe communism has not lost its relevance and credibility in Asia. Apart from other countries, China is still a communist country, in spite of its adoption of radical economic reforms and establishment of strong economic linkages with the Western Capitalist countries. While Russia failed miserably in its efforts to establish market economy in place of command economy, China has emerged a strong economic power due to economic reforms. No doubt South Asian countries have been moving towards establishment of democratic political system but at times doubts have been raised about its derailment because democratic traditions have not yet taken strong roots and there are some non-democratic centres of power that may wreck the process of democratisation. In this respect, apart from other countries, the survival of democratic system in Pakistan has always been under threat because time and again armed forces and the President sacked the elected governments. Though Prime Minister Nawaz Sharif has recently strengthened his position and humiliated his tormentors, yet there is still lingering doubts about the survivability of democratic system in Pakistan. Apart from India, in South Asia Sri Lanka has also embraced the democratic polity but it has suppressed minority rights much against universally endrossed basic principles of a democratic system. In other South Asian countries, the democratic system of governance has slowly been taking roots.

As in Europe Cold War began to end in the late 1980s with the dissolution of Warsaw Pact, election of non-communist government in Poland, demolishing of the Berlin Wall and cooperation in place of confrontation between east and west, there were some positive developments in South Asia as well because of removal of some irritants in the region. The Soviet Union withdrew its troops from Afghanistan and India pulled out its peace keeping forces from Sri Lanka. At the same time India also withdrew its armed forces from Maldives. The Indian President went to Pakistan to attend the funeral of General Zia-ul-Haq. Incidentally after the sudden death of Zia in an air crash, the parliamentary elections were held in Pakistan. Prime Minister Rajiv Gandhi visited Islamabad in connection with the Fourth South Asian Association of Regional Cooperation (SAARC) summit meeting in Islamabad. During his visit, Rajiv Gandhi had intensive discussions with Prime Minister Benazir Bhutto on bilateral and other issues of mutual interests. They signed three agreements amongst them one was on Prohibition of Attack against Nuclear Installations and Facilities.

Consequently hopes were raised about normalisation of Indo-Pak bilateral relations because of emergence of democracy in Pakistan. Rajiv Gandhi paid an official visit to Pakistan in July 1989. It was the first bilateral visit by an Indian Prime Minister since 1960 when Prime Minister Jawahar Lal Nehru had visited to sign the historical Indus Water Treaty. Earlier in December 1988 Rajiv Gandhi paid an official visit to China paving the way for "a new vitality and impetus to the development of India-China relations". Though some strains surfaced in Indo-Nepal relations after the lapse of the Indo-Nepal Treaties of Trade and Transit, they were removed after some wranglings.

No doubt there was a more conducive environment for development of India's relations with its neighbours but with the Soviet withdrawal of its forces from Afghanistan, Pakistan launched low-intensity war by means of terrorists in the Jammu and Kashmir (J&K). At the same time, Islamabad also generated religious hysteria. Since then Pakistan has not relaxed its unfriendly assistance to terrorist activities in J&K and the Punjab. Therefore it remains a serious irritant causing tension between the two countries and not allowing smooth improvement in bilateral relations. In fact Pakistan has been insisting on resolving the core issue of Kashmir before any improvement in the bilateral relations. According to Islamabad the Kashmir issue can be resolved only by holding plebicite and it believes that its outcome would be in favour of Kashmir joining Pakistan. In spite of India's insistence on keeping the issue as a bilateral one in view of Simla agreement but Pakistan never misses an opportunity to internationalise the issue. It also plays up the issue on the religious ground and wishes to win the support of Islamic countries individually as well as collectively with support of the Organisation for Islamic Conference (OIC). In this respect it may be pointed out that Pakistan exploited the demolishing of Babri Masjid in Ayodhya and launched a propaganda offensive against India.

In the early 1990s, the strategic environment changed with the disintegration of Soviet Union and the emergence of the United States of America as the sole Super Power. The former Soviet Union was a close friend of India and it had always supported India at the time of crisis. Though its successor state Russia promised to maintain the bilateral relations, it could not sustain its commitment because it had been passing through a long painful period of political and economic transition. Moreover, Moscow was aspiring to develop close relations with the West, especially the United States, Japan and China. No doubt India's relations with the USA and China improved, but both those countries remained closer to Pakistan. Moreover China continued to supply conventional weapons to Pakistan as well as assisted latter in its clandestine efforts to acquire missile and nuclear weapon production capability.

While it was appearing that the Indo-US relations were strengthening, the US Assistant Secretary of State, Robin Raphel, questioned the accession of Kashmir to India and trade and human rights issues caused tension between the two countries. Almost at the same time President Bill Clinton forced President Boris Yelstin to renege on cryogenic rocket deal concerning transfer of technology to India in July 1993. In this respect it may be noted that only a few months before President Bolis Yelstin assured India that he would never cancel the deal. Overall India's strategic concerns appeared to be growing but gradually India's relations with China, Russia and the US began to improve. India and China agreed to maintain peace and tranquillity along the line of actual control on the border. In fact both countries agreed to improve their bilateral relations and decided that the border issue should not hamper in normalisation of their relations. Prime Minister Narasimha Rao introduced economic liberalisation and went with an economic agenda to the US in March 1994. Subsequently American investment in India increased by manifold. Rao and Clinton issued a joint statement calling for establishment of nuclear free world. They also talked about Asian security issues. Later the US Defence Secretary visited India and agreed to Indo-US defence cooperation.

At the same time, the Indo-Russian relations were also strengthened. Russia reiterated its support to India's position on Kashmir. President Yeltsin also expressed his support to the case of India becoming a permanent member of the United Nations Security Council. The Moscow Declaration of 1994 stressed on protecting the interests of multi-ethnic, multi-lingual and multi-religious states. Moscow assured New Delhi that it had neither supplied military equipment to Pakistan nor it would do so in future but it had established military linkages with Beijing that was a strategic concern for India. In fact President Yeltsin paid his visit to China before visiting New Delhi in January 1993. Moreover Moscow and Beijing have also formalised their political, and economic relations and strategic understanding much before Moscow and New Delhi stabilized their relations.

In the meantime India established relations with all the Central Asian Republics (CAR) while Pakistan was not much successful in exploiting common Islamic religious bounds against India in the region. However Pakistan's association with the rise of Talibans and subsequently their command over major part of territory of Afghanistan has been a cause of security concern for not only CAR but also India. At times the Talibans talk about interfering in the resolution of Kashmir issue. Though some irritants between India and its neighbours persisted, they were cordially resolved except with Pakistan. After withdrawal of Indian peace keeping forces from Sri Lanka, both countries established friendly relations, especially with assumption of presidentship by Chandrika Kumaratunga. India's relations with Nepal were further cemented with the signing of a treaty on the development of Mahakali rivers. No doubt once Bangladesh attempted at internationalising the issue of river waters and the repatriation of Chakma refugees from India to Bangladesh but with the signing of a landmark Treaty on sharing of the Ganga waters at Farakka (1996), the Indo-Bangladesh relations have greatly improved. Both countries reiterated their determination not to permit their territory to be used by insurgents and undesirable elements. In the recent past Pakistan has enlarged its areas of nefarious activities in India, including north eastern region. It also reportedly established bases for its operation from Nepal.

In spite of adversial and confrontationist approach of Pakistan as well as its efforts to spoil India's relations with its other neighbours, India gave priority to strengthening its relations with its neighbours. Consequently India could establish friendly neighbourly relations with all countries, except Pakistan. India has also improved its relations with China and strengthened its relations with Russia. At times there were some irritants between India and Myanmar but India has improved its relations with South East Asian countries and it has been associated with the ASEAN Regional Fourm (ARF). However, there were some serious differences between India and the US on the issue of nuclear weapon proliferation and comprehensive nuclear test ban agreement. India opposed the indefinite extension of Nuclear Proliferation Treaty (NPT) as well as signing of Comprehensive Test Ban Treaty (CTBT). India also expressed its concern over a one-time waiver to the Pressler Amendment and allowing the supply of advance US military equipment to Pakistan. Nonetheless the Indo-US relations were further developed. President Clinton proposed a meeting with Prime Minster Inder Kumar Gujral during the latter's visit to New York for addressing the United Nations General Assembly Session in 1997.

Both countries engaged themselves in the strategic dialogue. In the Post-Cold War period, the strategic dialogue between the two countries means that they exchange views on emerging new world order. They make efforts to understand each others view on major flashpoints and procedure to be adopted for resolving them. Since economic interests have assumed precedence over the military concerns, therefore economic relations between them also figure prominently in any strategic dialogue. At the same time it was widely believed that the American tilt to Pakistan had gradually been reducing. Washington began to judge the Indo-Pak bilateral disputes more judiciously than it used to entertain. But with the declaration of the weaponisation of Indian nuclear programme in May 1998, India's relations with both of its immediate neighbours — Pakistan and China became tense and major industrialised countries decided to impose some sanctions against India and Pakistan for challenging the international nuclear control regime. However Pakistan made frantic efforts to project itself as an aggrieved country which was forced to weaponise its nuclear programme because India took initiative to become a nuclear weapon power. In fact the Prime Minister of Pakistan, Mian Nawaz Sharif expressed his helplessness in desisting from conducting nuclear tests in the face of popular demand after India became a nuclear weapon power. In reality Pakistan weaponized its nuclear programme way back in 1987 and India responded with its own nuclear weaponization in 1990.

Nuclear weaponization of both countries has brought forward openly their power equation. The major casualty of this development was the process of normalisation of Sino-Indian relations. In fact, a few weeks before India conducted its series of nuclear tests, the Indian Defence Minister reportedly called China as number one enemy of India. And after conducting of its nuclear tests, India justified its decision on the ground that it faces nuclear threat from China.

In this background, we would discuss India's strategic concerns especially after India declared itself a nuclear weapon state. For the last many years India has been expressing its concerns on growing Sino-Pak collaboration in nuclear field and Pakistani clandestine efforts to acquire nuclear weapon production capability. In fact Pakistan's secret efforts to acquire the nuclear capability was generally detected by the Western countries, especially the United States. Though Washington took action against China and Pakistan for violating terms of the international nuclear control regime, yet it has never realised that their nuclear collaboration and their joint or individual nuclear threat can be a strategic concern for India.

Be that as it may, the Indian weaponisation of its nuclear programme and its declarations and statements on the subject have brought its two adversaries China and Pakistan --- more closer and strengthening their military ties, especially aimed against India. At present China is the only dependable strategic friend of Pakistan. In the last few years India had improved its relations with China who even advised Pakistan to resolve its differences, including Kashmir, with India bilaterally. A set of confidence-building measures adopted by India and China in the recent past. It was widely felt that the prospects of China's involvement in any future Indo-Pak armed conflicts were remote. But with the weaponization of Indian nuclear programme the strategic environment around India has changed. Unlike the former Soviet Union, Russia is not a super power which can change the course of confrontation between India and China. In short, China has become more pronounced strategic concern for India since New Delhi announced its nuclear weapon status.

At the same time Pakistan's hostile activities against India have not declined after India conducted its nuclear test in May. Pakistan is not likely to give up its policy of engaging India in low intensity conflict and nefarious activities of its notorious ISI. In all probability India will not follow the policy of hot pursuit to capture terrorists and destroy their bases in Pakistan and Pak-occupied Kashmir, not withstanding the Home Minister L.K. Advani's high sounding pronouncements to that effect. Pakistan is likely to build its sufficient nuclear weapons might to deter India from taking any nuclear initiative. In other words, India's recently declared nuclear weapon capability has not reduced its strategic concerns.

Pakistan may gain some strategic advantages because of its recently acquired nuclear weapon states. It may raise its status amongst Islamic countries because Pakistan is the only Islamic country which has nuclear weapons. It may also strengthen fundamentalist forces in Pakistan and some other Islamic countries, it is felt in certain quarters. In this respect Pakistan's role in strengthening of Taliban's domination in Afghanistan may be significant. In case the fundamentalist forces finally achieve victory in Afghanistan, they would not only increase their interference in Kashmir but may also challenge secular base of India. This is a cause of strategic concern for India.

In the recent past, India has improved its relations with its neighbours and weaponised nuclear India is likely to maintain good neighbourly relations with them. Apart from Pakistan, which has been engaged in low-intensity war with India, China may renew its assistance to insurgents in north-east India. This may also become a cause of concern for India if Sino-Indian relations are not normalised in the near future.

Apart from India's strategic concerns emanating mainly from its two large neighbours, the United States' attitude towards weaponisation of Indian nuclear programme is also strategic concern for India. The United States has not only imposed economic and military sanctions against India but it has prevailed on some of its major allies to follow its policy as well as deny economic grants to India from major international economic grants funding agencies. However leaders of both countries want to engage each other in dialogue and reduce tension. In all probability the US leaders would not like to isolate India considering its growing vibrant economy, its military might, its pre-eminence in the subcontinent and functioning democracy. It appears that the US leaders have not been properly briefed about India's strategic concerns aggravated because of Sino-Pak collaboration in production of nuclear weapons and missiles as well as their ulterior designs against Indian security interests. In such circumstances China cannot play a neutral role in reducing tension in the region, as the US leadership suggested recently. Moreover India has consistently been opposed to any third party involvement in resolution of bilateral Indo-Pak disputes.

India has been confronted with numerous strategic concerns which can be reduced by engaging leaders of the United States, China and Pakistan in constructive and regular dialogues. In this respect the prime minister of two neighbouring countries, Atal Behari Vajpayee of India and Nawaz Sharif of Pakistan took bold steps to repair the bilateral relations. The objective is noble but the path to realise the goal is treacherous and difficult to tread. For Sharif it appears to be much more difficult and risky then for Vajpayee because the Pak psyche is too hostile towards India thus any visible and publicized step taken towards mending of the bilateral relations may be politically suicidal for Pakistani leaders. Evidently under strong domestic pressure Sharif was forced to cancel his proposed plan to accompany Vajpayee on the return bus journey from Lahore to Delhi on February 21, 1999. The Kashmir issue may continue to be a stumbling block in establishing cordial bilateral relations. The Sino-Indian relations are likely to improve gradually. But there may be some setbacks in the Indo-US relations because of India's criticism of the US-led North Atlantic Treaty Organization (NATO) intervention in resolution of the Kosovo crisis. It may also vitiate international atmosphere because Russia and China have strongly criticized NATO's intervention. At present Russia seems to be India's true friend but it is a declining power which may change its course under the US pressure. In the changing strategic world order, India has to strengthen its economic and military base to meet any security threat. Unlike in Europe, there is no regional forum or military alliance that deals with security issues. The South Asian Association for Regional Cooperation (SAARC) cannot meet the challenge.

4

Changing Dynamics of the Post-Cold War European Union Hungary's Case for Membership

H. S. CHOPRA*

Today, different world regions are endeavouring to contribute in their own way and to the extent their objective positioning in the global setting permits them, to the shaping up of a new post-cold war global order following the collapse of the preceding one, which for nearly half a century had remained swayed by the bipolar adversarial structures of power. Europe has now a sound reason to feel relieved on its remission, for it itself had then been a prized area between the two belligerent Super Powers. Already in its evolutionary setting, the European Community, which could not be compared with any of the deeply integrated classical forms of political collectivities, such as the United States, Indian Union or even the Swiss Confederation, has been playing for more than four decades a leading role in the global eco-political system. However, the more challenging task for the EU following the end of the systemic divide has been how to help reshape and reconstruct political and economic institutions in the newly emerged independent states of the former Soviet bloc. These could be divided into three parts:

first the Baltic states, Lithuania, Latvia and Estonia, which even though they formed part of the Soviet Union, had not been given recognition by the West.

*H. S. Chopra Former Professor in Centre for West European & American Sludies SIS JNU New Delhi.

second Central European states such as Hungry, Poland and Czechoslovakia, which traditionally had close ties with the East particularly the Habsburgs; and

third the remaining states in South-Eastern Europe, which are likely to take more time to develop their political and economic institutions so that they could be integrated into the EU as also the NATO.

Most of these states had been covered under the EC's PHARE Programme. And subsequently under the Europe Agreements, they have been accorded the status of Associate Membership.

II

Since its inception, EC's distinctive role has been in the economic, scientific and technological domains. Apropos, we need to look back to see how the EC at the twilight of the new millennium has succeeded in accomplishing the task hithertofore considered somewhat utopian. In the preceding three decades, it has experienced many ups and downs. Yet, its progression in the twin domains of deepening and widening continued even if haltingly. And at some stage in its dialectical evolution, it leapfrogged on to a new stage of organic integration. It is worth recalling that in the late 1960s the EC suffered its first grievous setback, explained graphically by Jean Jacques Servan-Schrieber in his best seller study *The American Challenge*. In that context, the European Summit meeting that took place at the Hague in early December 1969, formulated plans (such as those of the European Political Cooperation as well as of the European/Monetary System) for further deepening as well as widening of European integration. Worth mentioning in particular is the role played by the West German (Social Democrat) Chancellor, Willy Brandt, who minced no words in making clear to the French President, Georges Pompidou, that the FRG, with its growing normalized state of relations with its eastern neighbours and the USSR, would no longer be a 'political dwarf, and with its increased political clout, could be balanced within the Community only with Britain's induction as a member into the EC.[1] It is this way that the long standing imbroglio on Britain's entry into the EC was resolved thereby facilitating European Community's expansion, increasing its membership from six to nine.

Equally noteworthy was the ground-work done in the early 1970s by the West German SPD-FDP ruling coalition for Europe-wide repprochement through its peace treaties with the USSR and other Central and East European neighbours such as Poland, Hungary, Czechoslovakia and others as well as Basic Treaty with the German democratic Republic, which eventually led to the conclusion of accords and institutionalization of the East-West detente in early August 1975. This occurrence stengthened the Europeanists' self-confidence in-as-much as that they lent no support to the US plan on the New Atlantic Charter (devised by the then US Secretary of State, Henry A. Kissinger) which aimed at refurbishing the Western solidarity, particularly because at about this time, it had suffered grievously owing to the US defeat in South East-Asia, and which also intended to rope in its fold Japan as a new member.[2] Europe then demonstrated its will not only to assert its autonomy, but also that European detente had its own framework which had to be strengthened with a view to boosting up the flagging European morale, without affecting in any way the western solidarity.[3]

III

The second major shake-up with its many ramifecations came in the late 1970s, owing to two energy shocks in the same decade, and the negative spillover of the Reagonomics. The Japanese challenge especially in the domain of industrial competitiveness in

---

[1]H.S. Chopra, "India and the Politics of the major EEC Powers", in Bimal Prasad, ed., *India's Foreign Policy Studies in Continuity and Change* (New Delhi: VIKAS, 1979), p. 354.

[2]Henry Kissinger, *Years of Upheaval*, (Boston, Toronto, 1982), p. 153.

[3]Walter F. Hahn, Robert L. Pfaltzgraff, Jr. *Atlantic Community in Crisis/A Redefinition of the Transatlantic Relationship* (New York: PERGAMON, 1979), pp. 20-21.

the same period further compounded the economic turmoil caused by the world-wide stagnation. Its performance in industrial competitiveness was found to be better than that of the US and of the EC including the FRG. Its growth-rate of GNP (4.8 per cent) in this decade was higher than that of the US (4.8 per cent) and that of the FRG (2.5 per cent). Its performance in the major manufacturing industries such as automobiles, steel, and ship-building was unmatched by any other Western nation. Its efficient use of technology was accompanied by faster growth of labour productivity (without any significant corresponding hike in the wages) than that of any other industrial power in the West. More serious than the Japanese penetration in the conventional fields (cited above has been their penetration into the well-established European as well as US markets in the high tech. domains of super computers, semi-conductors, micro-processors, and informatics.[4] In the early 1980s, it was surmised that Japan supplied more than 50 per cent of the equipment in the field of informatics to Western Europe and nearly 80 per cent of the semi-conductors for use in the US weapon systems. A ground reality: among the major European industry leaders, Phillips found itself in grave financial crisis, and Britain's largest computer MNC, ICL, was taken over by the Japanese Fujitsu. These developments raised the larger question not only of the new Japanese "yellow peril", but also there came about increasing perception of the US tilt towards the Pacific. Japan began to acquire the status of a world economic power.

The comulative effect of the foregoing syndrome was increasing realization in Europe that most of their 'world-class' industries were in the traditional 'Fordist' or 'smoke-stack' sectors, such as plastics, chemicals and heavy machinery, which were unable to compete effectively with the pressures coming from the Newly Industrializing Countries in East Asia. Indeed the European perception of 'sclerosis', as one well-known European specialist says, owed to the oligopoloistic markets dominated by large-sized MNCs, which

[4]H.S. Chopra, "Western Europe and United States vs. Japan: Controversial Debate on the Industrial Competitiveness", in K.V.Kesavan, *Contemporary Japanese Politics and Foreign Policy* (New Delhi, 1989).

were unable to initiate or respond or adjust to the fast global changes in markets and technical innovations. Besides, there was also realization that many of the transactional mergers that had taken place in Europe in the late 1970s in no way added to their global network. Their interaction had remained confined within Europe, and that too among similar companies, with little or no added capability for capturing newer markets outside Europe. Margaret Sharp and Claire Shearman believe that the concept of "strategic alliance" might perhaps explain why cooperation with Europe, as distinct from collaboration with Japan or the US turned out to be less attractive.[5] Within European business circles, there was a well-grounded belief that the critical threat to European competitiveness came from the fragmentation of the European market.

As such, in the late 1970s and early 1980s, Europeans discovered the ground reality in relation to their vulnerability vis-a-vis the US and Japan. In this period, then, the Japanese Challenge manifested itself in particularly in the high tech. domiain. Europe had therefore to embark upon its grandiose plan of intensification of integration, as well as refurbishing its technological muscle power. In pursuance thereto, the EC set up two streams of high tech. projects such as SPRINT, ESPRIT, RACE, BRITE etc. and the Framework Programmes. Besides, it contributed significantly to the strengthening of the EUREKA set up at the French initiative in response to the US-SDI. Interestingly, while the latter faded out with the end of the cold war, EUREKA continues to be a thriving enterprise. However, the most effective response to the European business proposition was the conclusion in the mid-1980s of the Single European act in 1986 that led to the establishment of the Single Enlarged Market since early 1993. Major objectives underlying these ventures have been to deepen European integration as well as to overcome its deficit in the economic and technological domains, relative to the other two global gaints. In any câse, let it be added here that Europe did not lose its self-confidence. For it

[5]Margaret Sharp and Claire Shearman, *European Technological Collaboration* (London: Routledge & Kegan Paul, 1987)-RIIA Chatham House, papers 36, p. 19.

was fully conscious of its lead over others in many areas of basic research. In the period 1980-89, it had won 27 Nobel prizes as against 2 and 42 for Japan and the US respectively. Its share in the world trade (20 per cent) (excluding intra-European Community trade) has been larger than that of the United States' (17 per cent) and Japan's (10 per cent). Therefore even if it had trailed behind these two gaints, it believed that it was in the thick of global competition. It is worth illustrating here a "special Report on the findings of the 1990 International Manufacturing Futures Survey" (published in *European Affairs,* June/July 1991) which showed that while the Americans are building a "Value Factory", and the Japanese a "Design Factory", the Europeans are engaged in shaping up a "borderless Factory". This report also indicated that while the large Japanese high tech. industries continue to be "performance leaders", the American counterparts have fought back and recovered the lost ground. And the European performance has also steadily improved in the areas listed here below:

- Improvement in Manufacturing Costs;
- Delivery Reliability;
- Customer Services;
- Manufacturing lead time;
- Delivery time.

Europe in any case, has yet to catch up with the other two giants in the following domains:

- Overall quality;
- Inventory turnover;
- New Product Development Speed;
- Product Variety.

It may thus seem that Europe has been endeavouring over the years to regain its leading position in the global economic triad. Edith Creson, a member of the European Commission while addressing the 1997 Conference on Industrial Technologies held in Toulouse, had acknowledged that the global European research effort has declined over the past years, reaching 1.9% of EU GNP. The figure is 2.7% for the USA and almost 3% for Japan.

In the Dossier on "Factory of the Future" it was then observed:

> "If there is any consensus on what the 21st century will be like, it is that it will be knowledge-based. This will be reflected in its products, which can be made smallest, both through micro-electronics and smart 'materials', which can vary their properties upon command".

In regard to the social dimension, it may have to be added that despite its multi-pronged strategies on industrial competitiveness, adopted since early 1990s, EU has yet to give evidence of its noteworthy success in overcoming nearly two-decade long problem of unemployment, with ever growing socio-political implications not only for Europe, particularly new aspirants in Central and Eastern Europe for its membership but also for other world regions as well.

IV

While the EU has been presenting itself more or less as a credible factor in the global economic and technological arena, its performance on the political and security fronts has been disappointing. It is amazing indeed that following the collapse of Communism in the erstwhile Soviet bloc, the EC seemed to have been caught unawares. Particularly for Europe, such a systemic change has not been new, a one-time experience. Indeed, since 1789, Europe has witnessed several political upheavals, twice in this century at least, excluding the latest one. It was expected of Europe to have foreseen the internecine feuds re-emerging (in the wake of the systemic change) on ethnic, religious and other obscurantist grounds, which had remained dormant during the Cold War epoch. Had some sound contingency planning been done, perhaps the Yugoslav crisis, which was the very first case for the European Community to establish its credentials as an effective crisis manager, could have been averted. But, then, as it assumed unduly explosive proportion, one could not attribute such a negative development only to the endogenous factors. For, if the question is only of national self-determination, it should, in that case, not be forgotten that in 1919, when following the end of the First World War, three major southern Slav Communities, Serbs, Croats and Slovenians, coalesced together, they had exercised their political will to set up their United Kingdom (a collectivity) with a view to safeguarding their hard-earned independence against any attempt on the part of any of their bigger neighbours to devour them one by one. Their tragic history spanning over nearly five centuries had then imparted a lesson to them that their strength lay in their unity.[6]

One question that has often been posed over the years by some Western scholars and its answer has eluded them is in relation to the *raison d'etre* of united Germany's role in the break-up of Yogoslavia. The FRG itself regained its unification in peace and freedom, more because of massive change in the Soviet approach to the German question, and, in any case, less to the application of national self-determination. But, once its own unification became actualized in 1990, it sought to attach undue importance to the principle of national self-determination. It is in pursuance to this erroneous application of this principle that it accorded recognition somewhat hastily to Croatia and Slovenia, even though the Robert Badinter Commission set up by the EC itself had expressed its reservation in respect to the former, which did not seem to fulfil the basic criteria for such an act on the part of the EC and its member states.[7] Also it is noteworthy that the revised constitution of the Socialist Federal Republic of Yugoslavia (1974) made no provision for secession of any of its republics, as had been the case with the constitution of the Soviet Union. Furthermore, the Hague peace conference under the Chairmanship of Lord Carrington had started only in early September 1991. In the midst of the chaotic situation engendered partly by the internal and partly by the external factors, its peace attempts were faltering.

---

[6]H.S. Chopra, "Ethnicity and the Break-up of Yugoslavia", *World Focus* (New Delhi), April-May 1994, 172-173 p.34.

[7]Sonia Lucarelli, "Germany's Recognition of Slovenia and Croatia: An Institutionalist Perspective", *The International Spectator,* Vol. 32, no. 2, April-June 1997.

The European Community in its Brioni Declaration (June 1991) had counselled both Croatia and Slovenia to go slow in regard to their demand for independence. James baker had also favoured keeping up Yugoslavia intact in howsoever loose confederal form.

Soon after Germany's recognition of the afore cited breakaway states, recognition by the other member states, under the pressure of the former and in the "larger Community interest", ensued. This is not all. Its implications were far reaching and did not remain localized. Samuel Huntington, in his controversial article, "The Clash of Civilizations", notes[8] that with the end of the systemic divide (following the demise of the cold war), which otherwise, was expected to have laid foundations for new European peace architecture, democratic pluralism suffered its first major jolt, with the revival of religion, *LA REVANCHE DE DIEU.* The Vatican showed no less zeal in according recognition to these to Roman Catholic states before even the EC could do. Thus, the seeds of religious fundamentalism, with its much debated negative spill-over effects in the relations between the two major branches of Christianity were sown, even if unwittingly, in Europe itself. With it, then, came the tragic break-up of Yogoslavia, accompanied by new challenges in tune with obscurantist rhymes and rhythms, to peace and stability in the Balkan region. This is markedly a retrograde move, return to the 19th century power politics. On the threshold of the new millennium, Western Europe, which, thanks to its regional integrative endeavours, had earned the distinctive salience of having turned itself into a conflict free productive peaceful zone for the first time in its history, finds itself helpless in confronting its own war lords dancing diabolically at its door steps.

The European Community's failure to manage the Yugoslav crisis and subsequently the Bosnian crisis enfeebled its confidence in its ability for conflict management. As a result, the US led NATO had to intervene with UN approval to find a *modus vivendi* matually acceptable to the concerned belligerents in the

---

[8]Samuel P. Huntington, "Clash of Civilization". *Foreign Affairs* (New York), Summer 1993, p. 26.

Bosnian conflict. The Yogoslav-Boanian and Kosovo tragic scenario seems to have projected a somewhat shaded image of the European Union in-as-much as it will have to make do for long with its circumscribed autonomy, particularly in the security-strategic areas.

It may thus appear that there exist contradictions in the policies pursued by the major member states of the EU. Under the Maastricht Treaty (1992), it is expected that in due course, there would be greater harmony in the foreign and security policies of the EU member states. As at present, however, there exist differences in their attitudes and practices on European integration, but then they are tolerant in the larger community interest. Another example worth citing is that now the French regime led by a Gaulist President, Jacques Chirac, and the Socialist Prime Minister, Lionel Josepin, France appears to extend cooperation to NATO, though selectively, as in the past. This, however, is not a one-way move. On the six French nuclear explosions conducted during 1995-1996, neither the US nor any of the major West Euroepan powers raised any voice of protest, as had been done by Japan, Australia and New Zealand. This then sets out a dualistic approach on their part. While the major nuclear powers would continue to upgrade their own status in the global strategic systems (disregarding indefinite extension of the NPT and the forthcoming CTBT), they would thwart any attempt on the part of any of the Third World aspirants to wriggle out of their security dependence stranglehold.

Nonetheless, fractions among the Western powers on various security issues continue to exist on many trends. In the case of the Bosnian Serbs, a western commentator opines that France adopted "a private approach at the height of the crisis in May-June 1995, offering to block NATO strikes in return for freeing its hostages". Similar had been the position of the French Socialist President, late Francois Mitterand, who asserted his independence in regard to the Gulf War in early 1991, and later when the Bosnian Civil War became accentuated he made a personal visit (in pursuit of his solo diplomacy) to Sarajevo. In all these matters he did so without any prior consultation with the NATO partners.

Equally important in this context is the fact that Russia evinced keen interest in safeguarding the Serb position both in the Serbo-Croat and then Bosnian Serb-Muslim conflicts.[9] All these diverging positions of the member states of the EU as well as of the concerned adversaries in the security domain brought it out clearly that each one of the major Western powers tends to attach greater priority to its national (narrowly conceived) rather than collective interests.[10] In regard to Russia, following the American position, European Union considered it as a "rival", and not as a "friend". An example cited in this respect is Russia's assistance (despite America's opposition) to Iran's civilian nuclear energy programme. Russia also extends support to the continued preservation of Kosovo within Yugoslavia. Perhaps, here EU's position in regard to the Kosovo's fight for its liberation and eventual independence is debatable. The US led NATO air strikes against Yugoslavia since 24 March 1999 seem to have complicated the conflict. The substantive point in this issue is whether such military action by the US led NATO against Yugoslavia is tantamount to an aggression against a sovereign country, which has not in any way threatened the security of any of the NATO allies. Moreover, this on-going aerial expedition in the Balkan region is not only violative of the UN charter, but also of the NATO pact itself. The only valid option that the US as also the EU could adopt was to persuade the Yugoslav government to continue political negotiations with the Kosovo insurgents with a view to finding out the extent of autonomy that could satisfy their demands. For any solution imposed by the US led NATO on Yugoslavia would have grave implications not only for the lasting peace in the Balkans, but also for the effectiveness of the UN Security Council in global peace and security.

In any case, in 1997 the US-led NATO has concluded with Russia an agreement called the "NATO-Russia Founding Act", which bears the EU support, but not without controversy.[11] In

---

[9]Hans-Joachim Hoppe, "Moscow and the Conflicts in former Yugoslavia", *AUSSENPOLITIK* (Hamburg) 3/97, p. 275.

[10]Gerd Koslowski, "Bosnia: Failure of the Instiutions and of the Balance of Power in Europe", *AUSSENPOLITIK*, 4/96, pp. 360-62.

[11]Gerhard Wettig, "NATO, Russia and European Security after the Cold War". *AUSSENPOLITIK*. 1/98, pp. 18-23.

framing this agreement, critical inputs have come from the US State Department and the FRG Foreign Office. It is pointed out that Russia's position in the negotiations leading to this agreement has not been equal to the other two aforementioned powers. In any case, Russia has acquiesced to this agreement but not without misgivings that this is perhaps a ploy to meet superficially Russia's objections to the eastward enlargement of the NATO. But then this agreement bears no legal validity in international law. However, this bears the possibility of institutionalized discussion on security-strategic issues of concern to the NATO as well as Russia. But then neither side has any veto power, which means that either side can have its way even if it is not agreed to by the other.

This is substantially borne out from NATO's rejection of Russia's mediatory propositions in bringing an end to NATO's air strikes against Yugoslavia in Spring 1999.

With the end of the systemic divide, the Soviet-dominated regional economic and security groupings, the WARSAW Pact and the COMECON were wound up. There thus occurred a power vacuum, which had inevitably to be filled. Germany, which had only then been united (in 1990) became a prime power that felt concerned with this void. This could either be filled by Germany in its individual capacity or through multilateral endeavours of the European Union. Initially, most of the member states of the former Soviet bloc were included under the PHARE programme for reconstruction and reorientation of their economies in accord with the principles of free market economy. Subsequently, under the Europe Agreements, they were accorded the Associate status.[12]

Hungary is one of the five Central and East European Countries, the other four being Poland, the Czech Republic, Estonia and Slovenia identified as select candidates for opening accession negotiations with them as full members of the EU. These countries already enjoy the associate status with the EU. As per the Mastricht Treaty (1992), any European state could be considered for membership of the EU but it is only in the Copenhagen European

---

[12]Commission of the European Communities, *PHARE: Assistance for Economic Restructuring in the countries of Central and Eastern Europe* (LUXEMBOURG, 1992).

Council meeting of 1993 that the criteria for accession to the EU has been spelt out.[13]

- Stability of institutions that guarantee democracy, the rule of law, human rights and respect and protection of minorities;
- Functioning market economy as well as capacity to cope with competition within the EU.
- Ability to take on the obligations of membership involving adherence to the aims of political, economic and monetary union.

In pursuance to the directives of the European Council meetings held at Essen (1994) and Madrid (1995), the European Commission examined the candidature of ten CEECs (Hungary, Poland, Romania, Slovakia, Latvia, Estonia, Lithuania, Bulgaria, Czech Republic and Slovenia) and opined that on the whole the applicant countries' constitutions fulfil the political criteria for membership viz. guaranteeing democratic freedoms, and "have also set up democratic institutions and independent judiciary and constitutional authorities, which permit different state authorities to function normally". Further, it is acknowledged that in these countries fair and free elections have been held regularly, enabling peaceful alternative of the political regimes, with opposition playing its normal role.

But, then the Commission points out that "some of the applicant countries....do not have stability of institutions. *All the applicant countries have flaws in the rule of law which they need to put right*". It further adds that "there is a lack of suitably qualified judges and guarantees of their independence. Police forces are poorly paid and there is the need for better training and discipline".[14]

In any case, bearing in mind the criteria fulfilment of the aspirant member states, European Council meeting at Amsterdam (1997) approved the opening of accession negotiations which Cyprus

[13]European Commission, *Agenda 2000 for a stronger and wider Union* (Luxemburg, 1997). p. 39.

[14]ibid., p. 40.

as well as with the CEECs within six months after the end of the inter-governmental conference.[15] The future of Cyprus as a "bicommunal and biregional federation" under the US auspices has yet to be settled between the two feuding communities, the Greek and Turkish Cypriots. In the EU's view, the present political fragmentation of Cyprus is not conducive to the stability of the island or the region. However, the political and economic benefits of the EU membership may perhaps induce the two communities to arrive speedily at a mutually agreeable settlement of the issue.

From among the five CEECs, Hungary is listed as No. 1 in the European Commission's recommendations for opening up of negotiations for its membership, which have since begun in April 1998. Hungary, Poland, the Czech Republic and Slovakia have historical ties with the West. That explains why Henry A Kissinger had also considered necessary that the EU and NATO must expand to cover these countries on a priority basis. It may be noted that Hungary, which had suffered for more than a century under the Ottomans, was conquered and included in the Habsburg empire in the seventeenth century. In 1867, after Austria suffered defeat in the Prussio-Austrian war of 1866, Hungary succeeded in attaining equal status with Austria in the Dual Monarchy which was instituted at the time. The latter could not survive Germany's defeat in the First World War. With the result, many of its territories, such as Croatia and Slovenia gained independence: they in tandem with Serbia, set up a united kingdom, which subsequently in 1929 adopted the nomenclature of Yugoslavia. Hungary gained independence as a result of the Treaty of Trianon in 1920. In the Second World War, it fought on the side of Germany. Following the end of the Second World War, Hungary formed part of the Communist bloc dominated by the Soviet Union.

Hungary was second only to the GDR in having rebelled against the Soviet hegemony in 1956, but it was ruthlessly quelled.

---

[15]European Commission, *European Union: Treaty of AMSTERDAM* (Luxemburg, 1997); Also see second edition. *A New Treaty for Europe* (Luxemburg).

In some political circles it is surmised that if the West had then extended vigorous support to the Hungarian cause, there was then the possibility of initiating a multi-party system in that country.

However, since 1968, Hungary has been gradually moving to market-oriented economic reforms. In 1982, it was the first Central European country to have joined the IBRD and IMF. Hungary experienced a major economic crisis in the early 1980s. With the weakening of, and frequent changes in, the Soviet political leadership since early 1980s, Hungary gained an opportunity in 1989 to rid itself of the communist regime led by Janos Kadar. Hungary earned Germany's sympathies in 1989, when it facilitated migration of refugees from the GDR to West Germany through Austria.

In 1990, Hungary held for the first time democratic elections in that country, and in the subsequent elections held in 1994 and 1998, alternatives of the political regime have taken place peacefully. Further, its democratic credentials have been corroborated in the aforecited elections, particularly because the extremist forces opposed to its entry into the NATO and the EU failed to gain representation into the Parliament.[16]

VI

Following the end of the systemic divide, Hungary, like other Central and East European countries, has evinced keen interest in forging relations with the EU as well as NATO. It has already become a member of the CSCE, later on redesignated as the OSCE (Organization for Security and Cooperation in Europe), of which it has been Chairman in 1995 and a year earlier, it had also hosted the OSCE summit in Budapest.

The Hungarian government has already established a coordinated institutional framework for dealing with European integration. As per the European Commission's assessment reports, bilateral relations between Hungary and the EU have been considered to be satisfactory. Obligations resulting from the European Agreements have generally

[16]Hungary's Ministry of Foreign Affairs, "Hungary and NATO: On the road to Membership'. *FACT SHEETS ON HUNGARY* (Budapest). 1/1997.

been met on time. Hungary has adopted a realistic negotiating position during bilateral discussions, which has greatly assisted the resolution of potential difficulties. During the period 1989 and 1995, EU imports from Hungary increased from ECU 2.6 to 8.7 billion (+335%), while exports to Hungary increased from ECU 3.00 to 9.9 billion (+330%). The trade balance has presented a steady deficit for Hungary.[17]

Its position with respect to human rights and protection of minorities, Hungary has satisfied the Convention on the prevention of torture and the framework convention on minorities. It has not as yet signed the European Social Charter. However, it is encouraging to note that it has since ratified the Framework Convention for the Protection of National Minorities of the Council of Europe as well as the European Charter of Regional and Minority Languages.[18]

The Hungarian law of July 1993 recognizes as a minority any ethnic or national group which has been living in Hungary for over 100 years. Reportedly 6% of Hungary's population consists of minorities, such as Germans, Slovaks, Croats and Romanians. An unusual, but intensely democratic feature: each minority has a national autonomous government, the members of which are elected by the minority communities themselves. A number of public foundations has been set up to facilitate minorities population in the decision-making at various levels.

However, the gypsies' social situation appears to be problematic. According to the government report, inequality of opportunity between the gypsies and the remaining population has increased in recent years. Gypsies' unemployment rate is four to five times that of the national average, and life expectancy is 10 years less than the national average. The gypsies are also discriminated in the labour market. It is however creditable that the government is fully seized of this sociological lag, and the gypsies' social and

---

[17]European Commission, Agenda 2000: Commission Opinion on Hungary's application for membership of the European Union (Luxemburg), Supplement 6/97, Supplement 6/97, p.13.

[18]Miodrag Mitic, "Protection of National Minorities in Europe", *Review of International Affairs* (Belgrade), 15 July to 15 August 1998, p. 4.

political problems are being addressed under the direct authority of the Hungarian Prime Minister.

On the national economy front, Hungary has made satisfactory progress towards adopting the norms and mores of the free market economy. But, then the EU expects that its entry must not jeopardize the EU's financial resources. It is pointed out that if the original four VISEGRAD countries join the EU, the annual transfers from the EU to them may cost the EU budget around ECU 50 billion, which would be unaffordable from the EU's point of view; it represents nearly 50% of the entire budget for the EU-15 member states.

As such, it is unrealistic that Hungary or any of the other CEECs would be able to enter the EU, as it is being suggested, by 2002 A.D. On the other hand, Dr. Miroslav N. Jovanovic is of the view that an optimistic scenario is that if all goes well, meaning smooth negotiations of perhaps around a decade and an adjustment process of another decade". He further adds that "it would take the most advanced transition countries (such as Hungary) some 20 years to become full members of the EU.[19]

> "A hypothetical early expectation for full membership of the most advanced transition economies is the year 2015! Nonetheless, the entry depends on the political will (and the funds) of the EU countries.... Hence, all official statements about (very) early entry to the EU, by around the year 2002, need to be taken with a pinch of salt".

Now, owing to the on-going US led NATO air strikes against Yugoslavia, EU's new liabilities on account of resettlement of the displaced persons as well as reconstruction of the damaged economies in the Balkan region, after the NATO war is over, may increase manifold, thereby upsetting the priorities on account of widening of European integration eastwards.

There is however a saving grace. Germany continues to be the

[19]Miroslav N. Jovanovic, Is the Eastern Enlargement the end of the European Union?" *Review of International Affairs* (Belgrade), 15 March 1998, p. 10.

driving force in relation to the deepening and widening of European integration. Since its unification in 1990, Germany has a certain perception of its pre-eminent role in managing post-cold war European affairs. In early 1991, the former US President, George Bush, had called upon Germany to assume the role of "Partnership in Leadership".[20] Understandably, this is in addition to the US-UK "Special Relationship", which during the later half of the twentieth century became proverbial. Germany's interest in Central-Eastern Europe becomes explicit in the Core Europe Paper of the CDU/CSU FRAKTION, presented in September 1994 in the Bundestag. It was argued that:

> "Never again must there be a destabilizing vacuum in Central Europe. If (West) European integration were not to progress, Germany might be called upon, or be tempted by its own security constraints, try to effect the stabilization of Eastern Europe on its own and in the traditional way".

Howsoever detestable the words "traditional way" used in the above statement may be, it is clear that the Eastward expansion of the EU will have to be expedited, even if the costs may be out of proportion to the resources at this time appear to be available. Germany in collaboration with the other major EU member states may have to garner necessary resources to attain the objective. Therefore, in our view, optimistic stance in regard to this matter bears validity. Though actualization of the East-ward expansion by the year 2002 seems to be unrealistic.

---

[20]Gerd Langguth, *In Search of Security. A Socio-Psychological Portrait of Today's Germany* (London: PRAEGER, 1995), p. 6.

5

Indo-Hungarian Ties in the Changing World Order

NIRMALA JOSHI*

As the present decade draws to a close, there is no doubt, that the nineties witnessed some of the most tumultuous events of this century. The bipolor structure of the world ushered in by the Yalta agreement of 1945 lasted for over four decades. An ideological divide was the hallmark of this bipolor world. The beginning of the end of the bipolor world was triggered off by the crumbling of the Berlin Wall in 1989. This was followed by the unification of Germany. The unification of Germany signalled the end of the socialist bloc in Eastern Europe. Subsequently, communism in the Soviet Union also collapsed leading to its disintegration into fifteen sovereign nations in 1991. Last in the series of events was the violent break up of Yugoslavia along ethnic-religious lines. The geo-political map of the world in general, and Europe in particular had been completely altered.

At the same time equally fascinating trends appeared in the sphere of international economy. The trend toward globalisation indicated greater inter-dependence and economic integration among nations. The Information and Communication revolution facilitated the process of globalisation. Paradoxically, regional organisations were also acquiring greater weightage in international politics. Perhaps the globalisation trend has provided an impetus to regional

*Prof. Nirmala Joshi, Director, Russian and Central Asian Area Studies Programme, Centre for Russian, Central Asian and East European Studies, School of International Studies, Jawaharlal Nehru University, New Delhi

groupings. Hence we saw the Post-Cold War paradigm of international relations undergoing a radical change.

A new world order had to replace the old one. It was only by the mid-nineties that the contours of the new world order began to emerge, though the transitional phase continues even today. The process of understanding these basic changes and adjusting to them continues among nations. The focus of this paper is to examine Indo-Hungarian ties at the political level in this changed context. A brief review of Indian and Hungarian perception of the changing world order would be in order.

The Changing World Order

The triumph of liberal democracy and a free market economy over an authoritarian political system and a highly centralised command economy led many observers and scholars to believe that an unipolar world had come into existence. The disintegration of the Soviet Union and Yugoslavia confirmed this opinion. There is no doubt that in the changed context of the nineties the United States of America has emerged as the leading military and economic power. American intervention militarily in the Gulf War of 1990 against Iraq and the lead it took in the North Atlantic Treaty Organisation's (NATO) strike in Serbia and Kosovo convincingly demonstrates that the United States is the only super power in the military sense. Importantly, the U.S. has also shown its willingness to use this power, if necessary. While the U.S. has superior military power, nevertheless in Indian perception the world is not an unipolar one. This is because in the changed context economic power has also come to occupy a centre-stage in international politics. From that perspective there are other centres in the world which are economically powerful. Nations which have sufficient economic power and an advanced technological base are in a position to play a decisive role in international politics. The rapid advances in science and technology have made the industrialised nations like the U.S., the European Union (EU) and Japan emerge as major centres of power and influence. In that sense India believes that it is not a unipolar world.

Besides, China is likely to emerge as another centre of power and influence in future. Its steady growth in economic and military spheres, coupled with its vast resources both human and natural, easily makes china a resurgent power of the future. The Russian Federation has the potential to emerge as another major centre of power and influence. Today Russia is perceived as a weak power facing tremendous economic difficulties and an unstable polity. However, given Russia's size, location – straddling Europe and Asia its vast natural resources, a strong base of scientific and technical personnel and its nuclear status, signifies that Russia would count in future as a centre of power and influence.

An equally important force to reckon with in the changed world order is the regional cooperation groupings which are playing a decisive role in international politics. This is especially so of the EU, which has already emerged as a major centre of power. However the developing countries deprived of the countervailing presence of the Soviet Union could come under greater pressure from the developed countries especially from financial institutions to adopt certain economic and political policies.

In the restructured world order the possibility of wars breaking out on a global scale has been considerably reduced. This is because rival ideologies no longer dominate international politics. The main challenges before the world are the possibility of regional conflicts erupting and soon acquiring a wider dimensions. The rise in ethnic and religious nationalism, the resurfacing of traditional rivalries and the control for vital raw materials such as oil and natural gas could be the root cause for the outbreak of regional conflicts. The rise in ethnic and religious extremism has provided a fillip to terrorism, drug trafficking smuggling in small weapons, organised crime etc. Besides, issues such as environmental security, energy security etc would confront the world order at some time or the other.

Viewed from the perspective of India's national interest, the rupture in its relations with the Soviet Union and its allies in the socialist bloc had a profound impact. For over thirty years India and the Soviet Union, including its allies, shared a wide area of compatibility of strategic interests which augured well for Indo-

Soviet relations. The substantial defence and economic cooperation led to a multi-dimensional relationship. The Indo-Soviet Treaty of Peace, Friendship and Cooperation of 1971 symbolised the special relationship India enjoyed with the Soviet Union. With the breakup of the Soviet Union and the initiation of a systemic transition by Russia, and other countries India had to adjust to these changes. The benefits it derived from the special relationship had disappeared and India had to find a new basis for its relationship with Russia and the countries of East-Central Europe, including Hungary.

For Hungary the collapse of the Berlin Wall leading to the complete alteration of the geopolitical map of Europe was a welcome development. It provided Hungary with an excellent opportunity to reassert its sovereignty and freedom of action in international relations. Hungary could now proclaim its European heritage. Domestically Hungary could express its belief in Christianity, rule of law, respect for human rights and assert its support for democracy and a free market economy. Adherence to these values also cherished by the West has made Hungary to identify with Europe and European civilization. Former Prime Minister Joszef Antall in his address to the first freely elected Parliament in 1990 stressed that the new government would be a European one in every sense of the word. In his statement he asserted "We stand for the tradition of democracy pluralism and openness. We want to return to the European heritage".[1] In view of its strong assertion that it belonged to Europe, it was but natural that Hungary aspired to join the EU, NATO and other European security structures. Its objective has been to integrate with Europe. As early as October 1990 Hungary was admitted into the Council of Europe as a full member.

It was in keeping with this tenor of thinking that Hungary's early foreign policy acts were in the direction of Europe. Its immediate concern was to seek admission into NATO. Initially. Hungary even thought of proclaiming itself a neutral state. This option was given up because the Hungarian leadership realised

[1]The Foreign Policy of Hungary, Member of NATO, *Fact Sheets on Hungary* No. 1, 1999, Ministry of Foreign Affairs, Budapest, Hungary.

that the end of the bipolar world did not immediately bring peace. Hungary was perhaps apprehensive of the unpredictability and political instability in Russia, the violent break-up of Yugoslavia created uncertainty on Hungary's southern periphery, and an united Germany. These developments led Hungary to seek the protective shield of NATO. In Hungarian view NATO membership would bring stability and that would have a beneficial impact on its economy. In the words of former Foreign Minister Mr. Laszlo Kovacs "In seeking to join NATO Hungary is not motivated by the fear of a military threat. Our determination to become a member of the Alliance is based on shared values and the desire to contribute to a favourable security environment. In our opinion NATO enlargement represents the eastward expansion of the region of security and stability in Europe. It is our goal to be part of this region and to enjoy the benefits of security that NATO membership guarantees".[2] Having being able to fulfil some of the conditions land down in the charter, Hungary along with Poland and the Czech Republic were invited to join as associate members of NATO in July 1997. Two years later at the Washington summit in February 1999 Hungary and others were made full members of NATO.

Hungary also perceives that the US is a superior military power and therefore its participation in NATO is essential. In Hungarian view "The tragic events taking place in former Yugoslavia have clearly shown that the European allies may cope with such crisis situations only with the active engagement of the United States.[3]

Since the prime oljective of Hungarian foreign policy is to integrate with Europe, its approach is highly Euro-centric. Having succeeded in securing the membership of NATO. Hungary's next goal is to join the EU. Therefore, Hungary's views of the world order that has replaced the bipolar world is similar to that held by

---

[2]Laszlo Kovacs, Minister for Foreign Affairs of the Republic of Hungary, "Hungary's Contribution to European Security". *NATO Review*, September-October 1997.

[3]n. 1. p. 4

the EU. Hungary's foreign policy is keen to project the view that its perception of world developments and events are in harmony with that of the EU.

Hungary's domestic agenda since the revolutionary changes of 1989 has been the systemic transformation of its socio-political and economic system from a socialist system to a liberal democracy and a free market economy. In Hungary the transition has been smooth and rapid, as in the past Hungary had experimented with economic reforms. It appears that the transition process in Hungary is nearly complete. At the political level Hungary has succeeded in building a vibrant democracy. Free and fair elections of the President and Parliament have been conducted. A major source of tension for the Hungarian Government however, is the issue of Hungarian minorities in Romania, the Slovak Republic Serbia and Croatia.

India and Hungary

India did not apparently anticipate the historic changes in East-Central Europe including in Hungary. But once the momentous changes had occurred, India welcomed the movement towards democracy and a more humane and a liberal system of governance. During his visit to Hungary in July 1993 President Dr. Shankar Dayal Sharma aptly expressed these sentiments at a banquet speech. He said "what has aroused our admiration is that the profound changes are being undertaken in your country with the consent and involvement of the people. History has repeatedly demonstrated that, only that achievement endures which is acceptable to the people. The people of India are one with the Hungarian people in their espousal of the democratic sprit and their commitment to the democratic system of governance".[4]

As the systemic transition got underway in Hungary, it was necessary for India to restructure the relationship on a new basis. In the past India had enjoyed friendly and close relations with Hungary. This was a helpful factor for India in its endeavour to

[4]*Foreign Affairs Record*. July 1993.

recast the relationship. It was helpful to the extent that it provided a sense of continuity for the future. However, before proceeding further a brief look at the past relationship would be useful.

In the past for India, its ties with Hungary were in a way an extension of its close and friendly relations with the Soviet Union. The main thrust of Indo-Hungarian ties was at the economic level. Hungarian technical know-how was available to India in areas such as hydro and thermal power generation, telecommunication, aluminium and glass industries. Among the developing countries. India was the main trading partner of Hungary. Trade was on a rupee payment basis. Hungarian economic assistance has played a useful role in building India's basic industries in the public sector. At the political level Hungary has readily extended support to India on issues of crucial significance to it. For instance, the Kashmir question, the problem of Diego Garcia, Indian role in the Nonaligned Movement, the liberation of Bangladesh etc. Exchanges of high level visits was another feature of Indo-Hungarian ties. Besides there were exchanges at the party to party level, which included the Indian National Congress also. The regular exchanges at the cultural level was another dimension of the relationship.

Despite the revolutionary changes of 1989 the history of the past relationship imparted a sense of continuity to both India and Hungary. However, as mentioned it was useful only in a limited way. It was important to remember that Hungary had asserted its independence and no longer belonged to the Socialist bloc. A new equation had to be found. A helpful aspect was the absence of differences between India and Hungary.

The democratic orientation in Hungary and the liberalisation of the Indian economy, and the economic reforms opened up a whole new vista for both the countries to cooperate with each other. They could recast the relationship in a new mould. The possibility for economic cooperation has definitely opened up. However, the priorities of Hungary have understandly changed in the new context. As already mentioned Hungary's prime goal is to integrate with Europe, pursue a good neighbourliness policy and to efficiently manage the issue of Hungarian minorities living in the neighbourhood. Consequently, promotion and strengthening of regional cooperation occupies the focus of Hungarian foreign policy.

In this regard Hungary has taken certain important initiatives at the regional level. The first attempt was in 1988 the Central European Initiative (CEI). The aim of CEI has been to surmount the socialist bloc structures and to develop economic and technical cooperation among themselves. This was followed by the formation of the Visegrad Group. The countries of East-Central Europe felt that their strength lay in unity among themselves. It was the answer to this aspiration that the Visegrad initiative was launched in 1990. The Visegrad Group's cooperation was helpful in dismantling the Warsaw Pact and the Council for Mutual Economic Assistance (CMEA). Another regional grouping is the Central European Free Trade Area (CEFTA) which aims at establishing a free trade area. In 1990 Hungary was invited to the Council of Europe. It was the failed *coup d'etat* of August 1991 in the Soviet Union that led Hungary, Poland and Czechoslovakia to seek the membership of NATO at their summit meeting in Cracow in October 1991. All the three countries that is Hungary Poland and the Czech Republic are now members of NATO. Since Hungary has consolidated its position in the new scheme of things, linkages with India should be srenewed with greater vigour.

In India greater affinity is felt towards Hungary not only because of the past history of friendship, but more importantly because of its espousal of democracy. Apart from cherishing the same values, Hungary has been supportive of the Indian stand on the Kashmir question. Hungary believes that this question should be solved at the bilateral level within the framework of the Simla Agreement. On the Kargil issue Hungary has been supportive of the Indian position and believes that Pakistan had violated the Line of Control. Hungary has also by and large been sympathetic to India's security concerns. There appears to be understanding of the challenges posed by ethnic and religious extremism to India's integrity. However, it must be remembered that as an aspirant for the EU membership, Hungary's foreign policy postures would have to be in consonance with that of the EU.

There is considerable potential for cooperation at the multilateral level in international fora like the United Nations on questions of disarmament, international terrorism, the World Trade Organisation etc. The number of high level visits exchanged between India and Hungary are on a regular basis. Parliamentary delegations of the two countries are exchanged practically every alternate year. In April 1991 President Gomez Arpad visited India, in 1993 which was reciprocated by the Indian President Dr. Shankar Dayal Sharma's visit to Hungary.

There is no doubt that a wide area of congruence of interests does exist between the two countries. However, differences on certain issues does exist. In Indian perception Hungarian aspiration to join the NATO would give rise to uncertainties and tensions. ".....the enlargement of NATO will inevitably have an impact on the evolution of European security structures and constitutes a matter of global concern as it could lead to revival of tensions and rivalries which have only recently abated".[5] India is concerned at the New Strategic Concept adopted at the Washington summit in February 1999, for it may go beyond the defence of the territories of member countries. The military involvement of NATO in Kosovo is a case in point. On the other hand on the question of nuclear non-proliferation Hungary is not supportive of the latest nuclear blasts conducted by India. In its view India should sign the Comprehensive Test Ban Treaty (CTBT) and other nuclear non-proliferation treaties. These differences of perceptions do not however, affect the friendly tenor of Indo-Hungarian relations.

In conclusion, the relationship needs an impetus. A wide area for cooperation exists especially in the economic field and this opportunity should be utilised by both the countries. For the present political cooperation is on a low key. However, it can be strengthened by a continuous dialogue both at the official and non-official levels. It is important for India and Hungary to understand each others perceptions.

---

[5]Annual Report 1993-94. *Ministry of External Affairs*, Government of India, p. 54.

II
Experience with Democracy

6

Democratic Changes in Hungary— Past, Present and the Future

SZILÁRD SASVÁRI*

Looking at the changes of political courses in Middle-Eastern Europe from a historical aspect, it can be said that they have taken a very short period of time. Given political systems usually change with such a quick pace only in revolutions or at after-war situations. Hungary tried to get rid of an unacceptable form of state (the communist dictatorship) in 1956. Prime Minister Nehru said in connection with the revolution and war of independence: **"These peoples felt that they had to do their own politics and not the politics of someone else, forced by necessity."**[1] Practically the change of system in 1990 can be summarised with the same sentence. In 1990 the historical opportunity was given that the change of system became possible. Since then the people of Hungary have elected new parliaments and governments – with different compositions – three times according to their free will.

During this period the political atmosphere that had developed made changes inevitable. The essence of these changes can be summarised as follows. Political institutional and constitutional changes proved to be necessary, which meant the legality of political freedom rights. We established a number of political and social institutions that had functioned in the western democracies for long. On the other hand we realised turning the soviet

---

*President of the Culture and Media Committee of the Hungarian Parliament, Member of the Hungarian Parliament, Vice-President of the Faction of Fidesz Hungarian Civic Party.

[1]Radio declaration of Prime Minister Nehru, 28th October, 1956.

modelled planned economy into a market economy required working out in detail the conditions for survival as well as and ensuring its legal status. We can say that these two inevitable requirements for the effective operation of the country were completed by the system changing parliament and government of 1990. For the first time people were allowed to elect their representatives in the parliament and the self-governments of their own settlements freely. The Constitutional Court was able to start their work and the task of the police was not to keep the citizens in fear but maintain the public security.

Let me begin with a background to the Hungarian political and economic reforms.

Hungary, after the Soviet invasion and before 1990 experienced two main periods: the '50s and the '70s – of course a bit simplified. In the '50s the parliamentary democracy was abandoned, the institutions of the market economy were wound up and the independent internal and security polities was also given up. The communist government annihilated the middle class that meant approximately 50 per cent of the population that time by nationalising their properties and destroying their parties and civic institutions (NGOs). Their intellectuals and politicians were compelled to emigrate or sent to prison or simply wiped out physically. Every member of the society was forced to become an employee – most of them employed by a state-run firm – which means that a dependency situation was created where everyone was controlled through the world of work. To use an analogy the whole country was like a high-rise block of flats where no detached houses were tolerated. Only a huge, single block with a lot of small rooms where people were forced to live next to another. Inside this building it was possible to move about quite freely, you contd buy basic consumer goods at very low prices regardless of quality. But in front of the main gate there were guard in the inner door there was a Hungarian soldier on the outside a Russian. This is practically how the life of Hungary was in the '50s. I should add that in the attic and cellar of this building were the secret police who tried to control and influence people by all means – foul and fair.

In the second period, from the '70s this situation started to change–some people could get passports but there was no currency to spend. People who were allowed to see the world outside and also inside they could express some "unofficial" thoughts. In the private sector a minor market economy came to existence which practically meant a small amount of private possession. Some people could produce fruit and vegetables to sell on the markets and that fact led parts of the countryside of Hungary to a semi-civic position. The middle class that was annihilated during the dictatorship of the '50s began to emerge in small members.

In the light of all these two more aims of the system-changing governments of the '90s become more understandable: the change of the politically and economically influential elite, destruction of the "good old" connections. The other important thing has been to build again a national identity and self-interest and to help the national culture.

The realisation of these two steps is the task of the present government; and it is only when that happens could we say that a transformation has taken place. The change of the elite could not be carried out during the '90s because it did not have a radical agenda. "The aims were radical but the changes happened on the basis of democracy and constitutional state. There was no 'x-raying', there was no clear reckoning of the past."[2] As it is said today in Hungary and in Middle Europe, the invisible region has not been discovered and calling of the responsible persons to account has not been achieved.

Certain vital system have not been corrected yet, which still causes great difficulties to detect black economy so that the old political connections continue. The former autocrat Hungarian Socialist Workers' Party have not given account of its properties as yet as there is no inventory. The parties did not have to compete, there were not equal opportunities, free elections could not be held. The political social elite did not see the solution in a total transformation. This generation does not have the slightest intention

[2]We want a competitive Hungary–interview with Prime Minister Viktor Orban, in: "Európai Utas" 1998/3, p. 5.

to be close to the radical Right, as it wants not only to maintain the institutions of democracy, but also to strengthen them.

An aim to be completed is to enforce the national self-interest, and to support the national culture. The former left-wing government did not take on this aim as they found it absolutely unnecessary. According to their view the state politics cannot have any value content, cannot have cultural content. In the consciousness of the Left the neutrality of the state is not a constant seeking along values, but a totally pragmatist, power-centred entity. On this field the present government has introduced vital changes, so that the two fundamental determining factors of the changes between 1990 and 1998, as mentioned above: the establishment of democratic institutions and the transition to market economy can gain ground.

Stability has been set up in the Hungarian political system, the legal institutions that provide constitutionality have been established. They are the Constitutional Court, the Ombudsman, the self-governments both working as territorial institutions and the representatives of the minorities. Agriculture has also started to improve. During this period commercial banks started to work, the Stock Market was set up, laws helped the free enterprises, and foreigners have been allowed to invest in Hungary. Privatisation has taken place which means that the state property has been demolished.

The new government operates these democratic institutions as parts of inner stability and its intention is to make them even more effective.

It follows independent foreign and security policy with the intention of stability towards outside. This position can not be reached by adjusting at all costs, but it has to be a predictable without loosing our own interests and has to be based on mutual partnership. The government wants to put the economy onto an increasing track, and intends to create social balance, to strengthen the middle class.

As a special point I would like to emphasise the importance of the system-changing generations. This is quite a unique approach, but it might be interesting for You.

There are three such "generations"[3]: the historical ones, the so called '68 generation and the young generation.

The conservative side belongs to the historical generations too, which practically characterises the '90 to '94 government when the transformation of the system was started by a conservative, nationally committed governing style. This generation relieved the communist generation of its leading position, those ones, who had been ruling the country, through various positions, of the society from the '50s and who had created the dictatiorship. Practically the generation of the dictatorship was displaced by this historical generation. To characterise them we could say that they wanted to form a conservative, nationally committed Hungary. Despite the fact that their representatives turned up later in several parties they had a unique view: their orientation of values and interests was determined by the thoughts and problems of the intellectual-political world of the period between the two world wars. Their political personality was formed during the Soviet influenced political crisis of the period 1945–48. Their anti-Bolshevist attitude was primarily motivated by the fact that they regarded the communist ideas unfamiliar to the Hungarian national character. At the revolution of 1956 they did not intend to humanise the socialism but they wanted to redress the broken historical continuity. During the socialism they were slandered, harassed or simply ignored because of their thoughts and behaviour.

The second big group is the '68 generation, the ones who like to call themselves simply "the big generation". They changed their views somehow and went on in two directions from the 70s. The reform-communists were formed from one of these groups those who got close to the power in the middle of the '80s. But the borders of reformability had appeared soon from stopping of the economic reforms all the way to the silence of the people regarded as persona non grata or to forcing some people

[3]In the present case I am going to use the word "generation" according to the classic idea of Károly Mannheim, written in 1928. Generation means the collection of such groups of the same age that were formed by the same historical experiences they assimilated them in a similar way and it became a kind of collective memory of that generation.

into emigration. The other group was formed from those ex-Marxists that worked as a "samisdat" (self publishing) opposition and fought against the system. We can say that these two groups originated from the same source and their courses of life from the '70s till '92 moved on different tracks. In '92 they found each other again in connection with the Democratic Charta[4] and they worked together again forming the MSzP[5] government from '94 to '98. If we examine the big generation we can say that in theory there was the possibility of becoming a political generation, but history has seen quick intervening events, and they were not given the opportunity of changing their elite and opted for a new way of thinking.

The third generation is the new generation that announced a different political attitude and their example was the Polish Solidarity. This could be described as a post-communist "protest" generation at the beginning. They, young people just having finished their studies at the universities represented and represent the most characteristic political current, as they were the ones to set themselves the most radically against the declared and undeclared compromises of the party-state. This generation is my generation, the civic right-centre that practically became the central power of the '98 Government.

In connection with the generations it can be stated that with the parliamentary elections and government changes three generations followed each other. The '98 turn was also a generation change with the specific meaning of age, and this generation leads Hungary at present.

The primary task of this government is to create a society that can operate a stable political system, social balance, and an increasing economy. For this aim it is inevitable to strengthen the middle strata, which can be practically connected to a dynamic model

---

[4]An umbrella organisation established referring to the danger of the presence of the extreme right–which was not verified by anything. The liberal democrats and the members of the former communist party cooperated in this organisation.
[5]Hungarian Socialist Party.

described by Gyula Tellér[6]. This model consists of three groups.

The great owners, the lower classes that are the most interested in the distribution and the middle stratum. The group of the great owners can reach a quasi-monopol position practically because of its economic power if the politics does not create a balanced situation for them. This means that they can gain power not only on economic grounds but also on every aspect of life. They strive for monopoly through politics so that they can take advantage from it and they compel this way of putting forward their interest through the media practically to the whole society. They can afford to support publishing books and productions of the press that reflect their thoughts and interests. They can defend their own interests through the institutions of the legal system easier, and if needed they are able to employ experts. This does not mean only political, communicational and economic power, but through being in possession of all these it holds groups power as well.

The second big group consists of the ones interested in the distribution. They try to carry out a re-distribution by centralising most of the incoming resources to the central budget in one hand, so that it serves the interest of the lower social classes. The elite of this group aims at invading the positions of re-distribution and through these positions it influences the parliamentary majority of the given government.

On one side with the power of money and ownership, on the other side with the power of mass, the purpose is to overcome the institutions of democracy and to maintain their dominating positions permanently.

Between these two social groups there is the middle class that is the most interested in democracy. This middle stratum can be characterised by intellectual and financial independence, they have got their own financial, intellectual and relational capital. If this

[6]Political scientist, sociologist, president of the Association of the Hungarian Civic Democrats, politician. One of the important representatives and experts of the changes in Middle Europe.

middle segment is bit enough then it can create an optimal balance between the monopol interest of the great owners and the group interested in the re-distribution. The wideness or narrowness of this middle stratum creates the dynamism that is characteriscs of a western society. The main property of this social group is that they possess enough financial, intellectual and relational capital so that they can maintain their own schools, civic associations (NGOs), organisations representing their interest and political views. The importance of increasing the strength of this class is on the one hand to put forward the idea of subsidiarity–solve problems as close to their source as possible,–but on the other hand to maintain balance between the monopoly of great owners and the exaggerated demands for the re-distribution. In this respect it's time to give up Marx's theory about the war of classes[7].

As a consequence of the preceding left-wing governing Hungary can be characterised by a bi-polar society. Almost two third of the population makes the group which is interested in the re-distribution,–and a lot of them can be classified as poor. The other end is made up by a very thin layer of the rich. The danger of the bi-polar Hungarian society is that "the property and the incomes accumulating more and more in the hands of a very small group of the society makes the relationships of the different groups with the institutions of social integration and democracy fundamentally unequal."[8] This is typical not only in Hungary, but in every country of Eastern Middle Europe having gone through changes recently: There exists a group forming a very thin layer, but possessing even more power, and there is another, wide stratum of people being less able to assert their interests. Power and group size are inversely proportional. The middle class has to be fit between these two poles and to widen the society into a three-polar system. It has got several methods. Those civic associations, clubs and societies which disappeared during the socialist era still attract people. The role of the family, the smallest unit of the

---

[7]He speaks basically about two classes : the capitalists and the workers.

[8]The Chances of the Two-polar Society and Democracy, in: Magyar Nemzet 23. September 1998. p. 12.

society has to be intended more important, which unfortunately, was not emphasised and supported enough during the former period.

Let me introduce you to the Program of the Government which aims to support and widen the middle classes in order to realise the purposes mentioned above. It holds the title "Approaching towards the Next Millennium". It puts the following aims and tools to itself:

1. To support families, that means, in a peculiar way opposite to the policy of your country, encouraging families to accept children, and in Hungary one of the greatest problems is the demographic decrease. The ratio of the inactive and active population is very big, ageing characterises the society. Supporting families is a primary aim though, so that more children are born and they grow up in communities: in families.
2. To guarantee a competitive knowledge through educational institutions. This is the only system of institutions where social inequalities can be cured in a preventive way. It means that everyone must have the chance to gain such knowledge that helps him/her to cope with the market economy and the world of work.
3. To support the national culture, to save and maintain traditions for the next millennium that are characteristics only of this nation. This is such a cultural investment that prepares us for the next millennium.
4. To create public security primarily against corruption and organised crime.
5. To support enterprises with a policy that helps small and middle enterprises to be able to get resources.
6. To decrease taxes. We are interested in helping Hungarian economy to become stronger by decreasing the withdrawals.
7. Economic and military integration. Joining the NATO we create a political integration with the western world, entering the European Union we make such an economic decision which–through NATO and the EU–can be an insurance against getting back into the sphere of interest of the eastern Bloc and the Russians.

I can tell you that Hungary is again on the way to freedom and we are using again the routes connecting us to Europe for hundreds of years.

1. Hungary is today a constitutional state bearing a stable political system that intends to create a social balance by supporting the middle strata and its economy can be characterised by prosperity and growth.
2. Hungarian politicians and the supporters of this politics think that by having decided to join the NATO and the European Union Hungary is following the right path.
3. In 1998 there was a change of generations and this new generation intends to complete the transformation of the political system.
4. This generation bears a vision of future and they have definite ideas about it having a wide supporting background from the society to realise their conceptions.

7

Constitutional Development and Democratic Politics in Hungary

SHASHIKANT JHA*

If we consider the experiences of Central-East European countries in the field of post-communist political evolution, we find the Hungarian example quite distinct in many ways. The Hungarian political development during the past one decade has shown remarkable characteristics of a smoothly functioning and stable democracy with almost all its concomitants—governmental institutions, electoral system, political parties, popular participation in the political process, socio-political movements, the organs of civil society like trade unions, self-governments and churches, etc., and political culture—media, nationalism as well as interrelations between majority and minority communities – being in place and working with impressive degree of maturity and efficiency.

The success story of the Hungarian political development may partly be attributed to a steady decline of legitimacy and authority of the ruling communist parties in the entire region, more so in Hungary, after 1956. The •decline had been caused by several factors—economic, political, social, ideological and moral. Each major or minor development, which continued happening at regular intervals in the East-Central European region, contributed to the sapping of the very foundations on which the ruling communist parties had sought to base themselves. Every subsequent attempt by these parties to arrest the decline of their social acceptability and discover new sources of legitimacy—for instance, when ideology

*Dr. Shashikant Jha is Associate Professor in the Centre for Russians, Central Asian & East European Studies SIS JNU New Delhi.

was no longer sufficient enough as a basis of rule, they began to legitimise themselves by orchestrating the economic performance of the state under their leadership–failed in the long run. Facing an incredible variety of unrelenting challenges from within the society, not to talk of external factors, the communist authority in the East-Central European region managed to survive with the Soviet support till the end of 1980s. The process of decline culminated in the final collapse in the wake of Soviet Perestroika, when the patron power refused to come to the rescue of ruling elite of these countries facing the mounting societal pressure. The Hungarian transition from communism to democracy stood apart from the rest of the region in that it was a non-violent and negotiated transformation. That Hungary could successfully escape some of the violent experiences of transition in the region was made possible by a long and steady development of pluralistic-consensual tradition in that country, specially after 1968, when it launched a bold programme of economic reform called New Economic Mechanism (NEM).

We attempt in this article to make a brief survey of the development of some of the major democratic institutions and processes associated with them in Hungary. The evolution of the structure and performance of these institutions are discussed within the broader framework of the evolution of constitution in Hungary.

Constitutional Development

Hungary has gone through one of the longest and gradual process of constitutional reform. The process had begun well before the final end of communism. The constitutional reform in Hungary, unlike that of Poland and former Czechoslovakia, was initiated by the 'reform communists' themselves, rather than the victorious opposition, as a deliberate part of its strategy of survival. As early as 1987, informal proposals for constitutional reform had begun to circulate and be debated. Following the rehabilitation of Imre Nagy, the slain leader of the 1956 reform movement, in June 1989, the Hungarian parliament began to dismantle the 1949 Stalinist constitution. But, more specifically, on 18 October 1989, more than one hundred amendments were adopted by the parliament that almost entirely transformed the basic character of the Hungarian constitution. The process of constitutional change was further concretised by the proclamation, on 23 October 1989, of the Republic of Hungary, in place of the hitherto existing "People's Republic".

The constitutional change had reformist character and open-ended nature. The 'reform communist' government prepared the introduction of a new pluralist political institutional setting with a series of laws and decrees, for instance, on the freedom of association and assembly, etc. The process of constitutional legislation continued with the bargaining at the Round Table, the results of which were accepted and legislated by the last communist parliament. The most important results of this period concerned the electoral laws and the law on the activity of the political parties. The third stream of constitutional change within the new political setting was a result of conflict and concurrence between the old and new political forces. It took the form of referenda, bargaining and agreements, as well as decisions made by the new, freely elected parliament.

Even though the 1949 constitution of Hungary had been massively amended, there was a need to enact and promulgate a new constitution that could reflect the democratic spirit of the post-communist Hungary in totality. This was not an easy task. The political spectrum in Hungary was fragmented with each party and grouping eager to push through its own priorities. This was the reason why the first parliament, elected in 1990, could not make much progress towards the enactment of a new constitution. Among the major political parties the opinion was sharply divided on the nature of the new Hungarian constitution. While in the beginning the 'reform communists' wanted to have a strong presidential system in Hungary, they lost the initiative in a close referendum forced by the more radical groupings, and their game plan for an early popular election to the strong presidency was defeated. This meant that the new system had to be a parliamentary system. Under the 1990-94 parliament, the major political parties arrived at a broad agreement among themselves which entailed a weak presidency and a relatively strong parliament, though there were twenty types of such legislation which would require two-thirds majority in the parliament to pass. Thus, in a piecemeal manner, and through the default process of mutual checks and balances, the contours of the new constitutional system in Hungary was put in place. In spite of these developments the first post-communist parliament of Hungary failed to enact and promulgate a new constitution.

The programme of the ruling coalition in the 1994-98 parliament contained a commitment to rewrite the constitution. The express aim of their programme was to consolidate, update and revise the 1990 text (a substantially revised vision of the 1949 constitution) in the light of experience hitherto gained. More specifically, the objective was to consolidate and develop the separation of powers by strengthening the executive powers of the government, the supervisory powers of the parliament, the independence of judiciary, and making the amendment of the constitution extremely difficult.

The new constitution of Hungary was drafted by a special twenty-seven member parliamentary Constitutional Committee (CC), established in June 1995. After much rambling and differences of opinion, it was agreed that the Speaker of the National Assembly would be the Chairman of this committee. All Standing Orders relating to the working of the CC required a four-fifths majority on the floor of the house that made the support of the several opposition parties indispensable. Each of the six major parliamentary parties had an equal delegation on the CC, no matter what was their parliamentary strength and each one of them had one vote. The vote of at least five of the six parliamentary delegations was required for every decision. There was no additional requirement that five delegations together must constitute at least two-thirds of the seats on the floor of the house, which gave both the ruling and the major opposition parties an effective veto. It was further required that, after the coalition parties agreed on a common position, the final result must be approved by the full house and then put to a national referendum.

The mainstream political parties favoured a gradualist and organic approach that involved tidying and building up on the

1990 amendment to the old constitution. On the other hand, the radicals, ultra-nationalists and populist wanted a radical departure with a stronger presidency and weaker government with direct popular election of the president, etc. Another quite significant side of the whole process was the greatly strengthened hand of the Constitutional Court, as its decisions could no longer in practice be overturned by any constitutional amendment, even though adopted by two-thirds majority in the National Assembly.

In spite of extremely complex and highly consensual procedures agreed upon in 1994 to draw up a new constitution, the 1994-98 legislature failed to adopt and promulgate the new constitution. The reasons responsible for this could be identified in a variety of factors that need not detain us here. Broadly speaking, the CC put forward a new draft with few modest proposals that could have been generally acceptable. These proposals included reducing the number of MPs from 386 to 352; increasing the number of signatures required to call a referendum from 300,000 to 400,000; increasing the term of the office of the constitutional court judges from seven to twelve years, etc. There were some minor ad hoc changes suggested on judicial reform, immunity of MPs, and limiting the number of issues on which referenda could be called, while making their outcome binding, etc. No more progress was made during the term of the 1994-98 Hungarian parliament. Nevertheless, the new Hungarian constitution is, in its amended version consolidated in 1990, and further added to in the following years, is in place that provides for the structure and functional principals of present day democratic political system of Hungary.

Major Institutions of the Political System

Under the new Hungarian constitution the following prominent political institutions have been provided for. A well balanced distribution and separation of powers are strongly rooted in the institutions of the Republic of Hungary. There is a balanced relationship between the National Assembly, the President of the republic, and the government. This arrangement is provided for as per the constitutional norms, in accordance with the principles of checks and balances. One of the most formidable elements of constitutional control in Hungary is the new institution of Constitutional Court. This court enjoys far greater powers than its counterparts in the entire East-Central Europe. The proposal for a presidential system, as it was rejected by a great majority of the Hungarians in a national referendum, has not found a place in the constitution. The political system of Hungary is, therefore, a parliamentary one compared with the models of Poland, Czech and Slovak republics, or even Romania. A new political system modelled on the types of Western democracies, especially the German model, with a differentiated and pluralistic system of institutions and a separation of the legislature, the executive and the judiciary as well as their powers and jurisdiction, nearly neatly defined, have been provided for in the constitution.

The President of the Republic

The President of the Hungarian Republic is indirectly elected by the parliament for a period of five years, that is one year longer than the term of parliament. Nominees require the support of fifty Deputies to stand that clearly restricts the number of potential contestants. A two-thirds majority is required to elect a candidate as the President. If, in the first two rounds, the necessary majority is not secured by any of the candidates, there is a run off between the top two contenders in the final third round. The whole process of president's election is required to be completed within just three days.

The institution of presidency Hungary, however, suffers from certain structural problems that have originated from initial controversies around the basic nature of the constitution. This was finally settled in favour of a parliamentary form of government and weak presidency. As a result, the Hungarian President has just few independent powers. He is more in the mould of a father figure of the republic, above day-to-day politics, than an active political personality. Nevertheless, depending upon the specificity of circumstances, his reserve powers can prove to be significant. The President nominates the Prime Minister, who must be elected by Parliament, though this power is severely restricted by the remarkable stability of the Hungarian party system and by the fact that three democratic elections (1990, 1994 and 1998) have produced clear majority coalitions. In reality, the President has no discretion in the appointment of the Prime Minister which has been amply demonstrated by the evolution of such a convention since 1990. The so called 'constructive no-confidence' system, borrowed from the German constitutional practice and introduced in Hungary in 1990, further indicates that the President would have no discretion in the event of no-confidence motion. He can dissolve parliament only after four successive no-confidence votes passed in twelve months, or if parliament has not acted on his nominee for Prime Minister within forty days. All the major appointment in the republic are made by the President, though in such matters he is bound by the advice of the Council of Ministers as per the ruling of the Constitutional court. But, in some very special areas, like the appointment of judges and heads of Radio and Television, etc. the President can, and indeed does, exercise certain degree of his discretion. In conclusion, the President of Hungary for larger political purposes occupies only a ceremonial position.

The National Assembly and Electoral System

The structure of Hungarian Parliament is unicameral. Proposals for a bicameral legislative body were not accepted in the final constitutional document. As a reaction to the emasculation of the Assembly under the communist system, its rights and responsibilities have been extended within the new constitutional context. The national Assembly is elected for a maximum period of four years. It is intended in principle to be fixed term parliament, though in highly exceptional circumstances it can be dissolved early. The electoral system is a mix of both proportional and majoritarian elements. As many as 176 members are elected in single member constituencies. The various counties and the capital of the country, Budapest, are apportioned a number of constituencies on the basis of their population. In each of these 176 constituencies a two ballot system is applied. In order to be nominated a candidate requires at least 750 signatures from a particular constituency from where he wished to contest. The parliamentary elections pass through two phases. In the first round, the electorate votes for a candidate in the Single-Member Constituency (SMC) and also casts its vote for a list. A candidate securing fifty per cent plus one vote is elected. In reality, very few candidates are elected in the first round. In the other constituencies, a second round is held two weeks after the first round. In this round, all those candidates winning a minimum of fifteen per cent of votes cast at the first ballot can remain in the race. In the second ballot, the candidates winning the most of the plurality of votes are declared elected. Since the second ballot is also mostly a three-cornered contests, a majority of MPs are elected with only about 30-35 per cent of votes. The practice of alliances and mutual withdrawals to facilitate a straight fight between major contenders does not exist.

Another 152 seats are chosen in twenty electoral districts to which between 4 to 28 seats are allocated on the basis of population. The city of Budapest, with 28 seats, is the largest district. In this round, a second list vote is cast by voters. Seats are allocated on the basis of these list votes by using a simple electoral quotient. A party list polling less than 4 per cent is not allocated any seats. As a result, this practice leads very often to a slight or heavier over representation of the larger political parties. On the other hand, there is consequent unrepresentation of the electorate, too. In 1990, for instance, 3.5 per cent of the votes went unrepresented. This figure rose to 7.37 per cent in 1994.

A third national list section of 58 seats is allocated to parties that have tabled lists in at least seven districts. The unused votes in each district at the end of election are cumulated and seats allocated to parties winning over 4 per cent of vote. Vacancies in the single member constituency are filled by holding by-elections and other cases by the next unelected candidate on the list. A regional list can be tabled only by those parties which put up candidates in at least a quarter of single member constituencies in that district.

Looking at the functional side, on the other hand, the process of legislation in the National Assembly result in its constant overloading. The challenges of transforming the system are enormous, and the dependency of one legal aspect upon another makes new legislation very difficult. All legal areas must be basically reoriented, and large number of laws must be enacted to cope with the enormous challenges of transition. The fact that a desirable progress has not taken place thus far is due to the lack of experience and the uncertainty which still surrounds the economic-social system and property ownership. The National Assembly enacts its own rules of procedure, but there are serious uncertainties in cases where no legal regulations exist to provide orientation.

Another important aspect has been the reduced parliamentary control over the government as a result of certain strategic agreement between the major parties of the Right and Liberal persuasion, immediately after the first free elections in 1990. According to this agreement, a "motion of constructive no-confidence" was introduced into the constitutional setting, thereby restricting the right of the National Assembly to control the government. Under this system, the government as a whole is responsible to the National Assembly, which may call for its replacement only if it proposes an alternative government. Only the government as an indivisible unit, led by the Prime Minister, can be challenged by a parliamentary no-confidence vote, but not individual members of the government. Such institutional innovations resulted in the strengthening of the government's position in relation to the opposition and the National Assembly as a whole. When combined with the stable majority of the governing coalitions this situation resulted in the significant reduction of the National Assembly's political role in the control of the government.

The Government

As indicated earlier, Hungary was the first country in the region to establish a fully parliamentary government, based on the coalition between several parties. The first government formed after the 1990 elections was a three-party centre-right coalition. The second government formed after 1994 was a two-party social-liberal coalition. And the present government formed in 1998 is also a three-party centre-right coalition which has drawn its constituents from either flank of the hitherto existing political divide as a result of the sharp decline in the fortunes of some of the major parties.

The Prime Minister is elected by the parliament on the proposal of the President of the republic, after debating the new government's proposed programme. The appointment of other ministers are subsequently made by the President on the recommendation of the Prime Minister. The government remains accountable to Parliament and may be dismissed by a vote of no-confidence. However, the system of 'constructive no-confidence', borrowed from Germany, makes the toppling of government for purely negative priorities just impossible. It requires that the motion of no-confidence must propose simultaneously an alternative Prime Minister. Consequently, very few no-confidence motions are tabled, and none has been passed till date. The basic understanding behind this position is that a government once in place will last for the full four-year term. The government remains accountable to the National Assembly and must keep it informed on all policy measures. It is also important to note that the extension of the role of government in the constitutional system has, in reality, contributed to the strengthening of the power and authority of the Prime Minister. Hungary has thus achieved a stable executive and tight party discipline along with clear and operative provision for alternation in government. This is indeed a sign of their political maturity.

Judicial Reform and the Constitutional Court

As in other areas of political system, and in contrast to the communist model of "political justice", the new constitutional norms require the introduction of an independent judiciary in Hungary. Form the 1960s onwards, the communist regime had tried to implement a "socialist rule of law." Under this practice, the political persecution and a political judiciary had a limited scope of operation as compared to the more authoritarian regimes of Czechoslovakia, Romania and the German Democratic Republic, though it could not be denied that persecution did take place in Hungary. More often the cases of political persecution were handled at the administrative level than at the judicial. Towards the close of 1980s, the continuing tradition of the rule of law made it possible to purify the judicial system from the supporters of the old regime amicably without launching an overall judicial reform. Thus the independent judicial control and supervision of the executive in Hungary, as elsewhere in the region, came into existence around 1989.

The post-communist judicial reform in Hungary has evolved along two lines–the institution of ordinary courts which perform day-to-day judicial functions and the more important Constitutional Courts. Besides sharing the judicial functions with the ordinary courts of the regular judiciary, the Constitutional Courts enjoy administrative jurisdiction in particular. Of late, this court has come to occupy the most prominent position in the Hungarian political system.

The first Constitutional Court was established in 1989 and became functional in 1990. The Court consists of a maximum of 15 judges, elected for a term of seven years by the National Assembly. The election of judges requires a two-thirds majority in the National Assembly, which, in other words, makes a broad consensus among various political parties within the Parliament an absolute necessity. Even though the ruling coalition at a time has enjoyed the required majority, a convention of consensus is evolving to elect the judges of the Constitutional Court. Nominations for the judges are made by a nomination committee composed of one representative from each parliamentary group, thereby providing for a role to opposition parties in the process.

The Court is required to have the function of reviewing 'the constitutionality of laws and statutes'. It has the power to strike down unconstitutional laws. The rulings of the Constitutional Court are not subject to any appeal nor can they be overruled by the National Assembly. The National Assembly can revise the constitution prospectively, but not retroactively. As per the constitution, 'anyone' can bring a case before the Court, allowing public authorities, institutions, corporate bodies, organisations and individuals, whether citizens or not, to bring cases before the Court. More importantly the President of the republic can and does refer bills to the Court.

The Constitutional Court has a wide jurisdiction. It can make a concrete judicial review of the constitutionality of laws, delegated legislation and even individual decisions, grounded in a specific case. In case a matter is referred to it by the President of the republic, the Court can exercise an abstract control before the entry into force of a low or a rule. The incorporation into the Hungarian constitution of the principles of the European Convention on Human Rights (ECHR) has further added to the powers of the Constitutional Court. The Court has thus the power to provide protection of core rights in accordance with general European standards.

The Hungarian Constitutional Court has an impressive record of independence. It has given its verdict against the President, suggesting that his discretion to reject nominees for official posts proposed by the government was quite limited. It has also gone against the government on appointments in the media that was contested by the President. Some aspects of the 1990 electoral law were reviewed and declared unconstitutional by the Court. It annulled a law seeking to introduce prescription for political crimes committed during the communist period, but it allowed the prosecution of other, non-political crimes committed during the same period. The whole matter had been referred to the Court by the President of the republic. A 1990 legislation had given the ordinary courts, too, a jurisdiction to undertake judical review over administrative matters.

The Constitutional Court has become a strong pillar of the defence of constitution and democracy in Hungary, as elsewhere in the region. In a short time, this court has many a success story to its credit. The Court has demonstrated its independence and capacity to develop a strong body of constitutional jurisprudence, which may go a long way to improve the functionality of the nascent constitutional system in Hungary. The Court has proved itself a worthy political-legal arbitrator and shock-absorber in the conflicts between the various branches of the government as well as a defender of the basic rights of the citizenry. In short, this court gives a highly encouraging assurance to the people at large that something has indeed changed for the better, and that anybody can have a reasonable expectation that justice and the rule of law will prevail.

Political Parties and Popular Participation

One of the major markers of the democratising efforts of the post-communist regimes was the emergence of political pluralism with free, open and competitive elections for parliaments and assemblies. A formidable challenge to the successful functioning of parliamentary democracy in East-Central Europe comes from the proliferation of political parties. No sooner had the communist regimes legalised political pluralism than there was a virtual explosion of new political parties, associations, and pressure groups to vie for a share in political power or, at least, for an opportunity to influence political decisions. Initially for a short while, in many countries there emerged broad fronts of anti-Communist opposition which included under its umbrella almost all shades of political opinion that were against the regimes. The Solidarity of Poland, Civic Forum in former Czechoslovakia, and National Salvation Front in Romania were some of the earliest examples of these broad anti-communist fronts. Beginning as mass protest movements against communist rule and led by a core of long time dissident activists, these fronts provided a focus for mobilisation of broad-based and spontaneous popular pressure against communist power. Programmatically vague, ideologically unclear, and organisationally fragile these organisations lacked stability and cohesion from the very beginning. At one stage in early 1990s there were as many as one hundred political organisations in Romania which styled themselves as political parties. The situation elsewhere in the region was not largely different.

To the extent that they play a definitive role in the democratic development of a polity, the value of the plurality of political parties may generally be accepted as significant. But in the post-communist East-Central Europe, this phenomenon has not been without its negative consequences. Because of a great multiplicity of political parties competing for popular support in parliamentary elections, the political spectrum has been incredibly fragmented with the result that no single party has been able either to dominate the political scene or win a clear majority of parliamentary seats. Thus, in order to ensure a majority for governance, the leading party/parties were left with no option but to form coalitions with smaller parties that involved a good deal of ***quid pro quo*** between them. The leadership in many East-Central European countries during the current decade "had to engage in extensive deal making to form a coalition, making them beholden to their coalition supporters." This meant that in the formulation and implementation of some controversial policies, which carried the potential of sharpening differences among the coalition partners and at times even disrupting the coalition itself, the prime ministers had to exercise maximum caution to maintain the political balance. Very often, therefore, with weak ministerial leadership, the new parliamentary democracies of East-Central Europe did seem ill-suited to the task of addressing themselves to the complex social and economic problems that required difficult and unpopular policies.

It has been argued that political parties in East-Central Europe, for a variety of reasons, have not had a robust beginning. The analysts have seen them as weak, fragmented and barely capable of sustaining viable governments. They have also been described as cliquish, divorced from the mass of the society, generally underdeveloped, unrepresentative of public interests, divisive, self-seeking, antithetical to the hopes of national recovery, and harmful to state interests. The idea of the emergence and development of political parties, as an integral part of the post-communist democratic process, has received only a reluctant recognition in the region. That is largely because diverse forms of social movement were instrumental in overthrowing the communist regimes and they, along with the institutions supposed to be representatives of civil society rather than political parties, were initially identified as the major vehicles of subsequent democratic development. Hence, the parties were seen by many as outmoded and largely irrelevant to the process of democratisation in East-Central Europe.

While broadly keeping in tune with the regional pattern, the Hungarian experience with the evolution of the multi-party system has been quite different. The fragmentation of the political space in Hungary has not so much affected the evolution of political parties which are organisationally strong, disciplined, and ideologically committed, Further, they have effectively participated in the three post-communist parliamentary elections as well as a series of other provincial and local elections. The political stability in Hungary has not been undermined by problems generally associated with coalition governments. The parties in Hungary mostly have a middle class base. They maintain quite strong organisational discipline with experiences of much lower percentage of defection, disintegration, etc. They have indeed played a major role in the consolidation of post-communist Hungarian polity.

In the entire region, it was Hungary that saw the earliest development of party organisations. Its transition from communist system followed by a peaceful and gradual course which has been described by analysts as a "negotiated revolution". As a result, in the East-Central European region, Hungary might today appear to have the best chances of developing and consolidating democratic political institutions and a multi-party system.

The transition process in Hungary produced well established parties and a developed party system. Parties came into existence along political and ideological lines. Each party had an organisation, party programme, membership, and party discipline similar to those in developed democracies. The organisation and structure of these parties resembled those of middle class parties more than socialist or communist parties. All of them were closer to mass-based parties than to cadre-based parties, but none of them became mass based party in terms of membership figures, which were rather low. In the early 1990s, the total membership of six parliamentary parties was 2.5 to 3 per cent of the electroate. These included catch-all parties like Hungarian Democratic Forum and Alliance of Free Democrats and parties with specific interest representation like Independent Smallholders Party, as well as parties organised along some ideological lines like Christian Democratic People's Party, etc.

In the aftermath of the first general elections in 1990, the political fragmentation of parliament was moderate. Three parties formed the ruling coalition, and the other three sat in the opposition. More or less, the same has been the pattern till date, though parties forming the ruling coalition has kept on changing with every new election. The nature of political cleavage in Hungary has been very different from those of other East-Central European countries. The main characteristics of the Hungarian party system during the term of the first Parliament may be summarised as follows : compared with other countries of the region, a relatively well-developed and stable party system emerged in Hungary. Unlike in Poland and former Czechoslovakia, in Hungary the communist/anti-communist cleavage was broadly replaced by the competition between the non-communist parties as the main dimension of politics at the time of first general elections in 1990.

The party configuration in Parliament has also remained stable after each of the three elections since 1990. Most of the six parties were able to retain their internal unity. Nor did the political composition of the parliament change significantly during the past one decade. Only a negligible number of MPs switched their allegiance to other parliamentary parties or chose to become independent. In contrast, fragmentation of established parliamentary parties characterised the early years of the new parliaments in Poland and former Czechoslovakia.

Party groups in parliament had considerable independence from the dominance of extra-parliamentary party organisations. Most of the parliamentary groups built a 'well-integrated internal structure, and they displayed a high level of party discipline. In spite of occasional friction between the coalition partners, the strong party discipline in voting behaviour created a stable government position in the slightly fragmented Hungarian parliament. The party unity in parliament remained constantly high, above 90 per cent on an average. This was indicative of the high degree of cohesion and strong party discipline contributing to the stability of the Hungarian political and party system. The main characteristics of the Hungarian party system, as it has evolved during the past one decade, may be summarised as follows:

- ⇒ At the more apparent level, there is a clear absence of predominant competitive ideologies as well as such political parties which could play hegemonic role in Hungarian politics. The political system is, therefore, fragmented, but not as fragmented as elsewhere in the East-Central European Region.
- ⇒ The fragmentation of the political spectrum has brought into currency the politics of coalition with a remarkable degree of stability. This has happened in spite of the fact that the neat division among the parliamentary parties into 3+3 and 2+4 configurations in the first and second parliaments respectively has become more complicated now. The continuing elite realignments have contributed to this phenomenon.
- ⇒ At the more general level, party politics in Hungary is still an elite affair. The well-known Hungarian political scientist, Mihaly Bihari, called it ***libego*** (meaning floating in the air) phenomenon that is insulated from the mainstream of politics and public affairs. The term points to the thus far only superficial integration of the parties into a broader matrix of what the Hungarian public have traditionally understood by politics. They are yet to accept political parties as indispensable to democracy and good government.
- ⇒ The public's traditionally low sense of political efficacy is still a major factor that adversely affects political participation and electoral turn out. The habitual absence of one-third to one-half of voters from the polls at national and local government elections, that has now become almost a pattern, certainly helps in keeping the six-seven party system afloat. But at the same time it raises new questions about the long-term stability of the post-communist system in Hungary.
- ⇒ In tune with the needs of a pluralistic democracy, Hungary's party system in coming times would be shaped by the interplay of newly surfacing social forces, the "invisible hand" of a slowly emerging market economy, and powerful remnants of the country's Kadarist political legacy.

⇒ Attempts to trim the social safety net have proved counterproductive for the incumbent parties. The results of the 1998 elections were a resounding verdict against the steadily declining living standards and snow-balling, since 1995, of widely publicised scandals involving the misappropriation and embezzlement of huge sums of money by the ruling party loyalists.

⇒ It is legitimate to recognise that political parties as the vehicle of nascent parliamentary democracy are slowly and gradually striking firm roots in the post-communist Hungary. The dynamics of their evolution is closely related to the socio-economic processes of the post-communist transition period. There are challenges and difficulties whose impact upon the parties can be clearly witnessed. Nevertheless, from the point of overall political and parliamentary performance, the track-record of Hungarian parties has been much better than their counterparts in other countries of the region. This is what makes the Hungarian experience, in the evolution of multi-party system, a unique one.

Conclusion

Constitutional development in Hungary has produced some definitive results. This has particularly been more conspicuous in the field of dissolution of the old institutional structures coming from the communist era. Elements of the rule of law and the separation and balance of powers among different institutions have been assiduously created. The parliamentary form of government enjoys predominance in the political system. The president of the republic is largely a ceremonial authority. The judiciary is entirely independent of political control, and it is still in the process of an ongoing reform. By far the most significant institution is the Constitutional Court with far reaching powers of constitutional review at its disposal. In a way, this Court is perhaps more important than any other single institution in the Hungarian political system.

The new constitutional framework is, however, far from finished; it is still in a state of continuing transformation. There are sharp social, political and economic conflicts that, for quite some time, will continue to both affect and shape the contours of constitutional democracy and polities in Hungary. It can not be denied, however, that in a short span of time the achievements made by Hungary in the field of constitutional evolution, democratic institution building and processes are quite impressive by any standard. Such achievements look all the more conspicuous when compared with rather dicouraging performance of some other countries of the region, where nascent democracies were quickly put on backward trail by authoritarian leaders of the post-communist era. We may count Slovakia, Romania, Bulgaria, Croatia, and Serbia among such cases where the instrumentality of state was utilised to curtail civic rights, gage the press and other sectors of mass media, suppress the independent role of legislature and judiciary and perpetrate ethno-national discrimination, among several other retrograde policies. That Hungary has escaped many of these negative experiences goes to prove the maturity of its political culture developed over a long period of time.

References

Bihari, Mihaly, "The Political System in Hungary". Attila Gergely, ed., *Almanach of the Institute of Sociology of the Hungarian Academy of Sciences*, (Budapest, 1991).

Bihari, Mihaly, "Parliamentary Elections and Governmental Change In Hungary in 1994", *Hungarian Yearbook, 1995* (Budapest, 1995).

Bozoki, Andras, Andras Korosenyi and George Schopfin, eds., *Post-Communist Transition: Emerging Pluralism in Hungary* (London 1992).

East European Constitutional Review (New York and Budapest), vol. 7, Nos. 2 and 3, 1998.

Eland, F.M., "The Polish Parliamentary Elections of October 1991", *Soviet Studies*, no. 44, 1992.

Fitzmaurice, John, *Politics and Government in the Visegrad Countries: Poland, Hungary, The Czech Republic and Slovakia* (macmillan, 1998).

Frentzel-Zagorska, Janina, "Civil Society in Poland and Hungary", *Soviet Studies,* No. 42, 1990.

Gombar, Csaba, et al., eds., *Question Marks : The Hungarian Government* (Budapest, 1995).

Haraszti, Miklos, "The Beginning of Civil Society : The Independent Peace Movement and the Danube Movement in Hungary", Vladimir Tismaneanu, ed., *In Search of Civil Society,* (London, 1990).

Jha, Shashikant, "Democracy, Parties and Politics in Hungary", *International Studies,* No. 3, 1999.

Korosenyi, Andras, "Stable or Fragile Democracy? : Political Cleavages and Party System in Hungary", *Government and Opposition,* Vol. 28, Winter 1993.

Kukorelli Iistvan, "The Birth, Testing and Results of the 1989 Hungarian Electoral Law", *Soviet Studies,* No. 43, 1991.

Nwuhold, Hanspeter, Peter Havlik and Arnold Suppan, eds., *Political and Economic Transformation in East Central Europe* (Westview Press, 1995).

Racz, Barnabas, "Political Participation in Hungary : The 1990 Elections", *Soviet Studies,* No. 43, 1991.

Schopflin, George, "Post-Communism : Constructing New Democracies in Central Europe", *International Affairs,* No. 67, 1991.

Szoboszlai, Gyorgy, ed., *Democracy and Political Transformation : Theories and East-Central European Realities* (Budapest, 1991).

Tokes, Rudolf L., "Hungary's New Political Elites : Adaptation and Change", *Problems Of Communism,* No. 39, 1990.

Tokes, Rudolf L., Hungary's Negotiated Revolution : Economic Reform, Social Change and Political Succession (Cambridge, 1996).

Tokes Rudolf L., Party Politics and Political Participation in Post-Communist Hungary", Karen Dawisha and Bruce Parrot, eds., *The Consolidation of Democracy in East-Central Europe* (Cambridge, 1997).

8

Hungarians in Central and East Europe

SHAMS-UD-DIN*

The history of the Hungarian people in Europe dates back to the late 9th Century when Magyar tribesmen from the steppes crossed the Carpathian mountains and settled in Pannonia. By the Western world they are 'not accepted as autochthonous European residents' but 'Considered Illegal Asian immigrants.' They speak a Finno-Ugrian language unrelated to the Indo-European languages. According to Western historian, the Hungarians were either peaceful settlers who colonised a deserted terrain or barbaric interlopers who forcibly expelled the indigenous population to establish their own exclusive military, political, ascendancy from the late Tenth century.

The kingdom of Hungary was maintained until the advance of the Ottoman Turks in the Sixteenth century when in 1526 King of Hungary was defeated by the Turks on the field of Mohacs. The Turks subsequently occupied the central portion of the kingdom and the Habsburg rulers of Austria claimed the remaining parts of the Kingdom. Over the succeeding two centuries the Habsburg pushed the Turks out of Hungary, eventually incorporating the entire kingdom within the Habsburg monarchy of Central Europe. Hungary resisted the Habsburg overlordship through repeated rebellions that culminated in the 1848 revolution. Though the Hungarian uprising was suppressed with Russian help, Hungary was awarded home rule in 1867. The Habsburg monarchy was

---

*Prof. Shams-Ud-Din, Chairman of Centre for Russian Central Asian and East European Studies, SIS, JNU, New Delhi.

refashioned as the dual Austo-Hungarian Monarchy, and Hungary was permitted to have her own parliament. About half of the population of Habsburg-Hungary were Hungarians the rest consisted of Romanians, Slovaki, Serbs, Croats, Germans, Rutherian and Jews. In the second half of 19th century Hungary however proclaimed itself a 'nation-state' and between 1867 and 1918 made continuous effort to transform the ethnic composition to its advantage. Forced 'Magyarisation' became the order of the day. Most of the Hungarian Governments particularly that of Prime Minister Baren Dezso Banfty (1895-1899) readily employed any means to assimilate the bulk of the non-Hungarian population. The Hungarian chauvinists legislated to 'magyarize' the name of cities and villages and exerted severe pressure in people to magyarize their often Slavic or German names. The influential author and journalist Jeno Raposi (1842-1929) widely published his dream of an empty of 30 million Hungarians in his popular *Budopesti Hirlap*, in which he called for forced magyarisation of the various national minority groups.

Forced assimilation also had strong Hungarian critics as Endre Ady, Oszkar Jaszi, Jaszi correctly assessed that forced dissimilation makes real assimilation impossible. He supported democracy and equality instead of the declared linguistic supremacy of the Hungarian Nation.

Internal criticism notwithsanding, policy of magyarisation was pursued vigorously in Austria-Hungary. At the end of the World War I Hungary much to its dismay, found the tables turned. Entering World War I on the side of Habsburg, Hungary emerged in 1918 defeated and diplomatically isolated.

The Treaty of Trianon is not only one of the most crucial turning points in modern Hungarian history but certainly a watershed in the history of Hungarian nation. Comments Peter F. Sugar, 'No. no, never' as the slogan all children in Hungarian schools were brought up reciting during the interwar period. For these generations mutilated Hungary was no country while the whole (original) Hungary Heaven.

After the shock of World War I and a series of major social and political aftershocks in 1918 and 1919 Trianon gave berth to a defensive protective interpretation of nationhood. Hungarian foreign policy throughout the entire period between the wars was based upon the philosophy and political strategy of revisionism. All political parties agreed that Trianon was unjust and forced upon Hungary by the overwhelming military and political power at the Paris Peace Conference. 'Treaty revision' became the official government policy.

This passionate irredentism made the same impact in World War II as one of the Hitler's strategic satellites. Romania and Hungary, in fact, constantly competed for Axis favour over Transylvania. Initially Hungary successfully outclassed Romania and regained its lost territories with Axis help between 1938-1941. However, as Rothschild observed Hungary's hope of exploiting German power to restore her historic frontiers while avoiding identification as part of axis camp was unrealistic and based on an overestimation of their own diplomacy. In the end as the Axis tide turned, Romania skilfully executed a volteface from the Axis to Allied camp and in Allied eyes enhanced their claim for the eventual revision of 1938 borders. It was a blow from which Hungary never recovered.

Thereafter though dissatisfaction with Trianon continued Hungarian official attempts at territorial revision were abandoned.

Thus while on the one hand contemporary Hungarian state with its 1.33 per cent minorities (1990 census) quite easily satisfies the cardinal requirement of a 'nation-state' significant numbers of Hungarian people live in all seven of Hungary's neighbouring states between 1.65 million and 2.1 million in Romania, 567,000-650,000 in Slovakia, 345,000-450,000 in Serbia, 158,000-200,000 in Ukraine, 70,000 in Austria, 20,000-40,000 in Croatia, 10,000-5,000 in Slovenia. Excluding the voluntary emigrants and involuntary emigre residents in Western Europe and America some 9.7 million Hungarians today reside within Hungary and between 2.8 million and 3.5 million in enclaves across the immediate geographical vicinity of Hungary.

The Hungarian minority problem as noted was a specific outcome of World War I Peace Settlements. She lost two-thirds of her territory and over 3 million ethnic Hungarians had to accept a new identity as citizens of different neighbouring states.

This had two consequences: First it became doubly difficult for Hungarians and Hungary to come to terms with this reality and secondly, they were never in a position to reverse and regroup and consolidate the Hungarian nation on the basis of mythology and tradition.

After World War II East Europe rapidly came under communist rule. The Communist government however, enjoyed little legitimacy. To overcome this weakness they realied heavily on nationalism which means that the minority question remained unresolved. Moreover, the fact that this great war was ended on a marked note of distrust and hostility towards minorities allowed these states to push these questions into the background. The skeleton measures that were initiated on and off, lacked meaning given the general absence of freedom and liberty that these systems suffered from.

In recent years the violent ethno-national resurgence which blazed across Soviet Union under the carpet. Union and East Europe after the collapse of Soviet empire has brought the issue of ethnic minorities to the surface again, posing serious threat to peace and security in the region.

The demand of the Hungarian minorities for autonomy at personal territorial and local level is an issue on which the minority and the majority are completely at odds. So far as Romania, Slovakia and Serbia are concerned the demand for autonomy is just a small step from complete secession and they perceive it as a threat to their very existence. However, neither have these states shown any inclination to concede other demands such as a bilingualism, right to pursue their own education by maintaining their own schools and having their own language as medium of instruction which is clear violation of international norms.

Of late Hungary has come to openly support the fight of Hungarians across the border for their demands and redressal of their grievances. The presence of Hungary is simultaneously a source of encouragement for the Hungarians in the adjoining states and a constant irritant for the respective states. Their 'passionate-irredentism' of the post Trianon years, is what perhaps even today makes the neighbouring states nervous when Hungary shows slightest interest in the affairs of Hungarian minority.

Hungary strongly holds the view that all Hungarians living outside Hungary constitute to be integral part of the Hungarian-nation and therefore, it is the duty of 'Hungary' to uphold and protect their rights. Article 6 of the Hungarian Constitution categorically states 'The Republic of Hungary assumes responsibility for the fate of Hungarians living outside the borders and encourages them to keep up their contacts with Hungary. However, emotional the issue of millions of Hungarians living across her borders might be for Hungary, it is well aware of its limitations. Border revision either with consent of the concerned states or with force, as a solution is completely ruled out. No country is willing to concede the Hungarians' demand and Hungary is not militarily capable to re-demarcate the map of Central and East Europe. Moreover, it is also not willing to accept the influx of Hungarians. The new citizenship law passed by the government on 1 June 1993 which defines Hungarian descent as the main criterion for citizenship and it requires the applicant for nationalization to have lived in Hungary for a minimum period of eight years instead of the earlier requirement of a domiclie for 3 years. Each country is well informed about the strengths and problems of each other and given the overriding concern of all East European states to integrate with Euro-Atlantic structures as NATO and European Union they are forced to tone down their reservations about each other and try and solve the problem through negotiations and dialogue. In spite of palpable tensions over the minority issue cooperation between defence ministers of Hungary-Romania-Slovakia was not affected. For instance, the Hungarian-Romanian agreement was signed in 1990 which called for wide ranging cooperation including cultural and scientific exchanges, a sharing of information between military historians, and the setting up of joint committees at various levels. A Hungarian Czecho-Slovak military agreement was signed in January 1991. Even when relations between the Meciar government was at its worst nevertheless military cooperation continued. On 18 March 1997 a military cooperation agreement in Budapest was signed between Yugoslav Chief of Staff and Hungarian officials. It aimed at cooperation in logistics and in airforce and to create direct relations between the two corps stationed on the border.

The problem of Hungarians in Central and East Europe has acquired extreme nationalistic overtones because of the particular way 'nation' and 'nationalism' are defined in this part of Europe. It is defined in ethnic and linguistic terms which necessarily excludes significant number of minorities who reside in the state. The problem is that to tide over uncertainty and hardship which accompany such fundamental systemic change that these societies are presently undergoing political elites are tempted to tress on the revival of mythological past, with its martial, cultural and ethnic glories and achievements. Extolling and talking in terms of Romanian Slovakia or Srebian nation would then exclude the Hungarian residing within their boundaries. Such a connotation of 'nation' also makes Hungary's interest and involvement unavoidable and vice versa.

Nations arguably can be defined in a number of ways. Nations can be defined either according to territories and the people who live within them or according to citizenship or according to ethnicity. Unlike territorial and citizenship nationalists ethnic groups which claim to be nations define their units by reference to history, myths, symbols and sentiments. In the complicated ethnic maze that East Europe presents accepting a purely political and legal nature of nation which is based on a written Constitutions with national membership defined solely in terms of citizenship irrespective of ethnicity would perhaps go a long way to check further ethnicity related conflicts and tensions.

Emerging from their recent communist past all states of East Europe are experiencing an aggressive re-emergence of nationalist sentiments and ethnic consciousness. The Hungarian spread out in considerable number across East Central Europe have managed to organise themselves effectively, fought elections and entered representatives bodies at national and local level. They have successfully drawn international attention to the problem and demands of their group. However, they should also abide by specific obligations to the state. Minority leaders need to recognize the state's constitutional and territorial integrity. While ethnic cultural and religious pluralism should be allowed to flourish, it cannot be allowed to fracture and undermine a democratic policy. Minorities thus should also shoulder the responsibility of strengthening emerging liberal democratic systems. Incessant demands on nascent democracies and opposing government on all counts may jeopardise such experiments and trigger an authoritarian turn around.

III
Economic Reforms in India & Hungary

9
The Systemic Transformation of CEE and Hungary

SÁNDOR SURÁNYI*

The transformation of socialist economies towards market-based systems entails an unusually wide range of tasks and problems. Studies of related topics of this transformation are rendered by the speed of changes and the lack of clear historical precedents. The study of the process and its analysis is all the more important, since on the one hand business is increasingly interested in exploring investment and marketing opportunities in these reforming countries in central eastern Europe and in other transforming economies, and on the other hand these economies are interested in foreign investments.

The restoration and functioning of the market and private ownership has become the major problem following the collapse of the communist systems in late 1980s. Since then—in spite of half a century long existence of the command economy—the transition economies have made significant strides toward the achievement of this goal, and CEE has been undergoing profound changes in all spheres of their economic and social life.

The effects of this transition are far-reaching for the international community as well. For instance, accelerated the process of globalisation, by diminishing the non-market based and non-democratic socio-economic systems in the world and created a more homogenous system of world economy and market. The transition is far from complete, and the process continues to exert a profound,—and from many point of views contradictory - social, political, and strategic impact.

*University Professor, Budapest University of Economic Sciences, Department of World Economy—Budapest.

The Transition from Central Planning to Market Economy, Differences and Similarities

Formerly these CEE countries usually were treated as integral part of the "socialist block". But in fact such a homogenous bloc has never existed. It contained very different countries (size, level of development, social structure, etc). It therefore is all the more unlikely that a common economic policy or receipt for the transition could be applied for them, Countries–in this respect too–cannot ignore their history and geography.

It is an important question what similarities or differences are there among transition economies shaping even the process of transition, not to speak about the possible (and desirable) peculiarities of the system that are being established. There are countries with considerable experience earned in the reformations of the rigid over-centralised system (for example Hungary's new economic mechanism since the late 1960s), while others followed tightly the orthodox - dogmatist model with much less room for private initiatives. This legacy profoundly influences both the importance of different market reforms and the way policy makers approach them.[1]

[1]Important to note that from the late 1960s economic reform attempts ahve been characterising to some extent every centrally planned economy. Hungary as a small and open economy faced the economic difficulties–created by the rigid, fully nationalised economy–earlier than the bigger and stronger ones. But we should not forget, that these early economic reforms–although some of them in Hungary were quite significant and substantially altered the original Soviet system of central planning and control–were designed for the preservation of socialist ownership relations and the one party dominance. They aimed at only an improvement of the command economy by the reintroduction of certain elements of market and commodity-money relations. The ones that were doomed to liquidation in the orthodox Marxist system as remnants of the "dyeing" capitalism.

But it has become clear, that these reforms (especially because of their half hearted implementation due to ideological considerations) failed to address the problems of inferior production quality and world market competitiveness, technological backwardness, growing idebtedness and economic stagnation.

Although the sudden collapse of the communist system and that of the forty-year Soviet occupation in Hungary came unexpectedly, most of the experts were fully aware of the weakness and the growing impotency of the over-nationalised and over-centralised party-state system and the corresponding command economy in a demanding world economy. The long-term deterioration of the Soviet economy paved the way for these events. The growing isolation caused more and more losses for the satellite countries, that the inefficient COMECON (CMEA) "*integration*" could never compensate–just contrary its own crisis has grown deeper and deeper.

In spite of the colourful composition of this group of countries there is often a claim for a "general transition theory", or at least a "standard prescription" for the transition.

As part of the post World War II, Soviet "Empire", the previous socialist countries have been subject of the largest experiment of a radical social change in modern history, namely the creation of a radically new socio-economic system, replacing the old outdated capitalist one. That experiment clearly failed, and on its ruins they inherited a command economy. Experience as well as scientific analysis unambiguously supported, that the command economies could not catch up and compete successfully with the market economies in the field of productivity, competitiveness, and technological innovations.

But CEE countries had to follow the ideological guidelines of the Soviet type "socialist economy" (nationalisations, forced co-operativisation, central planning, etc) which produced also essential similarities, therefore socialist economies share similar fundamental conditions from the point of view of the basic character of their former development, such as self sufficiency at bloc level, Soviet orientation of external economic relations, bloc level harmonisation of essential economic policy actions, Soviet control over external economic relations, application of imperative planning with the exclusion of the feed-backs (external and internal).

Establishing private property is another major challenge. Clearly defined property rights are necessary to generate an efficient response to market processes. The institutions that support market relations and shape ownership did not exist under central planning. The initial conditions in this respect were also different in the individual socialist countries. In some transition economies the need therefore to privatise has been more urgent while in others the process of growing private ownership in one way or another started earlier.

The replacement of a socio-economic system by another one and its complex unfolding is in itself a formidable task. At the centre in this case is the restoration of the market, from which all the potential and expected benefits of the transformation flow. In our case this task comes together with the corrections made on a structurally deformed economy on the one hand, and the creation of the conditions of a sustainable development on the other.

Following the systemic change the strategies and the performances of the individual countries are increasingly different. In this process the CEE (first of all Hungary, Poland and the Czech Republic) economies occupy a good position

Stabilisation and growth acceleration

Even if the environment for the market is restored, its signals cannot function in an environment of severe macroeconomic imbalances, for example with high inflation. Stabilisation therefore has become a vital component to transformation in fostering productivity and growth.

Another major challenge is to alleviate poverty, which is the most serious ill effect of the transition on vulnerable groups. An effective social policy may bring some compensation, but restoring economic growth is the most essential element in poverty reduction.

According to the experiences favourable policy reforms have been able to accelerate economic development, but we should be convinced that for the longer term, transition economies are not in need of just good economic policies, but strong and accountable institutions to support and implement the policies. Reforming legal and financial institutions as well as government itself, is critical.

The agenda for the transition economies depends on the stage of transition. If macroeconomic stabilisation and liberalisation have been largely achieved, the main tasks in CEE is the implementation of different institutional reforms in order to facilitate its integration into the European Union and entering into an increasingly integrated and institutionally harmonised world economy.

It is well-known that as part of the socialist bloc these countries have developed in isolation from the world economy, and their economic policy was based on autarky. Integration helps these economies to stabilise their achievements in the process of transition, and their membership in organisations such as the WTO, and OECD support their domestic institutional reconstruction and speed up their development. This latter is the major condition for the rising of the living standard to a level similar in advanced Western-European countries.

To close the gap between the standard of living and economic development as quickly as possible, it is necessary for CEE countries to attain higher production growth rates in comparison to developed economics. According to both practical experience and theoretical arguments it is possible by realizing as soon as possible an economic policy, similar–at least in its basic characteristics–to that of other rapidly growing economies in the world economy (highly efficient allocation of factors of production in the economy, combination of high level of domestic savings with inflow of FDI, create the conditions to rapidly adapt foreign advanced technology (with the help of FDI), support of education and investment in infrastructure, etc.

The Transformation and Growth Characteristics in Hungary

The socio-economic development of Hungary prior to the beginning of the systemic transformation in 1989 has been very contradictory.

As the most liberalised part of the Soviet bloc it has shown considerable stability after the 1956 revolution. But serious structural tensions have accumulated as a result of the rigidity of the planning, high investment, and the rapidly growing foreign indebtedness, which at the end of the 1980s stood at more than 50 percent of the GDP. A relatively acceptable (better than most of the bloc's average) living standard could be maintained only by increasing amount of foreign debts. This created especially unfavourable conditions for the beginning of the transition (similarly to Poland) while Czechoslovakia inherited much less foreign debt.

Structural deficiencies in the economy have been growing from the 1950s in the form of oversized mining, forced industrialisation with disproportional development of the heavy industry. Technology has become increasingly outdated with low general productivity and high cost level.

The countries export capacities have become non-competitive, the terms of trade deteriorated and had caused serious losses for the economy. The relative economic isolation was growing and the insufficient development of the so-called "socialist international integration" (COMECON) produced additional problems for the development and correct economic adjustment.

With the beginning of the systemic change in 1989 the centralised large production units in state sector started to disintegrate, and the number of small and medium scale enterprises grew rapidly. The share of enterprises having more than 300 employees decreased from almost 20% of the total in 1989 to less than 10%. The relatively rapid organisational changes at the same time were not followed by similar rate of structural changes in the economy. The GDP started to decline, while the country's foreign economic relations have been radically and successfully redirected towards the western world. In fact it was "simply" the restoration of the country's historical economic ties in Europe.

Fortunately, it has been supported by a rapid inflow of Foreign Direct Investments. A large share of the region's FDI has flown to Hungary and a structural change has been launched, which could start to narrow the gap from this point of view between Hungary and the Western market economies. It includes the increasing share of the services especially finance and banking in GDP, the dramatic decrease of the contribution of agriculture and mining as economically non-profitable activities.

The radical changes in the organisational structure can be illustrated by the fact, that the number of Joint Stock Companies between 1989 and 1996 increased from 307 to as much as 3186. Similarly, the number of LTD-s increased from 4485 to 102697 in 1996.

The share of the FDI in the enterprises having foreign investment increased from 61% in 1992 to 78% in 1995. It is positive, that in 1995 36% of FDI was invested in the manufacturing sector. (Palánkai)

The simplest definition of the *transformation* is *systemic change* a *self-liquidation* of the previous Soviet-bloc an the corresponding bureaucratic management of the economy. Its implementation takes a *period* of transition.

In the transforming countries this process is usually characterised by serious macroeconomic instabilities. The problems are many-sided and complex, partly objective and on the other hand subjective ("man-made") ones.

The suddenly opened possibility of transformation, and the idea of "creative destruction" invited over-ambitious expectations: instead of stagnation of the 80s there would come rapid economic growth, and narrowing gap between the development level and living conditions in Hungary and in Western-Europe.

After almost a decade of experience we may see the possibilities in a more realistic way. Considerable differences have been existing for long historical period of time between Hungary and West-Europe, and the systemic transformation is not for the immediate elimination of the gap between East and West Europe.

Another important experience is that the tasks of the transformation are complicated and time consuming. There has been no parallel task in the history of economics.

The long-term existence of the bipolar world system and the relative stability of the bloc policy of the great powers, did not encourage the scientific research and the theoretical preparations for the replacement of socialism by capitalism. The task has come suddenly and the territory was "uncharted", and the science was unprepared.

The macro-economic stabilisation has become a primary task in Hungary too without a considerable external assistance. (The only exception is East-Germany since it has received during the transformation not less than $700 billion from the western part of the unified country.)

In Western literature there were only textbook-like approaches based first of all on the experience of the Latin-American stabilisation or on that of other middle-income Western economies. They apply first of all the IMF standard prescription, a vision of the radical (shock) therapy. But here super-inflation, Balance of Payments, Trade, and Budget deficits faced by an economy having entirely different ownership relations.

The task therefore is more than that of a "simple" economic stabilisation, since this has come hand-in-hand with the unprecedented task of the transformation, *Internal* problems have come parallel with the deterioration of the *external* ones, namely with the collapse of the former COMECON export market. As one of the first consequences a serious decline came in the economy.

In view of the extent and the lasting character of economic decline, J, Kornai–one of the most prominent Hungarian economists –introduced the notion and term of "transformation crises", accompanying the switch to market economy.[2]

It has also been questioned whether it is just a transformation crisis with its specific tension, or it is the process of transformation itself, which has got into crises.

For a correct understanding of the economic decline we should take into account that the transformation in Hungary took place in a general crises situation, started in the early 1970s. Therefore in the transforming economies there is the process of transformation unfolding in a general crisis situation. The systemic change itself was the product of the crises. It was not only a part of the system, or some institution that faced crises, but the development pattern and organisation as a whole.

The consequences have been graver only because of inappropriate theories and policies. An important factor of the crisis–evolving on the basis of the heritage left behind by the post Second World War Soviet occupation and its ideological dominance–is the launching of the transformation without an appropriate theoretical foundation, correct strategy and external support.

In addition to this, the collapse of the Communism came at the time of international recession. There are difficulties, even with the correct assessment of the extent of the crises in quantiative terms. (Problems with statistics: price distortions, high share of black economy).

There is no room for the application of the anti-cyclical policy of the western countries for the transformation crises.

There have also been several external shocks after 1990, which imposed additional costs on transforming economies first of all

---

[2]Kornai emphasised the importance of the correct diagnosis as the most important precondition for the correct therapy. The identification of the crisis phenomena is a major step ahead, in comparison to liberal "transformation euphoria" of 1990-91. It is also essential for the formulation of a correct economic policy.

because of the geographical location of Hungary, and hindered the recovery of her economy.[3]

Due to the peculiar circumstances the economic policy of this period featured many examples of "copying". Instead of elaborating own transformation strategy, the government has been following in essence a monetarist economic policy emerged almost two decades ago in developed market economies under entirely different conditions. This approach is unsuitable to solve accumulated structural problems, and the effect of the deterioration of external conditions.

In 1989-90 Hungary alone chose the model of social market economy in the region, opted for a course of transformation and modernisation, setting out from peculiarities of the previous Hungarian development. But in the course of practical implementation emphasis was laid on copying dogmatic liberalism, which was unsuitable for addressing crises phenomena, and on one-sided treatment of institutional elements of distribution.

Therefore today there is an agreement that launching the transformation without appropriate theoretical base, strategic concept and preparation, with belief in spontaneity has increased social costs of transformation and the risk of destabilisation.[4]

The economic tasks are tremendous. The restoration of the fee market system include:

- the transformation of enterprises (from directive tools of state planning to risk-taking organisations with financial responsibility for their decisions, the introduction of different new forms of enterprises),

---

[3]For instance as a consequence of the Gulf War in 1990 caused a loss of important market and credit repayment. Similarly Hungary has also suffered losses due to the Yugoslav civil war and the embargo reaching $2.5 billion between 1992 and 1996 (loss in foreign trade, transit fees, unpaid debts.)

[4]Another area of conflict is the social expectation about the equality. It is a problem even in capitalist countries. But in the "socialism" an utopian apporoach was adopted with the idea of equal consumption. Because of the relatively low level of economic development, the shortages were unavoidable. The eradication of shortage has come with difficult consequences for the masses.

- the establishment of an appropriate banking system (two-tier banking: National Bank, commercial banks),
- establishment of commodity and stock-markets,
- reformation of the accounting system (providing reliable information for business decisions of the enterprises, instead of that for central planning). In respect of
- the elimination of the fixed price system together with the system of state subsidies, and the establishment of an economically rational price system based on correct taxation.

The establishment of ownership relations adequate for the market economy includes the privatisation, resulting in the creation of an ownership structure based on (domestic and foreign) private owners, replacing the dominance of the collective (state and co-operative) ownership characteristic of the planned economies.

The liberalisation (deregulation from state control) of the economy has special significance in the area of foreign trade, price formation, wages, and the allocation of resources. Important to note that liberalisation means the elimination of the open, administrative forms of government interference in the economy. The indirect forms of government regulations remain even in a liberalised economy.

A very important requirement is the modification of the structure of the production. It means the elimination of the autarchic structures, characteristic of the COMECON co-operation (resulted in technological backwardness), the replacement of import-substitution policy with an export oriented competitive development. It makes the integration into the most advanced parts of the world economy possible.

A comprehensive reform is needed in the field of the community consumption partly with the introduction of the self-bearing of burdens by the local communities, and the decrease of the re-distributive role of the state budget.

Economic consolidation and the correct management of the

foreign debts[5] involves the relative stability of prices, an acceptable level of the budget deficit (3-4%), operation of capital market, international liquidity and solvency, and the convertibility of the domestic currency.[6]

Experience of the transition proves that the social costs are greater and the time of economic stagnation is longer than it has initially been expected on the basis of the political assumptions.

The measures taken in different areas of the economy are in **inter relation**. It is very important to establish a correct order among them in order to avoid the neutralisation of each other's effect, or the creation of contradictory circumstances.

Foreign Economic Relations of Hungary: A Radical Reorientation Towards the Western European Countries

Hungary's foreign trade is different from the neighbouring small developed Western European countries in two respects : first, 20-25 percent of its export is of *agrarian* origin, which has a special

---

[5]For the correct management of the accumulated foreign debts it is of utmost important to take into account the requirements of the economic consolidation and modernisation. It should not cause economic shrinking not even stagnation, but rather growth.

[6]Regarding the transition, various approaches could be seen in different countries in the practice as well as in the literature. Two extremes can be observed, namely a quick dramatic leap into the market economy, and a gradual evolutionary transition, based on the hypothesis of the existence of a dual economy (market and planned parts).

One of our prominent economists J. Kornai elaborated an intermediary third one, namely a shock-therapy for stabilisation and a longer period for systemic change with privatisation.

The measures that are being taken are of different character. Some tasks require short term actions (for example applicaiton of restrictive monetary policy) but most of them are time consuming (privatisation, import liberalisation), taking several years.

There are aims that can be implemented in one step, but most of them can be fulfilled only gradually (a desired market order can be established by regulations, but the price mechanism or convertibility only gradually, through series of regulatory actions).

significance for her undisturbed economic development; second, in the industrial export, the share of Trans National Corporations is (although in recent years it is rapidly growing) relatively small, therefore the industrial policy must also encourage the competitiveness of large number of small enterprises.

The essential changes that has taken place in the economy as a result of the transformation are also reflected in the structural and relational composition of the external economic relations of the country.

Significant changes have taken place in the composition of imports. Due to the consequences of transformation and the need for structural and technological modernisation, the Hungarian economy (together with other Central European transforming economies) is characterised by relatively high import propensity.

As a result of import liberalisation rapid inflow of technologically advanced goods from developed countries took place. The value of import of OECD from CEE countries increased by 40% between 1990 and 1994, but its export to the region increased by as much as 80%.

This has unavoidably led to growing Balance of Trade and Balance of Payments deficits in the countries concerned. The accumulation of growing deficit in the transforming European economies continued in 1995 and 1996 too, except Hungary, where–as a result of a strict and successful programme of macroeconomic stabilisation - an export-led growth was achieved with 22 percent and 23 percent export growth respectively, which has further strengthened in 1997.

In the reforming countries, the opening started alongwith the internal reforms. The main steps in the reorientation of foreign economic relations includes the elimination of the state monopoly of foreign trade, and the liberalisation of imports. At the beginning of the transformation 41 large foreign trade state companies controlled 81 percent of the Hungarian foreign trade. Their share fell to 15% in 1992 and about 15,000 companies started to conduct foreign trade. In the field of imports they abolished licensing. The Hungarian import has been liberalised as early as in 1992-93 and domestic production has been exposed to import competition. Liberalisation

Relational Structure of Import

	1989	1995
Other transforming or non-market economies	44.3	24.0
Market economies	55.7	76.0
EU	29.0	61.5
3rd world	9.9 (1990)	5.5

Source: Hungarian Statistical Office

steps also included considerably tariff reductions, and drastic reduction of state subsidies. Due to the association to EU and other trade liberalisation agreements (EFTA, CEFTA, other bilateral ones) for at least 70-75 percent of the tariff should be *eliminated in a 10 years time.*

Some of the changes are of positive character in the sense that they are supporting the reorientation of Hungary's economic ties. But some harm to the economy of the country can also be identified, namely creating a new kind of one-sided dependence towards Western Europe at the expense of others.

The commodity structure of the Hungarian export in the past has been characterised by *low* processing level. There has been little change in this up to the middle of the 1990s. In the second half the decade there is a progress of manufacturing industrial export by Trans National Corporations. The share of this group of goods in total export has been about 35-38 percent.

The share of investments goods, machinery, transport means declined very ıapidly from 24 percent of total export in 1989 to 12.6 percent in 1991 and remained on this level. The main reason of this is the collapse of COMECON, which has been a traditional, although not a demanding market for the relatively obsolete industrial goods and transport means. At the same time powerful western companies offered loans and favourable payment conditions for these markets. It was also the error of the Hungarian policy makers that they lost their interest in Eastern (post-Soviet) markets. The share of Russia in the Hungarian foreign trade has decreased to a mere 5 percent in the export, and 9.6 percent in the import (later comprising mainly energy carriers).

Important new development on the export side was the increasing share of consumer goods, as a reflection of change in the production structure. Its share increased from 15.7 percent in 1989 to 26.7 percent in 1994. Similarly the share of foods and live animals increased from 20.5–26.7 percent.

The change in the import composition has been smaller. As a result of the import-liberalisation the share of machinery, transport means, investment goods, and consumer goods has steadily increased partly as a result of the previous shortages and the isolation of the country. Today in these fields there is a relative oversupply. The situation is the same as in western economies. But as a result of the sharp income differentiation in Hungary and the relative low level of income of the majority of the population no immediate further increase can be expected. The most important groups in the import side are the energy carriers (11%), materials, semi-finished goods, spare-parts (42%), machinery, transport means, and other investment goods (20%).

The export and import structure are illustrated by the following tables:

Relational Structure of Export

	1989	1995
Other transforming or nonmarket economies	47.3	24.4
Market economies	52.7	75.6
EU	24.8	62.8
3rd world	8.4	3.9

Source: Hungarian Statistical Office.

In the years 1996 and 1997 the process of integration of Hungary into the **European Union** has been continuing and its share in the Hungarian foreign trade has increased to 71 percent.

A special aspects of this radical structural shift is (an unnecessary) decline of economic relations with the 3rd World Countries. We earned quite a good reputation and positions (buses, electrical appliances, bikes, etc) and the restoration of the market position shall be more difficult. All the more so since there is a new situation with sharpening competition of developed market economies.

The changes are similar to that of the export structure. From the trade statistics of the 90s it is clear that there is a strong orientation towards the EU and within it towards the German economy. Austria has the second place in this respect and it is of characteristic, that China's share in the middle of the 90s was only 1 percent. The share of the USA and North-America is smaller than desirable (US share in import in 3.1 percent in export 4 percent).

Foreign trade reflects the transition. New positions are not very stable and the country has lost most of its previous markets in favour of new ones, where it will be difficult to restore the positions.

Profound Policy Modifications in Favour of Foreign Capital Investments

The joint ventures and foreign direct investments (FDI) play strategic role in the integration of the Hungarian economy into global world economy. Therefore the development in this field characterises to a considerable extent the process of transformation in Hungary and in other CEE countries as well.

Till the end of the 1980s the interest of the foreign capital as well as the possibility for investment was very limited in the whole region. The acceleration of investments started only after 1989 as a result of liberalisation measures and one of the most striking policy changes has taken place in respect of FDI. Between 1972 (the year of the first joint venture legislation) and 1984 only 30 joint ventures were set up.

The real liberalisation measures came only after 1986. In 1989, at the beginning of the systemic transformation the principle of "national treatment" was adopted in respect of foreign companies, and all internationally accepted enterprise forms were allowed to establish on the basis of a simplified procedure, without any sectoral or other limitations.

The *liberalisation includes* such measures as free profit repatriation and the tariff-free importation of the goods connected with investment and operation of the joint venture.

As a result of this the foreign investments in the CEE region grew from $2.3 billion to 56 billion between 1990 and 1996. In Hungary by the end of 1998 the cumulative amount of direct productive capital investments have exceeded $18bn in 25,700 ventures, the largest amount among the countries of the region, $1800 per person since 1989, almost twice the per capita share of the Czech Republic and nine times that of Poland. Companies in foreign ownership or foreign participation produce 32 per cent of GDP, 45 per cent of manufacturing value added and employ some 25 per cent of private sector workers.

The joint ventures are dominated in terms of number of enterprises by German and Austrian firms, but in terms of the volume of invested capital, the American companies are in a better position. In Hungary about 1/3 of total direct investment is American while about 2/3 of foreign trade is conducted with the states of EU and EFTA. This has a considerable stabilising effect on the Hungarian economy.

Convertibility as Means of Reorienting External Economic Relations

It has been a priority objective in several socialist countries already in the 1980s, and they were trying to create its preconditions during economic reforms. Changes that started in 1989 created new conditions for the convertibility too. Political and ideological barriers (systemic constraints against convertibility) have been rapidly eliminated. General liberalisation, "grey" and "black" currency markets, rapid opening to the West characterised the new tendency of development.

But the introduction of full convertibility and the establishment of a real market system have been an "uncharted" territory. No "instructions" for this were available from any existing theoretical models. The science was totally unprepared and previous reform attempts beyond certain ideological limits were mostly failures. Not even West European analogies could be used (EPU, etc)[7]. The unique situation was created by the fact that the tasks of stabilisation and liberalisation have emerged simultaneously, parallel with the need of economic restructuring and systemic change.

There have been varieties of actual convertibility attempts in the transforming economies.[8]

In the Polish and Hungarian cases the currencies as a first step were made only internally convertible (only for the residents). Foreign participants of joint ventures were considered as residents. Total free convertibility was only a longer-term goal, and the currency of Hungary is now practically freely convertible.

Introducing convertibility, governments have voluntarily submitted themselves to an objective external constraint, exceeding sometime even the "conventional" IMF requirements.

---

[7]In the socialist system the inflow of FDI was totally rejected first of all on ideological ground. In Hungary within the framework of economic reforms and the "opening" towards world economy foreign capital investments were gradually liberalised from the 1970s mostly in the framework of joint venture legislation. But these were fairly restrictive measures at the beginning.

[8]In practice four different paths toward convertibility can be mentioned:

A. Full convertibility through monetary union in case of East-Germany. It is not a model to be followed because of its unique character. But it is instructive in the sense, that it shows the macro-economic costs of a swift transition to the market relations.

B. Convertibility through shock-therapy. The textbook example of this is the stabilisation policy of Poland. The convertibility–started with hyperinflation–has played prime role in the shock-threapy.

C. Convertibility through gradual import liberalisation. This involves limited convertibility, as it existed in Hungary, involving full import liberalisation, uniform exchange rate, no "parallel" foreign exchange market.

D. Convertibility in the dual-track system.It is the cover name of a fairly heterogenous attempt as it exists in China. Two different foreign trade and monetary regulations coexist (currency "rationing" and liberal exchange). In a pathological case (for instance Poland in the peiod of hyperinflation) dual system may develop into a two-currency system, i.e. foreign exchange is used for internal transactions too.

Privatisation: the most important strategic element of economic transformation

Socialism was defined as public sector economy, and the Communist Party leadership rejected any privatisation until the end of 80s. On the ground of the Soviet model, over-nationalisation has taken place, and about 90 per cent of the agriculture has been collectivised.

But even in the most severe Stalinist system, elements of private sector survived. It prevailed in the 1980s in retail trade, in repair, services, and handicrafts, loose forms of co-ops were also developing in which the members could retain their ownership over their lands. Entrepreneurship in the public sector also increased (profit motives in management in Hungary was introduced and started to develop after 1956), joint ventures could gradually increase, not to speak about the black economy, which was obviously also based on private "business".

In the second half of the 80s leading economists came to the conclusion, that it is not possible to successfully create market relations without privatisation (even this is not new: Von Mises, von Hayek and others long time ago expressed similar opinion).

The privatisation in fact started in 1988-89 with the issue of the first generation of Privatisation Law in the framework of the new Company Law in 1988. It included the transformation of the former (State and co-operative) enterprises into joint stock companies. The limits for private employees were removed and full foreign ownership of firms has been allowed. The Law has established institutional and legislative framework for privatisation. In the second and third wave of privatisation the main target was to accelerate and complete the process in 1997-98, which in fact has been fulfilled. Recently 85 per cent of the GDP is generated outside of the government sector.

The essence of privatisation is the transfer or exchange of public assets to private persons. It should lead to the dominance of the private sector in the economy. We may distinguish real and the so called "surface" privatisation. In the first case private or legal persons obtain dominant position in previously state-owned assets. As for the second case there are several possibilities. Reciprocal cross-ownership of companies, all owned by the state in final instance, or transfer of state assets to holdings, or property management funds. In these cases only transitional new owner has been created, and the real privatisation in fact is still to come.

As we stress the result of privatisation, it is the creation of an efficiently functioning private economy. It must involve real owners who are ready to invest and take the risk, rational company structure, macro-economic institutional and legal framework for efficient and profitable economic activity, proper macro-economic conditions.

Its beneficial effects are supposed to improve the efficiency, increase the productivity, modernise the economic structure. The consumers gain through improved supply as a result of competitive environment, there are also direct and indirect budgetary gains, creation of financial markets, increase of competitiveness and better image of the country, attraction of further foreign investment.

Ways of Creating Private Sector Economy

There are four major ways: new establishment, foreign private investments and establishment of new firms (green field investments), privatisation. In Western countries it comprises the selling of companies or state stocks, sometimes auctions and tenders, or the so called initial public offering (IPO) is applied.

Here, the first step has been the transformation to join stock company (commercialisation). In Hungary this started in 1988, and was finished in 1993. In other transforming European economies there are several different forms of privatisation (central direct selling of assets, open tender, etc.) An important form is the manager and employee privatisation.

Management buy-outs were also broadly practised in the West "Manager" privatisation started in Hungary and Poland in 1988. In Hungary it was also called "spontaneous privatisation". Later this process was stopped as "nomenclature" privatisation by the newly elected (first democratic) government, saying that in this way the previous party and state-bureaucrats could acquire considerable state assets.

The "simplified" or expert privatisation has been launched by the 1995 Law. According to this, smaller enterprises (less than 500 employees) can be privatised by the managers and the employees in a decentralised way.

The voucher (or coupon) privatisation has been applied in a number of transforming economies in Europe and elsewhere, namely in Slovakia, Estonia, Lithuania, Mongolia, Romania, etc. In Hungary it has been rejected, but compensation bonds (introduced and applied in Hungary) can be considered similar to vouchers.

The vouchers in fact are securities, issued by the state. Once used in an auction, the voucher is cancelled. But in practice there are several problems with the voucher system. It is difficult to determine who is eligible, how should it be distributed, how can it be used. In most countries all citizens above 18 are eligible, but in this way no real and responsible owners are created.

Privatisation through selling companies to foreign firms was also broadly applied (in Hungary in the food processing industry such as sugar, alcohol, tobacco, paper industry), but in ailing and declining enterprises the foreign investors are not interested.

Re-privatisation is a returning of formerly nationalised companies into private hands. In transforming economies it means direct or indirect restoration of original ownership on nationalised or confiscated properties (this method could be applied mostly in Germany).

Lastly we may mention the simple shrinkage of state sector (bankruptcies, liquidation, cutting production, closing down factories), since some companies cannot be saved.

EU aid to the "East" for the Transformation

"Today it is the Kremlin's corridors that are crawling with western advisers"–wrote The Economist in 1993. One team advises V Chernomirdin, the prime minister, on economic strategy. Another is a powerful influence on Russia's State Property Agency's privatisation programme. Third team has drawn up a plan for streamlining Russia's central government and cutting down the number of ministries. Fourth helped to bring about last year's agreement among the republics of the former SU on the establishment of a clearing system for their trade. The European Union's "TACIS" programme pays for these and other advisers. The EU runs a similar programme named "PHARE" for Central East European transforming countries.

Both are managed by the European Commission, and supply about 70% of the West's technical aid–the transfer of know how, rather than cash or credit. But there are complaints about the Commission's bureaucratic and slow management, which deteriorated its effectiveness.

The EU gives priority to areas such as privatisation, banking, environment, food distribution, reform of the civil service. In Hungary on the basis of PHARE they established a network of advice centres for small business, a new stock-market trading system, a statistical office, a land registry, equipment for measuring air pollution, etc. The government could not have afforded all these projects. But both consultants and recipients are criticising the Commission's handling of its programme. It is slow moving since the commission's procedure for dispensing money is too long. First: it works out an "indicative programme" with the governments concerned, laying down priorities. Then it selects specific projects for an action programme, it hires consultants to manage each project, through public tender for the larger contract. Consultants typically have started works on projects 12-18 months after the process began. In 1997 and 1998 the amount of PHARE-aid was 104 and 87 million ECU respectively.

Bilateral aid schemes follow simpler procedures, and get off the ground quicker. Britain's Know How Fund sends in consultants 8-12 weeks after receiving a request.

The liberalisation of prices and trade started in 1992. The old economy was not so much underdeveloped, but miss-developed. It was over-industrialised, and so inefficient, that in the process of manufacturing it actually subtracted value from its raw-materials. The changes in the way of thinking can be illustrated by the fact that a few years ago a debate was about whether private property was a desirable thing.

Concluding Remarks

In the past forty years rigid over-centralised and over-nationalised economy characerised the so called socialist construction in Hungary and other CEE countries. A characteristic feature of the central planning was the ineffective allocation of resources, which had a negative impact on their growth potential. The principal aim of the systemic transformation in these countries was the restoration of the commodity and market relations, and the creation of prerequisites for higher and sustainable growth and the termination of their economic isolation from the international community. Although considerably achievements can be observed in this transition, the process has proven more difficult and complex, the necessary time is longer and the social costs are higher than it was previously expected. One of the most important problem is that there are no clear theoretical guidelines for the transition. The science was unprepared for this unprecedented task. The past almost a decade in this process provides evidences for the analysis of some of the conflicts and achievements of this transition, although–in spite of some basic similarities–the tasks and conditions are widely different from country to country. Hungary is one of the leading "reformers" and it earned valuable experience in the transition too, but in spite of this–similarly to other transforming countries–the first period of transition produced serious decline in the economic performances. These countries need not only to stabilise their economies but also to create the institutions necessary to the operation of a market system. The macroeconomic stabilisation therefore has become an urgent task. The Hungarian Stabilisation package put into place in 1995 and the structural reforms pursued since the beginning of the transtion began to bear fruit in 1997 and 1998 as growth accelerated, inflation and unemployment fell, while the fiscal and the external balances improved.

10
The Hungarian Economy: From Reforms to Transformation

GULSHAN SACHDEVA*

Introduction

In this paper an attempt has been made to look into the Hungarian economic transformation, the policies implemented by different governments and their outcomes. Since many of the economic reforms were introduced even before the demise of the socialist system, the first section of the paper briefly highlights reform ideas and some major reforms implemented before 1990. Separate sections also deal with privatisation, foreign trade and foreign direct investment.

1. Pre 1990 Reforms

The Hungarian socialist project used to be most innovative in Eastern Europe. The Stalinist model functioned in Hungary only between 1949 to 1953. As a result, despite a centrally planned system in place, we can find evidences of the beginning of the marketization process even in the fifties. Influenced by intellectual opinion during the so-called "first wave of economic mechanism debate" (Szamuely, 1982), some practical measures, like the abolition of compulsory deliveries in agriculture and some limited profit sharing for enterprises, were introduced. Later academic discussions (for scholarly discourse at that time see Berend, 1990, ch. 17; Swain, 1992, ch. 4; Szamuely, 1984) resulted in so-called New

*Dr. Gulshan Sachdeva is Assistant Professor, in the Centre for Russian, Central Asian and East European Studies, SIS JNU New Delhi.

Economic Mechanism (NEM). The 1966 conception and 1968 implementation of comprehensive reforms was a major turning point in Hungarian economic life when a serious attempt was made at combining the elements of plan and market. The reform was designed to make resource allocation more efficient by way of introducing market or quasi-market mechanisms while keeping the basic characteristics of a planned system intact. The reform blueprint envisioned autonomous profit maximizing state enterprises operating in a competitive environment. It was also aimed at limiting the role of central price determination and linking domestic prices to international prices. Although Kornai (1986) denies that Hungarian NEM was close to market socialism of the Lange type, yet Swain (1992) demonstrates that the "naive" conception of the "1968 paradigm" was totally in line with the market socialism ideas of W. Brus, T. Liska and Elson, where simple reproduction is left to the regulated market but central control is retained over extended reproduction. The applicability of a particular type of "market socialism" to the Hungarian model may be a problematic issue,[1] but no one can deny that this reform brought far reaching institutional and behavioural changes in economy.

Apart from reducing the influence of the state and the emphasis on competitive forces, the 1968 reform started new types of experiments in the economy. During the collectivization drives of the early fifties and 1959-61 period, members of cooperatives were allowed to keep small household plots, mainly for production to

---

[1]The standard text book model of market socialism is usually Oskar Lange's "general equilibrium socialism" which concentrates on the primacy of the roles of prices in resource allocation. However there are varieties of market socialist ideas which differ in their attitude towards the nature of the markets and competition. It ranges from the manchestertum viewpoint of market socialism as embodied in the 19th century models of E Duhring and T. Herztka, through the works of pre-war socialist thinkers such as M. Breit. O. Lange, H. Dickinson or E. Oppenhheimer (see Chilosi, 1992), to the post-war models of market socialism dicussed by Yugoslav and other East European reformers and a recent "competitive socialism" (Bardhan and Roemer 1992). As things are always different in practice than theory, the Hungarian model was later described: although not anarchic, yet neither plan nor market (See Richet, 1989).

cover family needs. By the end of the 1960s, many restrictions on these plots were lifted. This resulted in impressive food production and improvement in the supply of basic foodstuff in the cities. Encouraged by these results bureaucrats extended similar opportunities to other sectors, mainly housing construction, restaurants and small shops as the 1968 reform had already promoted a multi sectoral development as a lasting factor of the economy. As a result a relatively balanced consumer market remained a specific feature of Hungarian socialism, unlike many other CMEA countries in the seventies and eighties. The increasing tolerance for household agriculture from 1965 and small scale part time businesses from 1982 resulted in the birth, rise and flourishing of the *second economy.* The millions of semi proletarians, semi-entrepreneurs started creating a whole new economic system outside, under or above the state economy. The process of embourgeoisement which had been interrupted just two decades before, was revived (Szélenyi, 1990).

The evolution of NEM stopped in the early 1970's and some backward steps were taken. As a result, in the mid-seventies, what Antal (1979) called the mechanism of "detailing regulators" were functioning. This was a setback to the process of marketization because central interference expanded, the role of central investment became decisive, sectoral management revived and the number of central development programmes increased. However, surprisingly, *the second economy* was gradually expanding even in this period when the overall reform was facing serious political opposition. In fact the growing recognition of the deficiencies of the dominantly state owned economy, the need for better utilization of tangible and intangible resources and the pressures of striving after additional incomes convinced the leadership to tolerate these activities (Roman, 1992).

The centralization drive ended in 1978 and the country entered into the second decade of reforms (see Brada and Dobozi, 1989-90; Clarke, 1989) and the so called third wave of reforms (see Hewett, 1983) started. This wave was aimed towards the completion of the 1968 blueprint through introduction of a conclusive market building set of arrangements. New guidelines were adopted for "competitive prices" mainly to connect most producer prices to world market prices. Further, these producer prices were required to be tied to consumer prices via uniform turnover tax. Many industrial branch ministries were abolished for a single Ministry of Industry, mainly to end the disliked central interference. Independent foreign trade rights were given to many enterprises aiming at adjustable arrangements with the rapidly changing world market environment. Manifold exchange rates were already substituted by a unified exchange rate in 1976 to bring the Forint in line with other currencies. For strengthening competition, a few monopolistic state trusts were broken up and attempts were made towards the expansion of small scale businesses and cooperatives. Additionally, contract work associations were permitted to operate within state enterprises. In the mid 1980s, in an attempt to build "genuine" worker self management, a considerable portion of property rights were given to enterprise councils. Later the mono-bank structure was reshaped with the creation of many commercial banks. Some form of capital market was created with the introduction of government bonds. A bankruptcy law was passed in 1986 and the old tax system was replaced with the value added tax and personal income tax from January 1988 (for details also see Boote and Somogyi 1991; and Mizsei and Török, 1990).

Compared to the "golden age" of the first few years of NEM, these later measures failed to improve the measured macroeconomic performance of the economy though it did change the entrepreneurial environment. The second economy, which was responsible for some economic prosperity in the seventies and early eighties, had exhausted its energies. As Szelényi (1989, p. 224) asked, "how could one expect such a highly restricted second economy to rescue a mismanaged national economy? ... one cannot expect that part time farmers who produce tomatoes or lettuees after working hours on one acre family plots will integrate the Hungarian economy into the world market". The second economy opportunities were extended to the industrial sector through Civil Law Partnerships (PJT). Work partnerships (GMK) and Enterprise Worker Partnerships (VGMK) etc. (see Laky, 1991), but these activities "could not become the household plots of industry" (Mizesi, 1990, p. 8). The industrial sector continued to produce moderate quality products in unprofitable ways which resulted in consistently declining export market shares. Additionally, the state sector was unable to produce enough high quality goods even to absorb the incomes generated through the second economy. About a third or half of the money heavily borrowed from international markets was to be spent on Western consumer goods (Szelényi, 1989, p. 224).

Despite the measures discussed above, throughout the eighties, enterprise budgets remained soft, prices still suffered distortions, a truly competitive environment was still lacking, effective enterprise autonomy remained restrained and profits could not become the correct indicators of enterprises' efficiency. The disappointing economic situation of the 1980s compelled many economists to look beyond the canonized objectives of 1968. From the early 1980s onwards a new viewpoint starts to emerge: that the socialist system cannot grow intensively because intensively growing economies are not based on state ownership. Therefore a fundamental requirement to overhaul the economic system, it was argued, was the restructuring of the ownership pattern.

In fact, the important works which have overviewed the process of socialist reforms in Hungary like Berend (1990), Clarke (1989), Revesz (1990) and Swain (1992) have analysed the dynamics of an inherently contradictory strategy of reforms. These reforms were an attempt to reconcile one party rule with a fundamentally decentralised economy. Although never conceived and coordinated in its entirety, scholars started to question the pillars on which the state socialism rested. There was a lively debate on the structure of public ownership of the means of production (see Sachdeva, 1994), abolition of state monopoly of foreign trade, and giving up reliance on trade with the East.

As a result of all these debates the ground for transforming rather than reforming the socialist economy was already prepared in the late 1980s. From the final months of 1988, till May 1990, when the coalition government was formed, there was a period of transition. During these months of negotiation and the period between signing of the agreement on the organisation of free elections and the formation of new government, many new political parties emerged on the scene. Large numbers of intellectuals who participated in economic debates in the early and mid 1980s, found themselves very close to different political parties. In the spring of 1990 new political elites and economists found a unique opportunity to implement their ideas. Three radical programmes of transformation were prepared. The first one was a book by the famous Hungarian Economist Janos Kornai (1990)–*The Road to Free Economy*. The Second was the proposal of the Blue Ribbon Commission (1990). The third was the Bridge Group. This programme was never published in English. But two-thirds of the group assumed government position in the first post-communist government. All three programmes outlined pluralism into the economy and society, and argued for radical transformation towards a market economy.

2. Initial Conditions

As table 1 of initial conditions in Hungary shows, the country entered the post-socialist era in a relatively favourable position compared to other countries in Eastern Europe. But it had suffered double digit inflation since 1988, and government budget had been in deficit since 1985. The foreign debt, which had been stabilised in 1982-83, already then with the help of IMF, had again increased since 1985, and had become highest in per capita terms in Eastern Europe (see Lavingne, 1994). Moreover, the economy, though more "reformed" and "modified" than other socialist countries, was still a socialist economy with 90 per cent economy under state ownership including more than 80 per cent land under state or collective agriculture.

3. Systemic Transformation

When transformation started in Hungary, some Western scholars were asserting that arguments about ends of transformation could wait (Sachs, 1990); and there was no single declared road map which could guide the way to the new system (Fischer and Gelb, 1991). But Hungary was the first former Eastern bloc country where the concept of "social market economy" was proposed as a model for the transformation of the economic system (Hieronymi,

Table 1
Initial Conditions in Hungary

Population (in Million, mid-1989)	10.6
GNP Per Capita (in 1989 US$)	2,590
GNP Growth (average annual rate in percentage, at constant prices	
1970's	4.5
1980's	0.5
Real GDP 1979-1988 (%)	1.7
Average Inflation 1979-1988	8.1
Administered Prices (% of total)	15
State Ownership (%)	90
External Debt/GDP (1990)	65
External Debt Service Ratio (1990)	57
Exports to CMEA (1990)	
% of total exports	43
% of GDP	16
Govt's expenditure as % of GDP (1989)	61
Govt's deficit as % of GDP (1989)	–2.5
Unemployment rate (1989)	0.5%
Structure of Agriculture (1989)	
State Farms	
Number	128
Average size (ha)	7,598
Percentage of land	12
Collective Firms	
Number	1,270
Average Size (ha)	4,195
Percentage of land	70
Private Sector	
Percentage of total land	15

Source: Bruno (1994), Johnson (1997) and various publications of the UN, IMF and the World Bank.

1991, p. 28). This means an economy having market mechanisms, basic economic rights and freedoms, correction of market failures and a strong social policy. Many Hungarian scholars also shared the same view. For example, Csaba (1991) envisaged the end of post-socialist transformation as a modern social market economy. Bauer (1990) also felt that the Hungarian market economy must be *soziale marketwirtschaft*. But interestingly, the issue of "social market economy" is missing in the later writings dealing with Hungarian transformation.

By virtue of its early start and due to different political and economic reasons, there was a near consensus view rejecting the idea of shock therapy (Major 1991) and the country followed a policy of gradual changes (Mizsei 1993). Under the new political setting, many of the previously declared, but half heartedly implemented policies, needed to be reasserted rather than revised. This was true for both internal and external liberalisation (Hare 1991; Marer 1991).

In the fall of 1990, the Hungarian government adopted a comprehensive medium term programme designed to put in place the most important elements, including institutional framework, of a contemporary market economy. In march 1991, the government launched a four-year action programme for Stabilisation and Convertibility (*Stabilisation*...1991). The government committed to reduce the role of the State in the economy through privatisation and other measures, and through transcending the operation of the free market. Another crucial element of the programme was tight financial and budgetary policy.

One interesting point about Hungarian programme is that usually it is considered that unlike Poland and Czechoslovakia, it refrained from imposing a "shock-therapy", even though the core programme was almost the same. The only major difference was that economic activity was more liberalised in Hungary. As a result, the structural components were less radical. The Hungarian government played that card well. On the one hand, it projected to international community that the country was a leading reformer. And domestically, it was always stressed that a big-bang approach was avoided.

The success of this programme was uneven. Considerable progress was achieved with respect to price and trade liberalisation. Subsidies were reduced from 12 per cent to about 4 per cent in a few years. But progress proved very difficult in the areas of fiscal reforms, as well as in enterprise and bank restructuring[2]. During the early 1990's Hungary's fiscal position deteriorated remarkably, with the

---

[2]For details of fiscal problems see Kornai 1992, and for enterprise restructuring (see Chapter 5 of UN Economic Survey of Europe 1993-94).

deficit increasing to more than 8 per cent in 1994. The fiscal deterioration was also inflected in growing external current account deficit financed by official borrowing and capital inflows (Table 2).

Table 2
General Government Revenue & Expenditure in Hungary
(percentage of GDP)

	1989	1990	1991	1992	1993	1994
Total Revenue	**59.6**	**57.9**	**53.9**	**53.9**	**55.8**	**53.3**
Profit tax	8.1	8.2	5.6	2.5	2.0	2.0
Wage tax & social security contributions	19.8	19.8	19.9	21.0	21.9	20.7
Vat, excise & custom duties	18.9	15.6	14.0	14.9	15.8	14.9
Other taxes & non-tax revenue	12.8	14.3	14.3	15.5	16.1	15.7
Total Expenditure	**60.9**	**57.0**	**56.9**	**60.7**	**62.5**	**62.0**
Goods & Services	20.5	18.7	18.5	18.8	20.3	18.3
Interest payments	4.5	5.4	5.9	5.5	5.0	6.8
Social security benefits	14.4	15.7	18.2	18.3	18.1	17.6
Subsidies	12.1	9.5	7.4	5.5	4.3	4.5
Other current expenditure	2.9	3.1	1.2	4.8	7.9	8.2
Capital expenditures	3.3	2.8	3.7	3.4	3.3	3.1

Source: IMF World Economic Outlook May 1996, pp, 80-81.

Overall the country fell into deep recession in the first years of the transformation. GDP contracted by 17 per cent between 1990 and 1993. Following the "transformational recession", growth performance remained poor because recovery was started under severe external imbalances and initial stabilisation programme was aborted. These deficits were particularly dangerous as they occurred against a back drop of high level of external debt.

In March 1995, the new socialist-liberal coalition government started to address many imbalances in the economy and initiated a strong emergency stabilisation programme combined with an acceleration of structural reforms. The five chief objectives of the programme as agreed with the IMF were as follows:[3]

1. A substantial reduction in the government deficit, aimed (in concert with monetary, exchange rate, and incomes policies) at securing the Government's objectives for inflation and the balance of payments.
2. Monetary and wage policies targeted at a significant reduction of inflation and the maintenance of international competitiveness within the framework of the crawling-peg exchange rate policy.
3. Structural reform of the public sector–that is, improved fiscal control mechanisms, a more efficient public administration, a broadening of revenue bases so as to reduce distortionary elements of the tax system, and adjustments in the social security system to safeguard its viability while providing adequate assistance to those in need.
4. Structural reform of enterprises and banks to curtail the role of the State and increase the responsiveness of the economy to market signals–this will require primarily a renewed impetus to privatization.
5. And an external current account balance consistent with no increase in foreign debt, without relying on exceptional inflows associated with privatization.

The stabilisation package introduced in March 1995 included drastic cuts in social security payments, a reduction in real wages in the public sector by about 10 per cent, a large devaluation of the forint, including an initial devaluation of the forint by 9 per cent, followed by crawling peg devaluation of 1.9 per cent per month,. and an import surcharge of 8 per cent. These measures were aimed at reducing budget deficit of 8 per cent in 1994 to 3 per cent by the end of 1995. In addition the current account was expected to be cut from $3.9 billion to $2.5 billion.

The stabilisation package was successfully implemented by the socialist led government. The budget deficit (excluding privatisation

[3]IMF News Brief No. 95/14 (http://www.img.org).

revenues) fell from more than 8 per cent of GDP in 1994 to about 3 per cent in 1996. This impressive reduction was possible because of reduction in fiscal expenditure from 61 per cent in 1994 to 50 per cent in 1996. Wage restrain was also important as real net wages declined by 12 and 5 per cent respectively in 1995 and 1996.

The package also had its intended results: aggregate growth was weak but outright recession was avoided. While GDP growth remained slow in 1995 and 1996 due to contraction in demand and fiscal tightening, the growth reached 4.4 per cent in 1997. Inflation declined from 25 per cent in 1995 to 18 per cent in 1997, registered unemployment has fallen below 10 percent of the labour force (Table 3).

Table 3
Macroeconomic Indicators of the Hungarian Economy

	1990	1991	1992	1993	1994	1995	1996	1997
GDP Growth	-3.5	-11.9	-3.1	-0.6	2.9	1.5	0.5	4.4
Inflation	33	32	22	21	21	28	20	18
Industrial Output	-9.3	-18.4	-9.7	4.0	9.6	4.6	3.0	
Agricultural Output	-4.7	-6.2	-20.0	-9.7	3.2	0	5.0	
Unemployment Rate	1.7	7.4	10.7	11.0	11.4	10.6	11.0	10
Private Sector Share In GDP (%)	25	30	42	50	60			70
Govt. Budget Balance	0.9	-3.0	-6.8	-6.9	-8.3	-7.1	-3.1	-4.6

Sources: Publications of the Hungarian Government, IMF, The World Bank and the EBRD.

4. Current Economic Situation

A new liberal/centre right coalition has taken office in July 1998. The new government has expressed its intentions to continue the fiscal consolidation process and to continue to implement structural reforms in the remaining public sector. The preliminary figures from the 1999 budget suggest the similar trend. The budget expenditure is projected to cut further 1.2 per cent this year from the present 47 per cent of the GDP this year and by another 5 per cent in the next three years[4]. Although growth is projected to be around 5 per cent next year, inflation continue to be a worry. Estimates for 1998 and 1999 projections by the Hungarian government shows that growth is still weak and inflation continue to be in double figures. The persistence of inflation, with year to year price increase still running 13.5 per cent in August 1998, reflect a combination of inertia in inflation expectations, driving high nominal wage growth and a relatively high rate of decline in crawling peg of the growth.[5]

Table 4
Current Economic Indicators projected by the Government and Forecasters
1999 Forecasts

	1998 Estimates#	Kopint Datorg	GKI	1999 Forecasts Penzugy Kotato	Budapest Bank	Govt
GDP	4.7-5.5	4&4.5★	3&4★	3.8&4★	3.8&4.2★	5
Inflation	14-14.8	11&12★	11	11	10.2&10.8★	10-11
Consumption	2.7-4.5	2.5&3★	4&5★	3.8	2.5&3★	2&3★
Investment	9-12	10	8	7	7&8★	12&14★
Exports	16-24	10&11★	10	10	10&13★	11&13★
Imports	17-25	10.5&11.5★	13	12	12&15★	12&14★
Budget Deficit (as % of GDP)	4.4-4.8	4.5	4.5&5★	4.4	4.5&5★	4
BOP deficit (US$bn)	1.4-1.9	2	2.5	2.2	2.2	2

#Based on estimations by institutions appearing in the table and Plan Econ.
★Cautious Estimation

[4]HVG, 7 November 1998 (http://www.hvg/hu/)

[5]IMF World Economic Outlook, October 1998.

5. Privatisation

The basic objective of reforms in 1960s has been to increase the independence of enterprises. Decentralisation of state property rights took place in 1985 with the introduction of "self governing enterprises" forms. The main objective of this reform was to enhance enterprise autonomy by separating management functions from the ownership and regulatory functions of the state. In 1988, a new Company Law was adopted. It gave new legal framework for setting up corporations. Later Transformation Law of 1989 gave special rules for transformation of state companies into company form, meaning their corporatisation. Subsequently this law provided the legal justification for the infamous "spontaneous privatisation". It was an attempt to restructure large State enterprises organisationally and financially, rather than ownership change and the promotion of former managers into the positions of owners. This process lasted for two years between 1988 and 1990. This process was criticised by many people. Therefore the then socialist regime set up a central organisation, the State Property Agency (SPA), to control corporatisation and privatisation transactions.

The first non-communist government inherited an already opened privatisation box. A few deals were already completed and many others at different stages of completion. In 1990 the SPA was fully under government control and next two years saw a process of centralised privatisation. The government announced "First Privatisation Programme" in September 1990, the "Second privatisation Programme" in December 1990, and "Investor Initiated Programme" in February 1991. To counter mounting criticism of slow progress, the government also started the programme of "self privatisation".

In 1992-1993 there was a modification in the privatisation policy. A new State Holding Company (SHC) was created in 1992. The purpose of this agency was to control state-owned firms that were not to be fully or partially privatised in the short run. To be more effective, a new Bankruptcy Law was also enacted. The parliament also approved a bill on the Employee State Ownership Programme (ESOP). Domestic participation in the privatisation process was also encouraged. By the end of 1993, the process of small privatisation was almost complete.

Later the new socialist led government started accelerated privatisation programme as part of the stabilisation plan in 1995. The SPA and SHC were merged into Privatisation and State Holding Company (APV) in May 1995. The new initiatives resulted in self-off of about $4 billion (almost 9% of GDP) in 1995 alone.

Table 5
Privatisation Revenues in Hungary 1993-1996
(million dollars)

	1993	1994	1995	1996	Total
Cash					
Foreign Currency	1203	105	3274	597	5179
Forints	250	337	282	260	1128
Privatisation Loans in forints	236	279	32	15	562
Privatisation Loans in Forex	0	160	0	0	160
Compensation Coupons	159	611	240	262	1272
Total	**1847**	**1491**	**3827**	**1135**	**8301**

Source: Burns and Perasso (1997).

Privatisation was not restricted to manufacturing firms. The national telecom company was completely privatised, as were gas distribution companies and most banks. Minority stakes in electrical distribution sectors were also sold. Major privatisation programmes were virtually completed in 1997. The major commercial banks have been privatised and their governance has been improved.

6. *External Economic Relations*

The socialist system not only distorted domestic institutions, prices etc., but also the foreign trade relations. As Mizsei, (1991) has shown, the foreign trade monopoly was not broken up even significantly relaxed in the 1968 reforms. Despite pioneering in reforms among East European countries, too much opening up towards the west was regarded as something potentially dangerous both politically and economically. As a result in the 1970's, the CMEA was still Hungary's main trading partner, especially in exports. In the 1980's, scholars concerned with the economy recognised that negative influence of CMEA trade should be neutralised.

The new post-socialist government was the leading advocate of dismantling of CMEA trading system. Compared to 1987, in which 49 per cent of exports and 47 per cent of imports were settled in transferable rubles, the corresponding figure had already declined in 1990 to 26 per cent and 29 per cent. The system was dismantled form 1991, with almost all transactions thereafter being conducted at world prices and in convertible currencies. The new government intended to align its trade policies with those of European Community members. By 1991, about 90 per cent of total imports were free of quantitative or value limitations. In 1992 an association agreement was adopted with EC, agreeing for asymmetric timetable for the dismantling of trade barriers. In early years, external account performed better than expected. The country was successful in containing imports despite liberal rules. At the same time exports were redirected to western markets, and the share of industrial countries in total exports increased from 40 per cent in 1989 to almost 70 per cent in 1992. But in 1993 and 1994, with sharply falling exports and continued strong growth in imports, the current account moved into deficit of over $3.5 billion (almost 10 per cent of GDP, see table 6).

But as a result of stabilisation package introduced in 1995, the external situation has improved significantly. The strong growth in exports and weak growth in imports helped to shrink current account deficit from 3.9 bn in 1994 to 2.5 bn in 1995 to 1.7 bn in 1996.[6] The current account deficit has been reduced to 2.2 per cent of the GDP in 1997. The trade with OECD countries has

[6]World Economic & Social Survey 1997, p. 23.

Table 6
Balance of Payments in Convertible Currencies
(in million US Dollars)

	1989	1990	1991	1992	1993*	1994*
Trade balance	536	338	189	-50	-3247	-3635
Exports	6446	6408	9258	10028	8094	7613
Imports	-5910	-6070	-9069	-10077	-11431	-11248

*initial estimates.
Source: UN Economic Survey of Europe.

Table 7
Changes in Foreign Trade Value & Trade Balance by Partner regions in Hungary 1993-96

	1993	1994	1995	1996
Exports (Growth rates in %)				
World	-16.5	20.4	20.2	5.6
Transition Economies	-5.6	5.6	26.7	4.1
Developed Market Economies	-20.9	29.7	15.9	5.4
Developing Countries	-11.4	-12.1	52.4	14.8
Imports (Growth rates in %)				
World	13.7	15.6	6.3	-2.5
Transition Economies	34.7	-7.5	6.5	-1.1
Developed Market Economies	5.9	25.5	6.0	-3.8
Developing Countries	15.3	25.0	8.5	8.4
Trade Balances (in billion dollars)				
World	-3.7	-3.9	-2.6	-1.5
Transition Economies	-1.4	-1.0	-0.6	-0.4
Developed Market Economies	-2.2	-2.6	-2.0	-0.9
Developing Countries	—	-0.3	-0.1	-0.1

Source: UN Economic Bulletin for Europe, 1995 and 1996

doubled since 1990 and now counts for over 70 per cent both exports and imports. The Table 7 also shows the changes in the trade volume and trade balance by partner regions.

7. *Foreign Direct Investment*

Hungary has been one of the most successful country among the transition economies in attracting foreign investment. It received the highest FDI inflows both absolute and per capita terms, with its cumulative per capita flows between 1991-96, of $1256 among the highest in the world. Hungary created stable and transparent framework for FDI early in the transition following the adoption of a new investment law in 1988 itself. It adopted a policy of greater foreign participation in the domestic economy. The privatisation programme which involved selling medium and large companies to foreign investors played a major role in attracting FDI. As a result in these policies, FDI inflows increased from $300 million in 1990 to about $2.3 bn in 1993. But large declines were registered in 1993 (nearly $3 billion). The reduced flows were also because of declines in privatisation related investments.[7] Again when a revised privatisation programme was adopted in 1995, which aimed at selling large enterprises in energy, financial and infrastructure sectors to foreign investors, inflows peaked at more than $4 billion compared to about $1 billion in 1994. For example, FDI flows worth $600 million in 1996 (or 29 per cent of inflows) were received in connection with privatisations, compared with $3 billion in 1995 (66 per cent of inflows) in that year.

In recent years, however, there has also been an outflow of investment from Hungary. In 1996, the country experienced FDI outflow of $58 million. Only in the first quarter of 1997, more than $50 million FDI flows were approved. In 1996, the National Bank of Hungary registered 385 licenses and approved another 74 licenses for outward investment. Hungarian firms initiated new investments in 44 countries. The favoured locations for Hungarian FDI were Slovakia, Romania and Austria.

[7]World Investment Report 1997, p. 96.

Table 8

FDI Flows in Hungary 1985-1996 (millions of dollars)

1985-1990 (annual average)	345
1991	1474
1992	1471
1993	2329
1994	1097
1995	4410
1996	1986
Total 1991-1996	12767
Per Capita Flow 1991-96 (US$)	1256

Source: IMF World Economic Outlook, May 1997, p. 107.

Table 9

Hungary's FDI Abroad, 1996

(Millions of dollars and percentage)

Host Countries	No. of Licenses	Share of Total (%)	Value of FDI (mn.$)	Share of Total (%)
Central & E. Europe	217	58	14.0	24
Poland	23	6	0.4	1
Romania	106	28	4.9	8
Russia	22	6	1.8	3
Slovakia	37	10	5.1	9
Ukraine	29	8	1.8	3
Western Europe				
Austria	98	25	10.0	17
Germany	36	9	2.0	3
Netherlands	4	1	2.0	3
U.K.	21	5	2.7	5
United States	46	12	2.8	5
Others	24	6	31.4	54
Total	**385**	**100**	**58.2**	**100**

Source: UN World Investment Report 1997, p. 99.

Oil and Gas Ltd. (MOI), some pharmaceutical and ceramics companies are investing outside. The main reasons for their outside expansion are perhaps the small size of the Hungarian economy, their increased competitiveness and strengthened financial position after privatisation. In addition their cultural and personal links in the region also play an important role.

Concluding Remarks

Today Hungary is in a much better economic position than any time since the country started its transition towards a market economy. The country has made a substantial progress in privatisation efforts, restructuring enterprises as well as in implementing financial sector and public finance reforms. The country was relatively open even under socialism. But it has opened up further after political changes. As a result, OECD countries are today its major trading partners. The progress made in all these areas has placed the country where it should be able to exploit the benefits of a competitive, enterprise based economy. If these efforts are accompanied by sustained growth and low inflation, the Hungarian economy can look forward to a relatively fast membership of the European Union.

Annexure 1

The Building Blocks of Transformation in Hungary

Political Reform	
Free Elections to the Parliament (date of first elections)	March-April 1990
Previous Economic Reforms	New Economic Mechanism (1968, Revised in the 1990s)
Concept of the transition	"Gradualism"
Macroeconomic Stabilisation	Restrictive Monetary, Budgetary & Income Policies Launched by Steps, 1990 New Programme in 1995

Price Liberalisation	Gradual Since 1975
Privatisation	
Restitution to former owners	Partial Compensation
Private Ownership of Land	from June 1991.
Small Privatisation	Began in 1990 completed in 1993
Large Scale Privatisation	Began in Sep. 1990
Privatisation Institutions	State Property Agency (created in 1990), State Holding Company (created in 1994) Both merged into Priv. & State Holding Company (1995)
Banking Reform	Creation of Two-tier Banking System since 1987, Banking Laws (1991), Debt Consolidation Plan (1994), 2/3 Share Capital is Privately held (1997)
Capital Markets	Budapest Stock Exchange opened in June 1990
Exchange Rate Regime	Crawling Band vis-a-vis DM (70%), US$ (30%) basket +– 2.25%
Opening up of the Economy	
Liberalisation of the foreign trade (ending of state monopoly)	Completed in 1991
Single Exchange rate	Since 1981
Internal convertibility	Since 1990 (de fecto) Article VIII (1996)
New laws on Foreign Investment	1989, amended in 1990
Relations with International Organisations:	
IMF, IBRD	Membership Since 1982
GATT	Membership in 1973
EEC	Association Agreement (1991)
OECD	Membership in 1999
External Debt Situation	High Risk Rating, No Default

Sources: Compiled from various EBRD, the IMF, The World Bank and UN publications.

References

Antal, L. (1979) "Development With Some Digression: The Hungarian Economic Mechanism in Seventies", *Acta Oeconomica*, Vol. 23., Nos. 3-4, pp. 257-73.

Bauer, T. (1990) "Hungary: On the Way Towards a Market Economy" in Central and Eastern European Economies in the 1990s: Prospects and Constraints, *Nato Colloquium 1990*, pp. 77-86.

Berend, T. (1990) *The Hungarian Economic Reforms* 1953-1988. Cambridge: Cambridge Univ. Press.

Blue Ribbon Commission (1990) *Hungry in Transformation to Freedom and Prosperity*. Indianapolis: Hudson Institute.

Bruno, M. (1994), "Stabilisation and Reform in Eastern Europe: A Preliminary Evaluation" in O Blanchart, K A Frost and J D Sachs, *The Transition in Eastern Europe* Vol. 1 Country Studies, Chicago: University of Chicago Press.

Burns A and G Perasso (1997) Hungary: Progress in Structural Reform" *OECD Observer*, No. 207, Aug./Sep. pp. 35-36.

Boote, A. R and J Somogyi (1991) *Economic Reforms in Hungary Since 1968*, IMF Occasional Paper No 83, Washington DC.

Brada, J. and Dobozi, I. (Eds.) (1989-90) "Money Incentives and Efficiency in the Hungarian Economic Reform" *Eastern European Economics*, Vol. 28, Nos. 1,2 (Special Issue).

Chilosi, A. (1992) "Market Socialism: A Historical View and a Retrospective Assessment" *Economic Systems*, Vol. 16, No. 1, pp. 171-85.

Clarke, R. (Ed.) (1989) *Hungary: The Second Decade of Economic Reform*. U.K.: Longman.

Csaba, L. (1991) "First Lessons of Transforming the Economic Systems in Eastern Europe" *Acta Oeconomica*, Vol. 43, Nos. 3-4 pp. 231-50.

— (1992) "Macroeconomic Policy in Hungary: Poetry Versus Reality" *Soviet Studies*, Vol. 44, No. 6, pp. 947-64.

Fischer, S. and Gelb A (1991) "Issues in Socialist Economy Reform" in P Marer and S Zecchini (eds) *The Transition to a Market*

Economy, Vol 1 The Broad Issues, Vol 2 Special Issues. Paris: OECD.

Hare, P. (1991) "Hungary; Transition to a Market Economy" *The Journal of Economic Perspectives* Vol 5, No. 4.

Hewett, A. (Ed.) (1983) "Hungary: *The Third Wave of Forms" Journal of Comparative Economics*, Vol. 7, No. 3, (Special Issue).

Hieronymi, O. (1991) "The Development of the Social Market Economy in Hungary and Opportunities Resulting from the Future Entry into the European Community" *Revista di Politica Economica*, Vol 81, No. 6, pp. 275-88.

Johnson, D.G. (1997) *Economies in Transition: Hungary and Poland*, FAO Economic and Social Development Paper No. 141: Rome.

Kornai, J. (1986) "The Hungarian Reform Process: Visions, Hopes and Reality" *Journal of Economic Literature*, Vol. 24, No. 4, pp. 1687-1737.

— (1990) *The Road to a Free Economy: Shifting From a Socialist System. The Example of Hungary*, New York: W.W. Norton.

— (1992) "The Postsocialist Transition and the State; Reflections on the Hungarian Fiscal Problems" *The American Economic Review*, Vol 82, No. 2.

Laky, T. (1991) "Small Organization in Hungary: Past and Present" *Research Review*, No. 2, pp. 31-48.

Lavigne, M. (1994) *A Comparative View on Economic Reform in Poland, Hungary and Czechoslovakia*. UN Economic Commission of Europe Discussion Papers.

Major, I. (1991) "Credibility and Shock Therapy in Economic Transformation: The Hungarian Case" *Communist Economies and Economic Transformation*, Vol 3, No. 4.

Marer, P. (1991) Foreign Economic Liberalisation in Hungary and Poland" *The American Economic Review*, Vol. 81, No. 2.

Mizsei, K. (1990) "Experiences with Privatisation in Hungary" mimeo. Paper presented at the World Bank Conference on Privatization and Ownership Changes in East and Central Europe, June 13-14, Washington D.C.

— (1993) "Hungary: Gradualism Needs a Strategy" in R. Portes (Ed.), *Economic Transformation in Central Europe: A Progress Report*, London. Luxembourg: CEPR, European Community, pp. 131-86.

Mizsei, K. (1993) "The Institutional Framework of Foreign Trade Reforms in Hungary" in M Kaser and A M Vacic (Ed) *Reforms in Foreign Economic Relations of Eastern Europe and the Soviet Union,* UN Economic Commission for Europe Economic Studies No. 2. New York.

Mizsei, K. and Török A. (1990). *Modified Planned Economies at the Cross Roads: The case of Hungary*, Helsinki: WIDER.

Revesz, G. (1989) *Perestroika in Eastern Europe: Hungary's Economic Transformation*, 1945-1988, Westview Press.

Richet, X. (1989) *The Hungarian Model: Markets and Planning in a Socialist Economy*, Cambridge: Cambridge Univ. Press.

Román, Z. (1991) "Entrepreneurship and Small Business: The Hungarian Trajectory" *Journal of Business Ventures*, Vol. 6, No. 6, pp. 447-65.

Sachs J D (1990) "Eastern European Economies: What is to be Done?" *The Economist*, Jan. 13, pp 18-24.

Sachdeva G (1994) *Privatization as a Factor of Systemic Transformation in Central and Eastern Europe, With Special Reference to Hungary and Poland.* Ph.D. Thesis, Hungarian Academy of Sciences, Budapest.

Stabilization and Convertibility. A Three Year Programme of the Hungarian Government. *The Hungarian Economy*, Vol. 19, No. 1-2.

Swain N. (1992) *Hungary: The Rise and Fall of Feasible Socialism.* London, New York: Verso.

Szamuely, L. (1982) "The First Wave of Economic Mechanism Debate in Hungary (1954-57)" *Acta Oeconomica*, Vol. 29, Nos. 1-2, pp. 1-24.

— (1984) "The Second Wave of Economic Mechanism Debate and the 1968 Reform in Hungary", *Acta Oeconomica*, Vol. 33, Nos. 1-2, pp 43-67.

Székély K. and Newbery D. (Eds.) (1993) *Hungary: An Economy in Transition.* Cambridge: Cambridge Univ. Press.

Szelényi, I. (1989) "Eastern Europe in an Epoch of Transition: Toward a Socialist Mixed Economy" in V. Nee and D. Stark (Eds.) *Remaking the Institutions of Socialism: China and Eastern Europe*. Stanford California: Standard Univ. Press. pp. 208-32.

— (1990) "Alternative Future for Eastern Europe: The Case of Hungary" *East European Politics and Societies*, Vol. 4, No. 2, pp. 231-54.

11
Energy Resources and Transformation in Hungary

RAMA SAMPATH KUMAR*

Privatisation represents the reversal of the process of nationalisation. The nationalisation wave swept over most nations early this century. In communist nations of East and Central Europe it took shape soon after they assumed power after world war 1 & 2 and in Western Europe the process took several decades to take root and around 1930's took firm ground. "Nationalisation represented a cherished post-war European ideal to create large vigorous state-owned businesses that provided pools of public jobs and allowed European politicians to wield influence over their economies. A wide consensus of European politics held that a strong, government-owned industrial sector was necessary for prosperity and middle class stability"[1] In the 1930's Spain, the Franco government nationalized the state petroleum resources, which later emerged as Repsol–Spain's state oil company. The Mussolini government in Italy did the same and formed what was to become ENI, Italy's state petroleum company. Energy resources were nationalized at about the same time elsewhere in Europe–although in other nations often by more freely-elected governments. In other regions, nationalization often involved the expropriation of foreign-owned domestic petroleum properties. Russia was the first to nationalize its petroleum industry following the Bolshevik Revolution in 1918. In 1938, Mexico nationalized what was at the time an industry largely held by US, UK, and Dutch interests. Later waves

*Rama Sampath Kumar Assistant Professor, Centre for Central Eurasian Studies, University of Mumbai.

[1]"Economic Change Social Upheaval; Governments Cutting Welfare Benefits, Selling State-run Firms'" *The Washington Post* (August 7, 1994), p. A1.

of nationalisation (and expro priations) followed in the post war era in Latin America and the Middle East.

By the late 70's there was a change of attitude towards state ownership, and in the West, nationalized industries began to lose favour. Disenchantment with state ownership grew as government enterprises began to be perceived as bloated and inefficient. Privatization has also been driven by the increasing globalization of the world economy. Several decades of rapid growth in international trade and investment have made competitiveness in international trade an essential factor in a nation's ability to create jobs, raise real wages, and generate wealth. For many nations, privatisation has become the only effective method of raising investment capital on favourable terms. High levels of past public sector borrowing have saddled many nations with large levels of debt. As a consequence, these nations have had little recourse but to sell state assets to reduce debt, generate revenue, and raise investment capital.[2] In Britain it was Margaret Thatcher who first favoured large scale privatisation. But soon even the British labour party leader called for the abolishment of the labour party's constitution clause calling for the nationalisation of industry–long one of the bedrock's of the British labour movement's constitution.[3] In Western Europe, the United Kingdom was at the forefront of privatisation. Britain has raised $95 billion through the privatisation of formerly state-owned enterprises.[4]

Other liberal parties around the western globe also embraced privatisation. As a result of this companies such as Repsol and ENI-started on the privatisation process. Various businesses have been privatized besides oil. Indeed, the largest privatization to date has been the sale of Japanese Telecom for $73 billion.[5] In the United Kingdom, public housing has been privatized and, in the United Stats, many municipal services, such as waste disposal, have

---

[2]*The World Bank Report of 1994,* The World Bank (New York, Oxford University Press, 1995).

[3]"British Labor Party Scraps nationalization Clause, "*The Wall Street Journal* (May 1, 1995), p. A11.

[4]"Sale of the Century," *The Wall Street Journal* (October 2, 1995), p. R4.

[5]Ibid, p. R4.7.

been privatized. In recent years both mixed-market and former socialist economies are engaged in various privatisation efforts and there seems to be a growing awareness since the decline of socialism that free enterprise advances the wealth of nations better than nationalised industries and planned economies.

Even among still avowedly socialist regimes, such as China, a move to free market-based reforms and privatisation has been evident for several years. Among the developing countries, privatisation has also been widespread. With the exception of Cuba, virtually all of Latin America has adopted some form of privatisation. Chile-Latin America's pioneer at privatisation–and, later, Argentina, Peru, and Colombia have undertaken the most ambitious privatisation efforts. Among developing Asian nations, electric power privatisation has been most prominent in countries such as Pakistan, the Philippines, Malaysia, and Indonesia. China and India, have also embarked on various forms of energy privatisation. So as can be seen, countries as different as the United Kingdom and Chile have led the way in privatisation. Countries as different as Peru and Poland have followed. Between 1988 and 1993, roughly 2,700 state-owned enterprises in over 95 countries were transferred to private individuals, raising over $270 billion.[6] In the East and Central European countries, the collapse of Communism precipitated later efforts to adopt market economies and privately-held industry. The nineties started with the East European countries undergoing major political and economic structural reforms. After years of strong central government control, they started the decentralisation process, transforming their economies through various programmes including industry restructuring and privatisation. The state run enterprises were restructured, shifting from public ownership with state control to various types of private ownership. To facilitate this process, each country attempted to develop viable legal structures, contract laws, regulatory systems, capital markets, trade policies, and domestic bond and stock markets. Different countries use different methods to privatise state owned industries, but all of them are a movement towards a market

[6]Ibid, p. R4}.

driven economy, diminishing public ownership and control and increasing the private ownership and control. Hungary was the first to move towards reforms, starting in the late 1960s, Hungary's former communist regime began economic reforms along capitalist lines that continued until the end of communism in 1989. In the 1970s more freedom was given to state enterprises. In 1972 it was already possible to establish associations with foreign participation which to a certain extent could be considered a 'private sector'. Some academics estimate that Hungary was one-third on the way to capitalism in 1989. However, owing to the political dependence of the country and the lack of confidence in the political and economic situation, only a few joint ventures were registered (30 between 1972 and 1984). Today, more than 27,000 are registered and Hungary can be regarded as a functioning market economy. Liberalisation and privatisation have progressed considerably, and there has been strong growth of new private firms. Hungary has had a head start over other former eastern block countries due to its unique economic history and geographical closeness to the West, providing some experience of a market economy. Hungarian enterprises are already competitive in EU markets. Restructuring of banks and industry is well under way. Hungary's record of consistent commitment to steady market reforms and its ability to take difficult decisions when they are necessary is an important positive factor. It has had a consistently high level of foreign direct investment.

As the countries of central and east Europe have seen dramatic economic and political changes during the 1990's these changes have seen the countries also trying to adapt to new energy realities. With the ending of cheap energy supplies from the Former Soviet Union (FSU), all have had to scrutinize the economics of energy supply and use, future consumption trends and improving the environmental performance of the sector. In Hungary, a new Law on Privatisation, passed in May 1995, improved transparency and initiated a simplified process. Privatisation has progressed dramatically since late 1995, particularly in the energy, telecommunication, and banking sectors. Currently about 80 per cent of the country's GDP is derived from the private sector. The government hopes to complete the privatisation process by 1998, by which time the private sector should account for about 85 per cent of GDP.

Energy privatisation is a recent world trend, stressing the benefits of market forces and less dependence on governments in the allocation of resources. Although privatisation efforts differ substantially from country to country, there is a strong common economic rationale underlying the various decisions to privatise state energy resources. In general, nations have privatised state-owned energy industries to achieve one or more of several objectives. These objectives include: 1) raising revenue for the state; 2) raising investment capital for the industry or company being privatised; 3) reducing government's role in the economy; 4) promoting wider share ownership; 5) increasing efficiency; 6) introducing greater competition; and 7) exposing firms to market discipline.[7]

Energy privatisation is closely connected with the development of international energy companies, whose focus is becoming both more global and more multipurpose. Until recently, outside of the world's few major integrated oil companies, only a handful of energy companies were considered multinational. Currently, in addition to the scores of petroleum companies that can now be classified as multinational, the scope of many coal companies, petroleum pipeline companies, electric utilities, and power generation equipment and construction companies, has become increasingly global. Through consolidations, mergers, acquisitions, and strategic alliances, the worlds's energy companies have also become more integrated. Oil and gas companies have become electricity companies; domestic regional electric utilities have become multinational electricity companies; electricity distribution companies have become generation companies; and generation companies have become distribution and transmission companies.

Energy Resources

Before going into the details of energy privatisation in Hungary, it

[7]The objectives of privatization appeared in *Privatization: Learning the Lessons from the U.K. Experiences* (London, U.K. Price Waterhouse, 1989).

would be beneficial to have a look at the energy resources and the industries associated with it.

Oil

Hungary's relatively minor oil reserves are estimated to be 100 million barrels. Oil production in 1994 was 50,000 barrels per day (b/d), falling far short of the 168,000 b/d comsumption rate for refined petroleum products. Imports accounts for the difference.

As in the FSU, the Communist regimes left East European countries with bloated and inefficient hydrocarbon industries that suffered from decades of neglect, outdated technology, heavy debt, and environmental problems. Unlike Russia's large reserves, Eastern Europe produces little oil and natural gas–only Romania has a sizeable endowment of reserves. The eastern European countries are dependent on imports, mainly from Russia, to meet primary energy demand. Hungary is a landlocked country that relies heavily on the Russian Federation to meet its oil import needs. Russian oil is supplied via a pipeline that runs through Croatia, connecting with the oil terminal at Kurk Island in the Adriatic Sea. the pipeline has been closed since 1991 due to the conflict in the former Yugoslavia. Because of this, much attention is being given to the issue of developing secure energy supplies by developing infrastructure links with or through OECD Member countries.[8] All East European countries have refinery industries. Most are badly in need of restructuring and upgrading. The petroleum marketing sector is the fastest growing sector in East Europe's energy industry, partly due to the introduction of foreign competition in many countries.

Natural Gas

Natural gas reserves are about 3.4 trillion cubic feet (TCF). In

---

[8]The Organization of Economic Cooperation and Development (OECD) includes Australia, Austria, Belgium, Canada, Denmark, Finland, France, Germany, Greece, Iceland, Ireland, Italy, Japan, Luxembourg, the Netherlands, New Zealand, Norway, Portugal, Spain, Sweden, Switzerland, Turkey, the United Kingdom, and the United States.

1994, natural gas production was 172 billion cubic feet (BCF). To meet the domestic demand of approximately 356 BCF, Hungary imports natural gas from the Russian Federation.

Coal

Recoverable reserves of hard coal are 600 to 700 million short tons (Mt), reserves for lignite are 3,000 Mt; and reserves of brown coal are 1,000 Mt. Most coal is high in sulfur and ash. Production in 1993 for hard coal, brown coal, and lignite was 0.95 Mt, 6.91 Mt, and 6.71 Mt, respectively. The only reasonable possibility for increasing new coalmining capacity would be from lignite. Domestic lignite resources are estimated to be adequate to justify an additional 900 to 1,000 megawatts (MWe) of lignite-fueled electricity generating capacity.

Energy Infrastructure

Pipelines for oil and gas, road and railway networks, and a high voltage electric grid are well developed in Hungary and have significant potential value for regional energy trade. In 1992, electricity transmission lines of 750 kV, 400 kV, and 220 kV measured approximately 160 miles, 970 miles, and 900 miles respectively. A substantial 120 kV distribution system also exists.

Power Industry Overview

The total installed capacity of the Hungarian power system was about 7,500 Mw in 1995, of which the public power stations represented about 7,300 Mw and industrial power stations the rest. The capacity of oil- and gas-fired power stations is about 3,500 Mw, of which the ten biggest, 215 Mw condensation units, were built in the 1970s (at the Dunamenti and Tisza Power Stations). These cover about 28 per cent of installed capacity, the others are mainly smaller, heat supply, district heating power stations.

Hungary has coal-fired power stations of about 2,000 Mw. The biggest of these is the relatively modern Matra Power Station with an 800 Mw installed capacity, using domestic lignite. The other, mainly brown coal-fired power stations cannot be considered as modern, despite the refurbishments of the 1980s.

The only Hungarian nuclear power station is at Paks, beside the Danubue. Paks operates four VVR 440 type units, each with a 460 Mw capacity (with a V 213 type pressurised water reactor). Availability of the units is excellent, and the power plant operates safely (it is regularly examined by the International Atomic Energy Agency).

Due to the geographical location of the country, only small hydro-power stations exist, with a total installed capacity of 48 Mw.

Nearly every public power station in the Hungarian system supplies heat in addition to electricity. These power stations provide two-thirds of country's heat demand, for district heating and industrial purposes.

In 1991, Parliament accepted a long-term energy policy, to go beyond the turn of the millennium. The need for this to be realised efficiently meant the structural transformation of the power industry. The first step was the transformation of MVMT (the Hungarian Electricity Board) into a group of companies by 1 January 1992. This temporary model made the statutory privatisation of the electric power companies possible. Until 1992, the electricity industry was managed by the Hungarian Power Company–Magyar Villamos Muvek Reszvenytarsag (MVM Rt). In 1992, Hungary reorganised MVM Rt into a two-tier company structure. The upper tier, which remained MVM Rt, manages all trade in electricity. MVM Rt owns and operates the high voltage transmission grid and dispatching center. It purchases power from electricity generating companies and sells it to smaller distribution companies. MVM Rt controls the financial flow of electricity-based goods and sevices by the use of tariffs. It also manages all electricity-related import and export transactions.

The second tier of the utility system, as of 1994, was comprised of eight generating companies grouped regionally and according to fuel mix; six regional distribution companies; and one maintenance company for the basic network. The eight power station companies, six power distribution companies and the Magyar Villamos Muvek Rt. (MVM Rt., Hungarian Power Companies Ltd.) supply Hungary with safe and reliable electricity. The basic task of MVM Rt. is to control the operation of the power system, as well as to carry out distribution and wholesale tasks, including import and export.

Accepting the 1994 Act XL VIII on the Generation, Transmission and Supply of Electricity was a decisive step in a process of developing the new operational model of the power industry. At the end of 1994 the Hungarian Government made a decision on the privatisation of the companies of the electricity industry. The main goals of privatisation are the efficiency improvement of electricity generation, transmision and distribution, as well as the reduction of costs, while maintaining continuous and reliable power supply in both the short and long term. Privatisation has to contribute to both the modernisation of the power sytem and the improvement of the state budget balance. The relevant governmental resolutions have established the operating and ownership structures of the electricity industry after privatisation.

With the elaboration of the details of this model, preparation for privatisation was finished by autumn 1995. In October of that year APV Rt (the Hungarian Privatisation and State Holding Company Ltd.) invited investors to bid for the minority package of shares in power plant and distribution companies. Minority shares of two power plants and all six distribution companies were partly sold in December 1995 and the majority of another power plant company in July 1996. The new owners are European power companies, or consortiums formed therof. Privatisation of three power stations and MVM Rt. continued in 1996. However, progress towards privatization in the electric utility sector has been complicated because two State entities with differing privatisation policies are participating in the privatisation process. These two entities the State Asset Management Company (AV Rt) and the State Property Agency (AVU) both have held interest in MVM Rt the generating companies, and the distribution companies.

In spite of this move towards privatisation in the power sector, most energy enterprises are still publicly-owned and government-run. But compared to other countries of the region Hungary has done better. For example, Hungary has sold an 18.8 per cent stake in its vertically integrated petroleum company, MOL. (The Czech Republic leads in this area and has merged its two largest refineries and sold 49 per cent to IOC, a western consortium.) This is because Hungary's economic reforms during the Communist era gave it a head start on the privatisation process particularly in terms of attracting foreign investors. Hungary has accounted for about half of all foreign investment in Eastern Europe since 1989. As mentioned earlier, since 1990, the Hungarian government has been transitioning to a market economy following earlier attempts at partial economic reforms, but it was only in June 1995, the Hungarian parliament passed the Privatisation Act. After a promising beginning there followed several attempts that turned out to be unsucessful, the first wave of energy sector privatisation went forward with a "combined offer" during October/November 1995. Companies in western Europe, Russia and U.S. competed for stakes in Hungary's oil, gas and electricity business. In November 1995, Hungary sold an 18.8% stake in MOL, as mentioned earlier, the first time ownership in an East European oil company.[9] The government has made progress in adapting its energy industries to a market economy. Hungary has embarked on one of the most ambitious of privatisation schemes. Hungary is the only country in the region to build a vertically integrated company, the Hungarian Oil and Gas Company (MOL).[10] MOL was founded in 1991 and is Hungary's largest utility segment ranks as one of Europe's top 15 oil and gas utilities. Currently, Hungary produces about one-fourth of its oil and half its natural gas needs. MOL accounts for 90 per cent of the nation's oil and gas production, refining capacity, and reserves.[11] Political uncertainty in the Ukraine and continuing problems with pipeline access to the Adriatic has jeopardized secure energy supplies. As a consequence, MOL has

---

[9]Privatizing in Hungary: A Door Reopens, "*The New York Times* (October 17, 1995), p. D1

[10]"MOL Issue Priced at Bottom of Equity Range Equity Offerings" *Financial Times* (November 22, 1995), p. 35.

[11]n. 9 p5.

sought to diversify its gas suppplies and to develop oil and gas reserves abroad by acquiring exploration licenses in the Former Soviet Union, Algeria, and Tunisia. In 1994, MOL and OMV, Austria's state oil company, agreed to jointly construct a 120-kilometer pipeline linking Baumagarten, Austria, and Gyor, Hungary, providing Hungary with its first access to western gas.[12] Germany also has agreed to sell western natural gas to the company.[13] In addition MOL is seeking joint venture partners in oil and gas exploration and production. After several postponements, the first bids for domestic exploration were offered in 1994, with the five concessions being awarded to a consortium of Blue Star, Coastal, and affiliates of Occidental and Mobil.[14] Before privatising, MOL began restructuring. In May 1995, the assets of Mineralimpex (previously Hungary's gas importing monpoly and, at the time, the country's second hydrocarbons trader after MOL) were transferred to MOL.[15] Both MOL and its new Mineralimpex subsidiary have been cutting staff, and MOL expects a profitable 1995.[16]

Foreign investment and competition have been visible in the retail sector for some time. Two decades ago, Shell Hungary was allowed its first franchised filling station through a local agreement with the state trading company, Interag.[17] By 1993, the company was 100 per cent Shell-owned. By 1994, Shell had 15 per cent of all service stations and held a 20 per cent share of product sales. MOL still leads the retail gasoline market in Hungary, with 50 per cent of the service stations and a 35 per cent share of pruduct sales. Other major gasoline marketers in Hungary include Mobil, Exxon, Conoco and Total, with each holding about 5 per cent share of the country's gasoline market.[18]

---

[12]"Hungary's Privatization Program Advances," *Oil and Gas Journal* (September 11, 1995), p. 26.

[13]"Eastern Europe–Reluctant to Sell; Special Report: National Energy Companies–A New Era; Industry Overview," *Petroleum Economist* (September 1995), p. 22.

[14]Ibid.

[15]"MOL Announces Nine Months Results," *PR Newswire* (December 15, 1995).

[16]"Privatizing in Hungary: A Door Reopens," The New York Times (October 17, 1995), p. D1.

[17]Hungary Prepares for Gas Sale with Privatisation Law," *East European Energy Report* (May 22, 1995).

Eastern Europe under central planning was virtually closed to foreign investors. Foreign capital could play a pivotal role in helping diversify energy supplies, increase energy efficiency through modernization, and improve the environment. Although foreign direct investment has increased in these areas, inflows remain modest. Foreign direct investment has been slow to materialize due to continuing macroeconomic instability and insufficient institutional reforms. To date, most foreign investment has been through joint ventures. Foreign investment is higher in the countries where reform has made the most progress, namely the Czech Republic, Hungary, and Poland. The diversity of reform among the countries in Eastern Europe–which includes voucher sales, direct sales, and National Investment Funds–is related to how each country addresses the issue of sovereignty over strategic national assets. The foreign capital inflow to Central Eastern Europe has accelerated, particularly in the past three years. Hungary has kept pace with the moves since 1990, during which time it has remained an attraction centre of the region to the foreign working capital. The political and economic stability of Hungary, together with the institutional and ruling system, are gradually resembling that of Western Europe. Hungary has joined international organisations which is beneficial too. Hungary's ability to attract Foreign Direct Investment (FDI) has been impressive Hungary has the largest inflow of FDI in the reigon, attracting 40% of the total FDI in Central and Eastern Europe. This has helped to reduce the foreign debt and contributed to the restructuring, privatisation and modernisation of Hungarian industry.

Foreign direct investment has a key role to play in the reconstruction of the Hungarian economy.[19] Three important elements determine the transformation of the economy: one is changing the owners of the companies, the second is foreign direct investment (a major component of capital inflows) and the third is changing the markets. These events are taking place in parallel and at an unusual speed. Foreign direct investment has

---

[18]"Hungary Petroleum Privatisation Limited by Economic Concerns," *Oil and Gas Journal* (July 4, 1994),. pp. 24, 27-8.

increased dramatically. Hungary alone attracted half the foreign direct investment invested in Eastern European countries as a whole. Foreign direct investment amounted to more than US$14 billion at the end of 1995. Hungary is rebuilding a market economy by changing owners on the basis of strong political motivation and new political possibilities.

Privatisation proved to be the principal attraction for capital. In the last seven years the country attracted working capital to the amount of nearly US$16 billion, of which an amount of $8 billion was collected directly from the privatisation of domestic companies. Foreign capital inflow in the region was the largest in the top year of privatisation, i.e., in 1995. In Central Eastern Europe, APV Rt. (Hungarian Privatisation and State Holding Company) was the first to privatise strategic companies, companies of public service belonging to the large supply systems of the national economy. Foreign investors acquired business shares in power stations, in the Hungarian Oil and Gas Company (MOL Rt), the Hungarian Telecommunication Company (MATiV Rt), in addition to the gas and electricity supply companies. The latter company in the listing, (MATiV Rt), was the first company in Europe, the shares of which were admitted to listing on the Stock Exchange in New York. The particularly high value of foreign capital per capita is worthy of attention. According to the data of 1995, in this respect Hungary is twice as good as the other 'star country' of the region, the Czech Republic. This data provides a good basis for Hungarian hopes, according to which the trust and interest of the investors remain on a long-term basis, even if those with the intention to invest no longer receive 'ready' factories, banks, or large plants. As they slowly reach the end of privatisation, the privatisation of some particularly importnat companies like MAHART (Hungarian Shipping Agency) or MVM (Hungarian Electric Works) is still incomplete.

Thanks to its geographical situation, Hungary is attractive and continues to remain attractive in order to gain foreign capital in the future. The Government recognises this situation and would

[19]"The development of the investment market in Hungary", Andras Sugar President, Hungarian Joint Venture Association).

like to use it to the benefit of both the country and foreign investors. In the eastern gate of Hungary a great number of incentives are offered to those intending to invest, namely those companies which are interested in involving themselves in Eastern Europe. Effort to place Hungary at the heart of Europe, not only in geographical terms but also in an economic terms should take priority. This will provides the economic integration between East and West.

The transition process in the Central and East European countries, including Hungary, has been under way for more than seven years. During this period very real achievements have been made, but the transition to a market-based economy is a very complex process, and so will take sometime before they can compete with West European countries.

12

Growth and Development of the Indian Economy: From Crisis to Reform and After

ALOKESH BARUA*

I. Introduction

This paper aims at analyzing the fundamental constraints to the growth and development of the Indian economy and the factors which eventually contributed to the dismantling of the import-substiution strategy of development that India had been following since the inception of the First Five Year Plan in 1950-51. In July 1991 India was virtually compelled to introduce a series of reform measures to resolve the acute current account balance of payments crisis. Of course, the need for economic reforms to achieve a higher rate of growth in the long run within an open economy environment has always been suggested by both economists and policy makers. The failure of the import substitution strategy of development to remove poverty and large-scale unemployment through achieving higher growth rate has long been recognized and attempts have been made since 1966 to gradually deviate from that path but without much success.[1] The other

---

*Alokesh Barua is a Associate Professor in the Centre for Diplomacy, International Law & Economies, SIS JNU New Delhi.

[1]The following observation by Tendulkar may be noted in this context: "While the reforms introduced without much public debate or discussion in the face of the foreign exchange liquidity crisis of the mid-1991, the basic cmpulsion arose from the need to overcome unsustainable fiscal dificits and the need to put the Indian economy on a higher growth path by removing the constricting shackles of the earlier direct discretionary control regime.There had indeed been unsure and halting steps in this direction between June 1966 and July 1991". See, Tendulkar, S. (1998), "Foundational Propositions Underlying the Indian Economic Reforms", in Agarwal, Barua, Das and Pant edited ***Indian Economy in Transition : Environment and Development Issues***, Har-Anand Publications, New Delhi p. 29.

objective of the paper is to review the strategy of the reforms and its impact on the performance of the economy since 1991. But before I do this I would like to contrast the Indian experience with the Hungarian experience not only because this paper is to be read on the occasion of the seminar on **"India and Hungary : Perspectives on the Changing World Order"** but also because the two economies share certain remarkable similarities in their experiences with development and economic reforms.

In comparison with Hungary (10 million population in 1994, an area of 93 thousand sq. kms. and $41 billion GDP in 1994) India is a large economy (913.5 million population in 1994, an area of 3288 sq. kms and $293.6 billion GDP in 1994). Hungary is a resource poor economy while India has a wide variety of natural and environmental resources. During 1994-2000 period Hungary's population is growing at a negative rate of -0.6 per cent while during the same period Indian population is growing at a rate of 1.6 per cent per year. Hungary is a relatively developed and industrialized economy. Its per capita GNP in 1994 was $3840 in contrast with India's $320 in 1994. Apart from such manifold differences in per capita income, Hungary's record in human development has been substantially higher than India. In terms of the UNDP calculation of human development index while Hungary ranks 48 in the world while India's ranking is 138. In Hungary less than 15 per cent people are below the poverty line while the percentage of poor in India is near 40 per cent.

Hungary has a very high manufacturing orientation as its share of agriculture in GDP is only 14 per cent and industry and services shares were 36 and 50 per cent respectively in 1989. The corresponding figures for India were 30 per cent in agriculture, 29 and 41 per cent in industry and services respectively. Hungary is a land locked economy but yet heavily dependent on foreign trade as its share of trade (exports plus imports) in GDP was as high as 67 per cent in 1994. However, for almost four decades Hungary's trade has been geographically highly concentrated with nearly 50 per cent of its trade being conducted within the CMEA (Council of Mutual Economic Cooperation) countries and most of this trade was settled in non-convertible currency. In contrast,

India has a vast sea coast on her western, southern and eastern fronts providing easy access to international trading opportunities, and yet her share of trade to GDP was only 19 per cent in 1994. But India's trade is geographically well diversified and except for the Rupee trade with the former Soviet Union and Eastern European countries most of India's trade was settled interms of convertible currencies. In economic and political terms India has very limited interaction with Hungary.

Yet the two countries share certain very remarkably common features in terms of their approaches to growth, development and reforms. First, both India and Hungary initially followed autarchic development paths. Second, bureaucracy rather than the markets played crucial roles in the decision-making processes in both the countries. Third, economic liberalization began in both the countries almost at the same time. In India it started with the devaluation of Rupee in 1966 while in Hungary it began in 1968 with the replacement of the earlier mandatory planning by "a system of macro-economic planning, under which targets were set for economic variables but were not enterprise-specific."[2] Fourth, major paradigm shifts towards market-based development process also commenced around the same time. Rajiv Gandhi's government in 1985 took serious effort towards economic liberalisation.[3] In Hungary "since 1985, about three-quarters of the total of some 1000 state-owned enterprises have operated under a system of 'enterprise self-management'."[4] As against India's major drive towards economic

---

[2]See page 5, Trade Policy Review, Hungary 1991, Volume 1, GATT.

[3]To quote Chadha and Paliwar in this regard: "A beginning was made towards liberaisation of India's trade policy regime during the late 1970s, and this liberalization gained some momentum during the later half of the 1980s. The committees led by P.C. Alexander (1978), Abid Hussain (1984) and Narasimham (1985) influenced Indian thinking on trade policy reform by emphasizing two major points: (1) there was a need to develop an efficient system which would make exports less costly and more profitable; and (2) there was a need to move away from a discretionary system of quantitative import controls to a system based on tariffs. The Long Term Fiscal Policy (LTFP), announced in 1985, envisaged the eventual removal of import licensing from all imports except consumer goods and also proposed simplification of the complex tariff structure.", p. 6.

[4]n. 2.

reform in 1991, privatisation programme began in Hungary in 1990 when Hungary experienced persistent decline in real GDP since 1988, high inflation and threats to large-scale unemployment. By January 1991, consumer and producer prices were, in principle, freely determined in Hungary. Finally Hungary's political life has been changed fundamentally since 1989 when the former one-party regime has been replaced by a democratic multi-party system. A new government was formed in May 1990. I hope the scholars from Hungary present here will shed valuable insights to the Hungarian experience. Let me therefore turn the focus of my attention to the Indian experience.

II. The Indian Crisis of 1991

The Indian economy was in the grip of an unprecedented crisis in 1991. The crisis was both economic and political. On the economic front the major issue of concern was India's foreign exchange shortfall leading to a serious payment crisis, that is, how to finance its current account deficit which was around $9.7 billion (3.5 per cent of GDP). Private borrowing in the international capital market was not feasible as India's credit rating had dropped to a very low level for reasons to be explained later and its own foreign exchange reserves–only $1 billion in the summer of 1991 were not even sufficient for a month's imports. The fiscal deficit rose to 8.4 per cent of GDP, the public debt went up to nearly 70 per cent of GDP and the economy was close to defaulting on its external debt of over $75 billion. Inflation was in double digits–17 per cent and GDP growth was less than 1 per cent.

The economic crisis was accentuated by the political crisis with the collapse of the Janata Dal government and the assassination of Mr. Rajiv Gandhi in May 1991. The rise in casteism and the growing regionalism had created a political vacuum and threatened the political stability and integrity of the country. As a result of this instability and uncertainty regarding the outcome of the General Election to be held in June 1991, India's credit rating in the international market had collapsed and the inflows of remittance income from the Middle East had also dried up due to the Gulf conflict. The NRI (non-resident Indians) deposits had started to be withdrawn in the first half of 1991. The inflow of direct foreign investment was also quite meager due to the disincentive policies of the government.

The June 1991 election has brought the Congress Party into power although it was not in absolute majority. The minority government led by Prime Minister Mr. Narasimha Rao was virtually compelled to introduce a series of reforms measures to resolve the crisis. The aim of the reforms was to dismantle the past development policies in which the 'bureaucracy' rather than the 'market' was expected to play the crucial role in economic decision-making. There had been attempts in the past, though with much caution and hesitation, to liberalize the Indian economy. But the philosophy of market oriented liberal economic reforms was not seriously taken as a desirable policy goal in India.[5] Comparing the earlier efforts of liberalization with the present one, the distinguished Indian economist Jagdish Bhagwati writes : " 'Reform by storm' has supplanted the 'reform by stealth' of Mrs. Gandhi's time and the 'reform with reluctance' under Rajiv Gandhi".[6]

It is true that, in contrast to the earlier efforts, the reform measures initiated in 1991 have a clear direction and are 'forceful and explicit'. But it is worth noting that it was the foreign exchange crisis rather than the political will of the ruling government that was responsible for India finally embracing economic reform in 1991. The need for economic reform had been felt in India for a long time but the 'pro-reform' forces were not strong enough to make it possible politically to carry out any full fledged reform programme. The situation in 1991 was different for the following reasons. First of all, there existed no other feasible alternative for the government but to draw loans from the IMF to resolve the crisis even though the loans required the government to take firm

---

[5]Before 1991, close to 93 per cent of all the local production of internationally tradable goods was protected by some type of quantitative import restriction. See Pursell, 1996.

[6]Bhagwati, J., India in Transition: Freeing the Economy, Oxford Clarendon Press 1993.

action both to control and reduce the budget deficit' and also to undertake structural reform. To that extent, India's commitment to liberalize the economy was more of an externally rather than an internally generated phenomenon.

The minority government of Mr. Narashimha Rao had been successful in diverting the attention of his political opponents from the caste-based issues which rocked the economy and brought down the Mr. V.P. Singh opposition government in 1990 towards the more fundamental issue of economic reform. This has indirectly helped in stabilizing the political system. Secondly, with the collapse of communism around the world and the Chinese attempts to introduce market reforms and globalize their economy, the environment has become more conducive for the initiation of reform measures in India. Thirdly, the emergence of an articulate and influential middle class, which wanted economic reforms in India for their own interest, has helped in accentuating the reform process. Had Indira Gandhi or Rajiv Gandhi been confronted with a similar situation, they too perhaps would have responded the same way that Mr. Narasimha Rao did in 1991.

In the past 'anti-reform' forces comprised mainly the agricultural class dominated by the '*kulaks*' (rich landlords) and a small industrial lobby whose interests were better served in a protected market and under governmental support.[7] These forces dominated the political scene in the early epoch of Indian development. However, over the years there has been a substantial expansion of the middle class whose aspirations were to increase their levels of income and consumption. At the same time there has also been a growing enterpreneurial class who sought expansion of their business horizons both domestically and internationally. These are also the groups who have been more vocal and influential. These forces constitute the 'pro-reform' forces and they cut across all political parties. Undoubtedly since the 1970s these forces contributed to a great extent to the gradual deviation from the Nehruvian policies, and

[7]Agriculture is still protected in India from any kind of import competition. For example, exports of most agricultural products are controlled by canalizing agencies and this policy was not changed even till 1991.

they seem to have marginalised the anti reform forces in the new political equilibrium that was established in the 1990s. Also, as noted, the collapse of communism helped in marginalizing the 'anti reform' forces and also in legitimizing the reform programme. At the same time, it helped in discrediting the past policies of controls. The economic crisis of 1991 thus provided the necessary support and boldness to the 'pro-reform' forces to carry out the reform programme.

III. The immediate cause of the crisis

The Indian economy had to face many uncertainties in 1990-91. The Indian Government's Economic Survey, 1990-91, notes: "The effect of the political situation at home, and the persistent fiscal imbalances were accentuated by the Gulf crisis which intensified strains on an already weak balance of payments position". While India's trade balance was always in deficit, the surplus on invisible account helped India to manage its overall current account deficit. For instance, in 1980-81, India had a trade deficit of $7,383 million and a surplus of $5,451 million on invisible account which has brought down the current account deficit to $2,095 million. However, the surplus on invisible account has been declining since then, and, in 1990-91, India observed for the first time a deficit on invisible account of $242 million and a current account deficit of $9,680 million. The immediate issue in 1990-91 was consequently how to finance this unprecendent deficit.

The Gulf War was one of the causes of the current account deficit in 1991. It adversely affected remittance earnings and India's exports to the Middle East. The third-oil shock in 1990-91 also resulted in a sharp rise in India's import bill for crude oil and petroleum products. The rising fiscal deficit also played an important role in causing current account deficits in the balance of payments. The rise in foreign borrowing was also a major component of the fiscal crisis. The external public sector debt as a proportion of GNP rose from 10 per cent in 1980 to almost 21 per cent by 1987/88. As a consequence, debt service as a proportion of exports increased from 7 to 32 per cent. The deterioration in the savings performance of the public sector was another important factor underlying the persistent fiscal imbalances. The year 1990-91 ended with a fiscal deficit of 8.4 per cent of GDP. The deficit then had to be financed either by running down of foreign exchange reserves or through additional external borrowings. The postponement of the regular budget in February 1990 and the subsequent domestic political developments affected confidence abroad in the Indian economy, and it became more difficult to borrow in the international capital markets. Receipts under NRI deposits also decelerated. All of these factors led to a sharp decline in foreign exchange reserves and forced the Government to borrow from the IMF. In January 1991 the Government received an IMF loan of $1.8 billion under the modified Compensatory and Contingency Financing Facility (CCFF) and the first tranche of the standby facility. By October 1991 the borrowing was increased under arrangements that required the Government to reduce the budget deficit and undertake structural reforms. Thus the crisis situation called for urgent and effective measures to correct the structural imbalances which had led to a chronic balance-of-payments problems.

While the Gulf crisis appeared to be the immediate cause of the crisis in 1991, a careful analysis of the Indian economy suggests that the crisis was, as argued by Buiter and Patel, purely home made.[8] The public debt-to-GNP ratio increased through the 1980s and towards the end of the decade it reached almost 60 per cent of GNP.

The factors responsible for the above situation are (i) the failure of the public sector enterprises to generate investible resources and (ii) the explosive growth of the Government's current spending. As a consequence the budget deficit rose from 6.4 per cent to 9 per cent of GDP in the 1980s. The rise of foreign debt was also an important component of the crisis. The macroeconomic crisis was further accentuated by the bureaucratic controls on the economy which resulted in the misallocation of resources and concomitant micro-economic inefficiencies.

---

[8]J Bhagwati (1993) on this For a discussion on the role of debt on BOP crisis, see Manmohan Agarwal, "India", in Padma Desai edited Going global: Transition from Plan to Market in the World Economy, The MIT Press, 1997.

Of course political instability was also responsible for the macro-level crisis. India had been witnessing a crisis in politics since 1975 when Prime Minister Indira Gandhi had declared emergency rule, thus bringing to an end the democratic foundation of the country. Democracy was revived in 1977, of course by Indira Gandhi herself. But the Indian voters had rejected totalitarianism en masse and reaffirmed their confidence and faith in democracy. Indeed Indira Gandhi was defeated in the election of 1977 and an opposition led government for the first time since independence was formed in the centre. However, political instability has become the hallmark of Indian politics since then, and this instability was mainly responsible for the lack of fiscal discipline and continued rise in government deficits.

Thus the micro-economic failings caused by the 'irrational economic policies' and the macro-economic crisis caused by 'growing political indiscipline'—both contributed to the unprecedented crisis in 1991. In this connection, Bhagwati has noted: "...it is hard to imagine that micro-economic reforms now being undertaken would have been attempted with serious resolve unless there had been a compelling crisis, such as the macro-economic crisis at the end of the 1980s, that would clear the economic and political fog and permit a clear view of the inefficiencies of India's micro-economic policies".[9]

IV. The long-term cause

The strategy of economic development that Jawaharlal Nehru (the first Prime Minister of India) initiated during 1950-51 was to attain self-reliance through a democratic development process. The ultimate objective of this strategy, of course, was to remove the abject poverty of the vast Indian masses by means of rapid and sustained economic growth. While democracy was assumed to provide equal opportunity and initiative to every individual for participation in the development process, self reliance was seen as the key to maintain national sovereignty by keeping at a minimum India's dependence on other countries. In fact, self-reliance limited the degrees of

[9]See Bhagwati, J. 1993, India in Transition : Freeing the Economy, Oxford: Clarendon Press.

freedom in the formulation of trade policy because the logical conclusion of self-reliance was to produce 'everything' locally at whatever the cost. Since resources for development were limited and domestic consumption difficult to restrint in democracy, a complex system of quantitative controls came into being with the formulation of the Industrial Licensing Policy of 1956. The inward looking strategy of development with an elaborate control regime and government's active and increasing role in production and distribution were thought to be adequate to attain rapid growth and social justice. The Indian development planners never thought that it was necessary to examine whether the objectives and the instruments they used to achieve those objectives were consistent and viable.

Nehru's vision of development and self-reliance also guided his foreign policy. It was the hey day of the Cold War. Nehru decided to maintain a safe distance from each of the two power blocs and he initiated his foreign policy of non-alignment. He believed that non-alignment was the best strategy for India to get the maximum help and aid from each of the blocs of countries. The Nehruvian strategy was indeed a remarkable success in providing the country with a stable and functioning democratic political institution. Nehru could foresee that there was no better alternative to democracy to unite as vast and heterogeneous a society like the Indian society. And history proves that Nehru was right. Democracy turned out not to be a serious hindrance to the mobilization of resources for development. The gross domestic savings of the country increased from about 10 per cent of GDP in 1950-51 to 23 per cent in 1991-92. The democratic experiment in development also succeeded in increasing the life expectancy of the Indian people from about 32 years in 1950-51 to 60 years in 1990-91. Similarly, the literacy per centage increased from 18 per cent in 1950-51 to 52 per cent 1990-91. Technological progress in agriculture was undoubtedly impressive, making India almost self sufficient in food. These are no mean achievements.

Yet, on the economic front, the Nehruvian strategy failed badly in achieving its main economic development, that is, removal of poverty. Although there are studies showing that the poverty ratio, as estimated by Planning Commission, declined from about

51.5 per cent in 1972-73 to 38 per cent in 1987-88, the poor still constitute more than a quarter of India's 900 million population. Further, we can also observe increasing inequality in personal and regional income distribution over the years. These developments in income distribution, particularly in regional income distribution, have threatened increasingly the democratic polity on the one hand and the stability and the unity of the country on the other hand. Nehru wished to produce an economic miracle with the help of now discredited economic doctrines' which partly explain why his strategy of development failed to bring about the desired results. India's comparative growth performance during the entire post independence period is shown in Table 1.

Table 1
India's Annual Average Growth rates of GDP at 1980-81 prices

Period	Growth rate
1961-62 to 1970-71	3.5
1971-72 to 1980-81	3.1
1981-82 to 1990-91	5.6
1990-91	5.4
1991-92	0.8
1992-93	5.3
1993-94	6.2
1994-95	7.8
1995-96	7.2
1996-97	7.5

Source: Economic Survey, 1997-98, Government of India.

The growth rate is indeed disappointing if one looks at the growth of savings and investment. Total savings have increased from about 9.3 per cent of GDP in 1950-51 to 26.1 per cent at current prices in 1996-97. Similarly, gross capital formation increased from 10.2 per cent in 1950-51 to 27.3 per cent at current prices in 1990-91. This disproportionately between low growth and savings-investment rates must be explained. The Mahalanobis model of development in India was based on the basic premise that savings were the major constraint to economic growth. Therefore the planners' view of economic growth centered mainly around increasing the rate of investment via increasing national savings (and external assistance). The subsequent experience of economic development in India demonstrated that the planners went totally wrong in putting the entire burden of development on savings alone. That is, savings were not the major constraint to economic growth. Rather, the fundamental problem of Indian economic growth turned out to be the disproportionately crisis : high savings (and investment) and low growth.

V. The Causes of Low Growth

Several studies have shown that the basic cause of low growth has been the decline in the growth of productivity. In particular, the productivity of capital alone may explain the poor growth performance of Indian industries. While there are many reasons for this, in short, it at least shows that the Nehruvian planners were wrong in framing Indian development strategy by assuming that savings alone were the major constraint to growth.

The three basic reasons for the low productivity growth in India are: (i) extensive bureaucratic controls over production, investment and trade; (ii) inward-looking trade and foreign investment policies; and (iii) a substantial public sector. According to Bhagwati these "three sets of policy decisions broadly set strict limits to what India could get out of its investment".[10]

(a) Internal competition

Bureaucratic controls over entry of firms into industries and also over firms' decision on capacity and investment prevented healthy economy competition within India's internal market. It led to all kinds of rent seeking and productive inefficiency at the level of the firms. There was no incentive for technical innovation as can be seen, for example, from the fact that the same passenger car was sold for half a century without any major modification! Industrial

---

[10]Ibid.

development has been associated with a rising trend in capital intensity and a decline in productivity growth. A capital poor country like India certainly cannot afford to have the luxury of a industrialization process based on rising capital intensity. Along with rising capital intensity, it was also observed that there has been a rise in capital output ratios. These two factors partly explain the disproportionately crisis–high investment and low growth–as discussed above.

Distinguishing between technical change and firm level efficiency change, Barua and Das[11] have observed that there was no technical progress in Indian industries after 1974, and Indian industries have witnessed over the years a secular decline in efficiency.

(b) External competition

Apart from protecting the industries from internal competition, Indian industries were also protected from international competition by high tariffs and various non tariff barriers. Similarly, India's trade policies were biased against exports, which possibly grew out of the export pessimism of the 1950s. As a result India's export performance has been steadily declining, and its share of world exports declined from 2 per cent in 1960 to 0.5 per cent in 1990-91. The distorted export-import policies not only contributed to inefficient industrial structure within India's protective environment but were also responsible for India's chronic balance-of-payments problems. India was clearly unable to realize the gains from booming world trade like the East Asian tigers especially had done.

(c) Public sector

Finally, the inefficient functioning of public-sector enterprises adversely affected their contribution to the economy and created a condition of rising fiscal deficits that resulted in a serious macro-economic imbalance. Tables 2 and 3 show performance of India's public sector enterprise.

---

[11] n. 1.

Table 2
Profitability Profile of non-Departmental Central Government PEs, 1990-93

	1990-91	1991-92	1992-93
Number of Operating Enterprises	236	237	237
Profitable	125	135	133
Loss-making	111	102	104
Profit of PEs (Rs. billion)	54	61	73
(% of GDP)	(1)	(1)	(1)
Loss of PEs	31	37	40
(% of GDP)	0.6	0.6	0.6

Table 3
Profit margins in Selected Sectors (per cent of sales)

	1990-91	1991-92	1992-93
Steel			
PEs	-3.9 (9)	-5.8 (9)	-1.7 (9)
Private	2.4 (164)	2.9 (151)	2.4 (92)
Fertilisers			
PEs	-8.5 (8)	-7.5 (8)	-11.29 (8)
Private	6.9 (25)	5.9 (22)	4.5 (13)
Chemical & Pharmac.			
PEs	-2.9 (20)	-3.1 (20)	1.5 (20)
Private	4.3 (181)	4.7 (175)	5.0 (109)
Heavy Engineering			
PEs	-3.0 (16)	-2.7 (16)	-2.3 (16)
Private	3.4 (82)	3.7 (80)	3.6 (57)
Other Engineering			
PEs	1.5 (23)	1.3 (23)	2.3 (23)
Private	3.5 (169)	3.4 (166)	3.5 (102)
Textile			
PEs	-16.7 (14)	-23.7 (14)	-39.2 (14)
Private	3.9 (186)	2.3 (174)	2.2 (108)

Note: Number of enterprises in the sample in parentheses. Profits are net of taxes.
Source: India: Recent Economic Developments and Prospects. A World Bank Country Study.

(d) Instruments of controls

Several regulations and laws empowered the government to give the public sector the exclusive privilege of investing in the key sectors of the economy. Private investment was regulated even in sectors where it was permitted. Private investment in housing in urban areas was affected by the Urban Land Ceiling Act of 1976, which subjects all sale of urban land to state government approval. In agriculture, private investment in storage was controlled indirectly by a ceiling on the amount for which commodities could be stored, bans on future and forward trading in agricultural commodities, and directly by licensing restrictions in agro-processing. In manufacturing, any investment in a registered industrial firm (responsible for 3/4th of manufacturing) for expansion or diversification of production required prior government approval. Additional restrictions applied to foreign investors. The Foreign Exchange Regulation Act (FERA) of 1973 (amended in January 1993) prevented companies with more than 40 per cent of foreign equity from borrowing funds or raising deposits in India, taking over any business interest from an Indian resident, acquiring or disposing of any physical assets (including land) within India, appointing technicians or managers without RBI (Reserve Bank of India) clearance, and using their trademark without RBI clearance. It is indicative of the restrictiveness of the foreign investment regime that as recently as early 1993 there were only about 80 firms in India with foreign equity exceeding 40 per cent.

VI. The Strategy of the 1991 reform

The strategy of the reform program has been to reform the economic structure in a sequential manner through a set of policies relating to the investment regime, trade policies, the financial sector, taxation and public enterprises. The major objective of the reform process was to reduce the capital intensity of India's growth process and lessen reliance on the unsustainable expansion of the public sector, thereby translating the country's relatively high investment rate into high and sustainable growth of output and employment.

The success of any economic reform process within a democratic framework requires an overwhelming support of the people and therefore public debate on the essentials of the reform policies constitutes an important ingredient of the reform process. Since July 1991, the government has appointed several high level committees of experts to formulate reform proposals such as the Narasimham Committee on the financial sector reform, the Chelliah Committee on taxation, the Goswami Committee on exit policies, the Rangarajan Committee on disinvestment of government equity holding in public enterprises and the Malhotra Committee on the insurance industry. These were followed by other committees to examine the technical aspects of reforms. Based on the recommendations of these committees the government prepares its policy papers. The reports and government papers have been made public and amply discussed among academics, industrialsts, and unions. This approach helped the Government build consensus around its economic program, anticipate public reactions to reform measures and avoid reversals. It also helped the Government to avoid errors in sequencing of reforms.

(a) Sequencing of reform

Broadly speaking, economic liberalization in India began with the liberalization of the product markets through the dismantling of industrial and import licensing policies which regulated both investment and trade. This was followed by the liberalization of factor markets which was achieved partly by the liberalization of financial markets.

A sharp devaluation (in July 1991) preceded the lifting of quantitative restrictions on imports of intermediates and capital goods which had in turn preceded reduction in tariffs.

(b) Liberalization measures

Over the period 1991-92 to 1995-96, the Government has introduced numerous measures which have effectively dismantled the previous system of controls and opened most areas of the economy to the private sector. Only insurance, railways and postal services are now the exclusive monopoly of the government. Private investment in power is now unrestricted with up to 100 per cent of foreign equity. The banking sector is being gradually opened as part of the financial sector reform. Lifting of restrictions on private sector participation in the insurance industry is under consideration. Private airlines have already captured one third of the domestic airline industry. In manufacturing investments licensing ceased to be a constraint both for domestic and foreign investors, except for private investment in agro-processing. In addition, the January 1993 amendment of the FERA Act now eliminated virtually all differences between foreign and domestic private investors. India allows foreign investment in the mining sector up to 50 per cent of equity while mining is reserved for domestic investors in most East Asian countries. Further, companies with foreign equity investment of any size are treated essentially at par with domestic investors.

(c) Trade regime

India's trade regime was characterized by an extremely complex import licensing system based on twenty-six lists of commodities that classified all importables with different approval procedure for each list and 10 different types of licenses applied to over 4,000 of the approximately 5,000 codes of the Harmonized System of classification used in the Indian tariff schedule. There were export controls over 440 items, agricultural commodities accounting for half of the restricted items and the exchange rate was a crawling peg fixed periodically by the RBI.

Licensing requirements on imports of intermediates and capital goods have been eliminated. Several rounds of tariff cuts have reduced maximum tariffs from 400 per cent in 1990-91 to 50 per cent in 1995-96. The government has also indicated that over the next few years remaining licensing restrictions on imports (of consumer goods) would be eliminated. Export controls have been reduced. In addition the Government has liberalized the foreign exchange regime. The rupee was floated in March 1992 and near full current account convertibility established in March 1994.

(d) Financial sector

The discretion of financial institutions over portfolio composition has increased and incentives for efficient use of funds improved. Control over the lending decisions of banks have been relaxed. Interest rate controls have been relaxed and restriction on access of firms to capital markets removed. Public banks are being made more autonomous and their capital base is being strengthened both through direct budgetary support and changes in legislation enabling them to mobilize resources from the market.

(e) Tax system

Five taxes account for 95 per cent of India's total tax collection which are 16-17 percent of GDP: customs, excise, sales taxes, taxes on corporate income; and personal income. All these taxes suffered from the common problem of high and highly differentiated tax rates falling on a narrow base. Together with several hundreds of exemptions, the opaque and highly differentiated tax system complicated tax administration encouraged litigation. In addition sharing revenues with the states from the personal income tax and excise has led to serious allocative inefficiencies. Over the last six years Government has simplified and rationalized the complex and opaque tax structure. The thrusts of the policy are simplification, lower rates and greater buoyancy.

(f) Public Enterprise

There are about 1000 non-financial public enterprises (PEs) in India, of which 300 are owned by the Central Government and about 700 by state governments. PEs have been the Government's most important vehicle to channel resources to key sectors of the economy.

India's PEs mange 55 percent of the economy's capital stock (excluding households) and generate one-fourth of the country's non-agricultural GDP. In July 1991 the central government announced a three-pronged strategy to improve PEs' weak finances and economic performance consisting of : (i) eliminating PEs' privileges such as protection from external and domestic competition and preferential access to budget and bank resources (through forced holding of government debt); (ii) restructuring potentially viable PEs, liquidating others and establishing a safety net program to cushion the social cost; and (iii) providing PEs greater autonomy and the mandate to become profit oriented.

VII. The responses to reform

The economy has responded positively to the reform measures. The balance of payments has shown a steady improvement since 1991-92 with exports covering a larger proportion of imports than in the earlier years. The export-import ratio has increased from 0.65 in 1990-91 to 0.83 in 1997-98. The current account deficit has also declined from 3.2 per cent of GDP in 1990-91 to 0.4 percent of GDP in 1993-94 which has now increased to 1.5 percent of GDP in 1997-98. Of course, severe import compression policies also helped in containing imports to a large extent which indirectly affected industrial growth. This was particularly true for two years after 1995. However, improvement in the BOP position has resulted in an unprecedented buildup of foreign exchange reserves, as can be seen in Table 4.

The unification of the exchange rate and the removal of exchange restrictions on imports through the abolition of foreign exchange budgeting in the beginning of 1993-94 constituted the first major step toward current account convertibility. In August 1994, India accepted its obligations under Article VIII of the IMF, under which, India is committed to forsake the use of exchange restrictions on current international transactions as an instrument in managing the balance of payments. These developments are a reflection of a shift from a foreign-exchange constrained control economy to a more open, market-driven and liberalized economy.

As a result of the policy change, net capital inflows from abroad have risen from about $4.3 billion (including IMF transaction) in 1992-93 to $9.2 billion in 1993-94. The share of foreign

Table 4
India's Foreign Exchange Reserve
(in million US dollars)

1990-91	$2236	1 month's import
1991-92	$5631	3.4 month's import
1992-93	$6434	3.5 month's import
1993-94	$15068	7.8 month's import
1994-95	$20809	9 month's import
1995-96	$17044	
1996-97	$22367	
1997-98	$25975	

Source: Economic Survey, 1997-98, Government of India

investment flows in the total capital flows rose from $585 million in 1992-93 to $4.1 billion.

The composition of these flows has also changed towards equity and away from debt. Similarly, external assistance, external commercial borrowing, IMF loans and NRI deposits have declined progressively from 85.8 per cent of net capital inflow to 40 per cent in 1993-94. The DFI was on the order of $150 million in 1991-92. It has increased to $620 million in 1993-94 and to $756 million during April-December of 1994-95.

The annual increase in the stock of external debt declined from a high of $8.1 billion in 1990-91 to $0.7 billion in 1993-94. The proportion of short-term debt in total external debt fell from 10.2 per cent at the end of 1990-91 to 4.0 percent at the end of 1993-94 with a further decline to 3.1 percent by the September 1994. The proportion of concessional debt has remained unusually high at 47 percent compared to other developing countries with large debt stock such as Brazil (2%) Chile (16%), Indonesia (28%), Mexico (1%) and Russian Federation (5%).

India's External Debt
(in billion US Dollars)

	Debt	Debt Service Ratio	Debt/GDP
1990	$75.9		
1991	$84	35.3	30.4
1992	$85.3	30.2	41.0
1993	$90	28.6	39.8
1994	$92.6	26.9	35.9
1995	$99.0	27.5	32.7
1996	$92.2	25.7	28.7
1997	$92.2		
1998	$92.9		

Source: Economic Survey, 1994-95, Government of India.

The year 1994-95 saw the fastest growth of the Indian economy in the last four years, that is from 0.9 percent in 1991-92 to 7.8 percent. The economy has been growing above 7 percent during the periods of 1995-96 and 1996-97. This has been so despite a negative growth of agriculture in 1995-96. However, agriculture has been growing at a record rate of 7.3 percent during 1996-97. During the years of 1994-95 and 1995-96, manufacturing, electricity, construction and gas and water supply had been growing above 10 percent per annum. But the growth rate of this sector has declined to only 6.8 percent in 1996-97. The growth of GDP in 1978-98 has declined to 5 percent due to sharp fall in agricultural growth and deceleration in the growth of industry. One of the major reason for this is the demand slow down in the export market.

VIII. The future of the reform process

The liberalisation policies have succeeded in stabilising the economy to a remarkable degree. However, the fiscal deficit continues to remain high and is the major cause of inflationary pressure. The borrowing requirements of a high fiscal deficit are the source of pressure on interest rates and adversely affect the availability of resources for productive investment. There are still many bureaucratic barriers to competition. Continued dismantling of barriers to competition must be a key element of further reform. Substitution of tariffs for quantitative import restrictions will improve efficiency and check smuggling.

It is necessary to phase out unnecessary legal and bureaucratic impediments which impose time delays and costs on producers, without contributing to efficiency. Finally the role of State governments is critical because land use, water power generation and distribution and roads come under the purview of State governments.

The future of economic reform and the speed with which the reform measures will be implemented will depend on political stability as well as on the speed with which the government carry out the reform measures. There is still a large area virtually untouched by the reform measures. The crisis of 1991 showed clearly that fiscal excess, political instability and governmental inaction can combine to have a serious consequences. But what we have learnt from our recent past history is that political inaction cannot be taken for granted. The philosophy of economic reform has now been accepted by the people of India in general and also all the political parties have taken a positive view towards the need for economic reform for rapid economic growth. This gives an element of certainty towards the continuity of the economic reform process in India.

13
Transnational Companies and Indian Industry‡

ARUN KUMAR*

1. Introduction

The Indian economy started its recent process of opening up to the rest of the world in June 1991 in the face of a crisis[1]. Problem were encountered on several fronts, like, the BOP, budgetary deficit, unemployment and inflation. Most critically, the country was about to default on its international payments obligation (due to a loss of confidence by the international financial community). This was not only due to the adverse trade scenario but also because of the actions of NRIs and Indian businessmen. Indian capital has used NRIs as fronts to park funds siphoned out of the economy through under and over invoicing of trade and parallel banking channels, like havala. In 1990-91, Indian capital at home and abroad speculated on the value of the Rupee and magnified the extent of the crisis (See Kumar, 1991b-6).

Globalisation implies allowing two way flow of capital and goods. Proponents argue that foreign capital is essential to upgrade technology and make the economy 'efficient'. Opening up forces the adjustment of the economy to the external environment. The

---

‡This article is a revised version of 'New Economic Policies: Prospects for the industries sector, Exam growth and social change, Sept. 1993.

*Dr. Arun Kumar is an Associate Professor in the Centre for Economic Studies and Planning, SSS JNU New Delhi.

[1]Earlier phases when the Indian economy was opened up are the pre-independence period and starting with the Asiad in 1982 and accelerating with the Rajiv Gandhi period. However, the phases of openness differ substantially from what has been initiated in 1991. There is a paradigm shift both nationally and internationally.

size and influence of global capital can be gauged from the estimated daily transactions of $500 billion in early nineties (133% of the South Asian GDP). This sum dwarfs the national economies so that in today's context, opening up forces the adjustment of national economies to the interest of global capital.

Ownership of global capital is dominated by the TNCs and 90 per cent of them originate in the advanced nations (Table 1). Consequently, these countries further the interest of the TNCs[2]

Table 1
Number of Parent TNCs and Foreign Affiliates, Early 1990s

Area/Economy	Parent Corp Based in Country	Foreign Affiliates Located in Country	Year
Developed Countries	33,500	81,800	
Germany (FRG)	6,984	11,821	1990
Japan	3,529	3,150	1992
USA	3,000	14,900	1990
Developing Economics	2,700	71,300	
Brazil	566	7,100	1992
China	379	15,966	1989
India	187	926	1991
S Korea	1,049	3,671	1991
World	36,600	1,74,900	

Source: World Investment Report 1993. An Executive Summary pp. 2-3.

[2]It is often argued that today capital respects no boundaries so that it is not tied to nation state. This argument is incorrect since TNCs or mutual funds originate in specific countries and their governments represent their interests in world fora, like, the WTO or when they face problems like when Enron was in trouble, the US government intervened with the Indian government. Korten (1995) quotes US Treasury officials as saying that for every $1 the US Government contributes to the World bank, more than $2 comes back to the US. (p. 167).

which require (amongst other things) increased access to markets for accelerated growth. The WTO, the IMF and the World Bank, dominated by the advanced nations represent the interest of global capital. The advice tendered by these agencies to nations facing BOP problems and seeking their assistance is to open up, whether or not this is in the interest of the country being advised. This is the context of India's opening up-under pressure from global capital.

A country going for Globalisation of the IMF and the World Bank variety is required to modify its economic policies so as to facilitate the functioning of international capital. WTO has carried this process a step further. In India since TNCs have been operating for a long time (perhaps East India Company was the first of them) and by 1990 over 900 of them were present in various forms (Table 1), a base for global capital has existed. With NEP changing the policy regime, a new chapter has opened up for the functioning of TNCs.

Capital is not just an abstraction or a number but carries with it social, political and economic relations. It brings with it a paradigm of 'consumerism' and 'development'. It effects fashion, art and culture. It has a profound effect on family, environment and individual's notions of success and so on. While this may represent greater interaction across nations which is not bad, one way influence is not desirable. With few exceptions, this is what is happening in much of the Third World.

Globalisation has strengthened international capital and TNCs since it is forcing the Third World Nations to compete with each other to obtain a share of the considerable global capital[3]. The carrot dangling before each nation is that even a small fraction of it flowing in its direction can change the investment climate of that country. Consequently, TNCs are obtaining concessions not even available to local capital so that the terms of trade are shifting in favour of the advanced nations. The working of the WTO has

[3]Not only the nations are competing in India even the State governments are vying with each other to offer greater concessions to attract foreign capital. This has globally weakened labour viz-a-viz capital.

further aided this process by enabling a tighter grip over technology. How does all this impact Indian industry?

The industrial sector is affected not just by policies specific to it but also by fiscal policies, trade policies, labour legislation and other such policies. In other words, the New Economic Policies (NEP) as a whole effect the industrial sector. The impact of TNCs on Indian industry is also going to be multifarious; through competition, access to finance and technology, impact on labour markets, income-differential and uncertainty, etc. As such, to understand what is in store for Indian industries it is necessary to analyze both the specific new industrial policies and NEP as a whole.

To facilitate TNCs, FERA has been diluted and restrictions on repatriation of dividends and the requirements of indigenisation (PMP) almost eliminated. To promote marketization, planning has been down graded while licensing has been ended. Checks on the growth of monopolies are now non existent. A variety of tax concessions have been offered to the corporate sector, the upper income groups and to investments in the share market. Foreign investments are being given special concessions over and above those offered to Indian capital. Customs duties have been reduced drastically and the borrowings by the government and the public sector reduced so as to make more funds available to the private sector. To discipline labour, an Exit Policy is sought to be introduced along with golden handshake and VRS. (See Kumar, 1994).

Industry has never had it so good. Yet, all this has produced an uncertain result. The rate of industrial growth slumped in the period 1991-94 (lowest after 1979-80) then it rose sharply for two years[4] (to historically highest level) and again fell after 1996-97 (See Table 2 and for monthly data for 1985-95 see Kumar [1996]).

---

[4]There has been much attempt to present a brighter picture of performance of the economy and data have been repeatedly changed (See Kumar, 1994). Data change within the same document as in the Economic Survey, 1997-98 between pages 3 and 5. A higher growth of the industrial sector may be a result of the reporting of the previously unreported output by the private sector in order to dress up their balance sheets.

Table 2
Growth Rate (%) of Industrial Production

Year/Plan	Plan	Plan	91-92	92-93	93-94	94-95	95-96	96-97	97-98
Industry	7th	8th							
Manuf.	7.7	9.2	0.6	4.2	8.4	11.9	14	7.4	3.6
Industry	7.5	8.0	-0.8	4.2	6.6	10.4	12.5	6.4	4.2

Note: Figures for 95-96 to 97-98 are provisional
Source: Economic Survey 1997-98 pp 3-5 and CSO.

This uncertain growth in a period of massive concessions to industry needs analysis?

The structure of Indian industry is complex. It consists of an organised and an unorganised sector. The organised sector consists of the public and the private sectors. The private organised sector itself is made up of the TNCs and the Indian companies. Using scale as the basis, Indian companies can be classified as large, medium or small. The unorganized sector consists of the small scale sector, cottage and village industries. NEP affect the fortunes of each of these components in different ways–this needs to be understood to resolve the paradox.

To understand what NEP is attempting to achieve and whether it will succeed in doing so, it is necessary to analyse the performance of Indian industries in the period before NEP were launched. Though doubts about the quality of data exist, the average rate of growth of Indian industry at constant prices was close to 6.6% between 1980-81 and 1990-91. Yet, dissatisfaction was expressed with this performance since the East Asian Tigers, Japan and China were doing much better in terms of growth, exporters, technological dynamism and avoiding the kind of BOP pressures India faced.[5]

Proponents of NEP suggest that India's slow growth is a consequence of the shackles placed on Indian industry, export

[5]Problems have appeared in these countries since the last two years but it cannot be denied that they did considerably better than India in the Eighties and the first part of the nineties.

pessimism, inefficiency of Indian labour and the low level of prevailing technology. Government intervention is seen as the villain of the piece. The solution proposed under NEP was a reduced role of the State and incentives to industry (listed above). Protectionist tariffs and quotas are supposed to have made Indian industry flabby and MRTP and FERA had reined in those who were apparently rearing to grow. However, why did the private sector not expand in the international markets which are supposed to be free considering that there were not only few restrictions on exports, when a variety of incentives were available?

If Indian big business and TNCs operating from India were indeed dynamic and only reined in by MRTP and FERA, they could have expanded abroad. In India itself, they expanded into most areas, directly or through other means. Their average rate of growth was higher than that of industry as a whole (Kumar 1993a). If they had exported more, they could have grown even faster. It is argued that they were too comfortable in the domestic market and, therefore, did not make the effort abroad. In other words, they were not dynamic enough. Yet, NEP puts a great deal of faith in these entities. Would Globalisation make them dynamic?

2. *'Efficiency' and Labour*

'Efficiency' is the new buzz word. There can be no quarrel with making India more efficient. But it is not clear what is meant by this term or whether say, an 'Exit Policy' would help to achieve it.

One way of defining efficiency would be that with the smallest possible resource cost to society the maximum be produced for the welfare of *all* (not just a minority). This requires a redistribution of incomes in society and overall planning for the optimum utilization of the resources. A prerequisite for all this is a bureaucracy and an industry which will deliver what is desired by policy. These are conspicuous by their absence.

The proponents of NEP do not accept the above definition. They argue that one has to accept the income distribution as it exists and allow individuals to maximize their welfare. For them, the only policy should be to end policy and to let the markets as defined by the current distribution of wealth and political power operate. It is suggested that such markets, freed from government intervention, would be the 'most efficient' in the sense of improving the welfare of individuals as they themselves perceive it. This is a prescription for status quo[6].

If the theoretical argument for opening the economy under any circumstance was valid, the G7 nations should do this good to themselves before recommending it to others. Clearly, they do not believe in it but use the argument to get other nation's markets opened. The US in violation of the then existing GATT rules used to threaten its trade partners with action under 301 (Special and Super). It has not unilaterally opened its markets and used them to force others to comply with its conditions.

It is argued that one reason for inefficiency in Indian industry is labour indiscipline due to protection and manifests itself in high wages and over employment. Whereas the latter is certainly the case to varying degrees, the former is not. In fact, in spite of the latter, the Indian wage cost per unit of output is usually less than that of most other countries in the world. It is then unlikely that Indian labour costs are the reason for India's inability to compete globally or an indication of inefficiency. The share of wages, salary and bonus in the total cost has declined since the early Seventies (Sharma 1991).

In India, the wage indexation to inflation is incomplete even for those who are the best organised, the Government employees. In all the recent pay revisions, the idexation has been partial. Data are often quoted from the public sector showing that the average emoluments of PSU workers have risen faster than the cost of living index (Economic Survey).

This is misleading. It is argued in Kumar (1989) that employment

[6]Can Globalisation and entry of TNCs be called status quoist? The status quo referred to here is between the propertied and the non-propertied. If amongst the set of the propertied, new actors like TNCs become dominant at the expense of Indian capital this does not make policy less status quoist. It implies that Indian capital has been short sighted.

in the public sector has changed in favour of the managerial cadres and skilled employees. It is unclear what has happened to the age and the seniority structure but very likely, the increased skills of those employed should lead to a rise in the average emoluments. Finally, the product mix of the public sector has changed in favour of more sophisticated products requiring more skilled workers. Thus, raw time series data on emoluments are not suitable to argue that real wages have risen or that inflation indexation exists or that labour is inefficient.

Ajit (1992) shows that in organised manufacturing, capital labour ratio went up during the Seventies and the Eighties, productivity of labour rose but that of capital declined. It may be argued that labour productivity should have risen more and over employment needs to be eliminated but given the cost structure, reduction in employment will hardly lower costs; something else needs to be done. The black economy needs to be brought under check and management practices changed. In effect, inefficiency in Indian industry may have more to do with capital than with labour. While capital has indulged in malpractices, labour has responded through indiscipline, etc.

3. *TNCs, Globalisation and Indian Industries*

3.1 TNCs in India: Possible Benefits

Under NEP, great store is set by globalisation of the Indian economy to end many of the perceived ills of Indian industries. It is believed that TNCs would make available advanced technology and to introduce better management practices to upgrade Indian industry and enhance its productivity. They are for the consumers at lower prices. Great store is laid on the possible role in promoting exports and helping stabilise the BOP.

TNCs can be expected to do what is in their best interest but is it in their interest to promote Indian industry? Given the size of Indian capital and its technological backwardness why would TNCs help Indian capital, specially when they are being given easy access to the Indian markets. Some argue that since they are unfamiliar with the Indian markets they need Indian capital. Perhaps, but this would only be a temporary phase and cannot be a reason for TNCs to enable Indian capital to acquire any degree of independence of autonomy. With the marginalisation of the PSUs and Indian private sector lacking the capability to absorb and develop technology (with few exceptions) autonomy is unlikely even if access is allowed to technology. Maruti after 15 years still designs cars in Japan and does not manufacture gear boxes. TELCO has not been able to develop an indigenous truck in over thirty years.

TNCs may introduce modern business practices or advertising, etc., but lead to reduced employment, consumerism, inequity and cultural effects. The increased choice of products is only for the well off sections since TNCs mostly produce premium products. This is true even items of daily use like, cosmetics, detergents, soaps, etc. Soft drinks, Mcdonalds and KFC may be for the common man in the advanced nations but in India only the well off can afford them. The white goods sector and automobiles are clearly only for the well off. The high pressured advertising that accompanies products manufactured by TNCs trying to establish a toehold in India is promoting greater consumerism with attendant problems.

It is unclear that there would be greater competition in the Indian market leading to reduced prices for the consumer. As argued above the premium products introduced by the TNCs tend to be higher priced ones. Thus, for the bulk of the population there is no reduction in prices. Anyway, internationally, TNCs tend to have managed competition and they are likely to practice the same in India. Pre-1991, this was the prevalent situation in India with a large number of firms operating in most products but managing competition amongst themselves. Thus, nothing much is likely to change on this front, except the names may be different.

3.2 Negligible Global Weight

Globalisation would ideally have meant that while India opens itself to foreign influences it would be able to influence policies in other countries to its advantage. It has been argued by some that Indian economy has matured and can face international competition. But, India's weight in global GDP, Investment, S & T, Exports and Imports is negligible (Table 3). It can hardly affect international events (especially, economic) so that once the only card it had, namely, access to its market, is given away for free, none need concede anything to it. There is no bargain left, only a one way impact on India is likely.

Table 3
India and the World Economy in 1995: A Comparison

	India	World	Japan	USA	SKorea	China
1. GDP (Billion $)	324	27,846	5,109	6,952	455	698
2. Exports(")	31	5,145	443	585	125	149
3. Imports(")	35	5,246	336	771	135	129
4. Inv/GDP (%)	25	23	29	16	37	40
5. Pvt Cons/GDP (%)	68	63	60	68	54	46
Share in Total Household Consumption (%) in 1990						
6. Food	52		16	13	35	61
7. Consumer Durables	3		6	7	5	

Source: World Development Report, 1997 and 1990.

In the reckoning of the advanced nations, in economic terms, India counts for little. India would have to globalise on their terms. Capitalism has tended to increase concentration and centralization; amongst nations, within nations and within groups. International experience is consistent with this. Most of the Third World countries which came into the orbit of international capital in the Seventies and the Eighties have had to pay a heavy price[7].

[7]The success of the NICs since the Seventies needs to be viewed in the context of the fight of capitalism against communism. Without belittling their achievements, it needs to be stressed that access to technology and markets was allowed to these countries. Capitalism for its own needs allows certain regions to grow. Further, some of these countries acted in their own best interest and refused to succumb to outside pressures.

Economic drain from the Third World is going on apace (UNCTAD, UNICEF and ILO have documented this). They have had to give in to more and more demands from the advanced nations and the TNCs. Globalisation has drawn India also into this web.

NEP are based on the logic that economic agents do the best for themselves if left free by governments and this through the invisible hand leads to the betterment of society. If this is accepted then surely the TNCs and the G7 would also do what is best for them. Why would they not act on it? They know India is weak and willing to make concessions. Why would they be interested in a positive sum game viz-a-viz India when they could get more in today's situation? Since they do not constitute a whole with India, what is best (getting the maximum) for them is not the best for India but at a cost (Kumar, 1991b). Exports illustrate this.

3.3 Export Possibilities

Developing India as an export base would require significant increase in exports in certain sectors. This would mean increased international competition. Who would promote exports, TNCs or Indian capital? Table 4 shows that since 1991, only 8% of Investment proposals are for Exports and the foreign equity involved is 12%. In other words, exports from India are hardly a priority for capital –Indian or foreign.

The TNCs' interest is in the Indian market and in promoting the interest of their parent companies in the world markets but not in increased *net* exports from India. The strategy of the TNCs, controlled by the parent companies, would be to maximize their global profits and not only that of a subsidiary. For this, export from India need not be a priority. Opening up of markets leads to access to local markets and increased profits. Increased net exports from India do not ensure larger profits specially if world trade is growing slowly. Can this happen as a result of strategic tie up with TNCs? For, this India would have to become a part of the global production structure of some TNCs. This is a complex matter and would take a while given the state of Indian politics

Table 4
Industrial Investment (Aug 1991 to Oct 1996)

Category	Number		Proposed	Inv (Rs Cr)	Employment
	Total	Foreign	Total	Foreign Equity	
IEMs	27,743		5,37,926		49,53,916
LOIs	2,714		88,907		6,17,976
IEM+LOI	30,457	4,391	6,26,833	71,743	55,71,892
EOUs	2,810	956	50,224	6,248	4,91,176
GDR		36		10,196	
TOTAL	33,267	5,383	6,77,057	88,188	60,63,068

Source: SIA Statistics Vol II. No. 8, Dec. 1996, Min of Industries GOI, p. 2.

Note 1: Data reveals that upto March 1998. IEMs increased to 32,918 involving an investment of Rs 6.09.184 crore and employment of 56,51,000. LOIs were 3127 with an investment of Rs 1,01,774 cr and employment of 7,34,000 (Economic Survey 1997-98:101). 1995 was the peak year.

Note 2: IEM–Industrial Entrepreneur Memoranda
LOI–Letter of Intent
EOU–100% Exports Oriented Units.
GDR–Global Depository Receipts

and of infrastructure. It has not yet happened in the last seven years.

TNCs are also supposed to be afraid of loss of control over their technology if they do not have control over the firms. Hence they may prefer imports or assembly of goods to manufacture. Would 100% equity change this since then the TNCs would get the entire profit for themselves and would have no fear of loss of control over technology? Even then the argument for exploiting the Indian market would stand as a better option than increasing net exports.

Indian big business cannot export more unless they get access to foreign markets. In today's world, this is also dependent on the TNCs. If Indian businesses are unable to face competition from TNCs in their own preferred home markets it is unlikely they would be able to do so in the international markets. It is worth noting that in most foreign collaboration agreements (whether equity or technical or financial collaboration in India), there are restrictions on exports. Post 1991, conditions of collaboration have become more adverse since TNCs have gained the upper hand viz-a-viz Indian partners (Table 5).

Table 5
Conditions of Foreign Collaboration: A Comparison

Years	1988-90	1991-93
Category		
1. By Duration of Agreement		
a. Ten years and more	11%	36%
b. No duration	15.6%	0.4%
2. By Royalty Range		
a. 5% and above	24.8%	46.5%
b. 3% and less	61%	49.4%
3. By Export Clauses in Technology Agreement		
a. Differential royalty	15%	22.3%
b. 100% exports	15.12%	11.04%
c. Buyback	4.7%	1.02%
d. Export Oriented	36.2%	16.9%
e. More than 40% financial equity	4.8%	30.9%

Source: Subrahmanian (1996).

Table 5 shows that India is not gaining access to markets due to the restrictive conditions in collaboration agreements. Clearly, for the maximization of their global profits TNCs prefer to sell in the Indian markets. After all, a surge of Indian goods manufactured with cheap labour constitutes a threat to their global profits. Indian businessmen have got access to some intermediate level technology which will enable them to compete better with other

Third World countries. Table 6 shows that 90% of FDI is concentrated in 9 industries which represent intermediate technology or sectors, like, telecom and services which are not involved in exports. If significant exports take place rom the remaining sectors, this can only lead to the deterioration of India's and its competitor's terms of trade viz-a-viz the advance nations. Hence, even if Indian industry (not TNCs) export more, it may only be under adverse conditions.

Table 6
Sectorwise Approvals of Foreign Investment and Collaborations

Name of Industry	Total No			Amt. of FDI	% of Total Approvals
	Tot	Tech	Fin	(Rs Cr.)	
Metallurgical	385	229	156	5198	5.89
Fuels	261	107	154	17327	19.65
Electrical	1701	772	929	5326	6.04
Telecommunication	289	76	213	20016	22.70
Transportation	497	274	223	5760	6.53
Chemicals	1020	580	440	5561	6.31
Food Processing	542	119	423	5671	6.43
Service Sector	363	11	352	7780	8.82
Hotel and Tourism	187	65	122	2224	2.52
Grand Total (All)	**9761**	**4378**	**5383**	**88188**	

Source: SIA Newsletter, No. 1996 Min of Industries, GOI, pp 7-9.

3.4 Export led Growth and Agriculture

Under NEP, increasing *net* exports has become critical to reduce the current account deficit and the country's dependence on foreign borrowings. That would also enable the country to repay its debt and the interest on it. Increase in *net* exports will also enable the Indian economy to recover from recession; they constitute additional demand. This is termed 'Export led growth'.

As already argued, exports depend to a large extent on TNCs who dominate the world markets and on other countries allowing access to their markets. For instance, there could be greater trade with our neighbours–SAARC countries and China–due to advantages in transport costs. But each member of SAARC denies access to its markets to other countries of the region. Similarly, there could be greater trade with China but again, access to each other's market is limited. In brief, the prospects of export led access elsewhere is difficult, Indian costs are high in spite of cheap labour, under NEP subsidies are disallowed and quality is indifferent due to technological reasons.

What about increasing exports of traditional goods, like, agriculture and allied goods (20% share). Under NEP, with fewer restrictions on exports of agricultural produce and devaluation, agricultural exports should have spurted. However, international trade in these commodities is controlled by a few TNCs. According to Korten (1995) these companies dominate the US markets as well (p 224). Even if food processing sector grows and tries to export, the market is controlled by TNCs. Table 6 shows that this is not a priority area for TNC investment (6.43%) so that it is unlikely to boost exports. India would have to give more concessions to the TNCs to make it attractive for them to market Indian products and disturb their currently existing arrangements.[8]

Indian success in agricultural exports would cause an adverse shift in the terms of trade for its competitors, as has been the case with tea, coffee, sugar, cashew nuts, etc. In effect, the Indian farmers may benefit little since on the one hand the international prices are likely to drop and on the other hand, they would have to concede a bulk of the reduced profits to the TNCs. Two consequences would follow form such exports. First, Indian agriculture would be subject to the pattern of international demand and secondly, adversely affect India's food security. Indian farmers

[8]Perhaps this is the reason that Pepsi, when it entered India in 1988 promised increased agricultural exports from India but did not deliver on its promise. Post 1991, it requested that it should not be forced to export since Coca Cola was not required to.

may divert the best land towards plantation crops for exports and reduce land under basic foodgrains required by the local population. Under NEP, changes in land legislation to enable large plantations to come up is being envisaged. This will have adverse consequences for the rural poor and for industrialization.

It is not that the country should not try to increase exports but it should not only depend on this. There are two other problems with this strategy (Kumar, 1991b). First, all the nations in the world cannot achieve an export surplus simultaneously. Some have to have a deficit for others to have a surplus. The country should certainly try to have a surplus but with all the Third World nations simultaneously trying to have a surplus, prices of their exports would drop. The terms of trade would shift against the Third World, their current account would not improve and make repayments of debt more difficult.

Finally, it needs to be clarified that the old distinction between traditional and manufactured goods is not a good one in the modern context. India's exports are now largely of manufactured goods. The distinction should be made between goods produced with advanced technology or using intermediate and low technology. As technology changes, a former high technology good may become one of low technology. For instance, earlier technology differentiated between manufactured goods and raw materials but now the divide is between manufactured goods produced by the advanced nations and the rest. Technology and the new regime of intellectual property rights have become critical in this context.

3.5 WTO and Access to Technology

World Trade Organization (WTO) is a reality. It has not only redefined the international trade regime but even national laws to suit TNCs. It puts most Third World Nations on par with the advanced nations in matters of trade, like, market access and national treatment to foreign capital and has strengthened the control of TNCs on technology. If India had free access to international technology, it could be a threat to TNCs domination in the world markets. Today, high technology is closely held and not available. WTO governs the regime of intermediate technology and strengthens the control of TNCs over it (See Kumar, 1993b).

For Indian exports not to lower the global profits of the TNCs which give either the technology or access to markets or both, the terms on which technology (intermediate level) is to be made available to Indian businesses have to be stiffer (as Table 5 shows). Not only do TNCs profits rise, out go of foreign exchange from the country in the form of repatriated profits and fees of various kinds also rise. Additional outflow of foreign exchange occurs since foreign collaborators insist on their own consultancy and supply of plant and equipment. Finally, the mechanism of transfer pricing is used to siphon out undeclared profits and constitute further drain of foreign exchange. Indian business men's interest in stashing profits abroad makes them collude with the TNCs[9].

The advanced nations have typically not allowed access to high technology. The recent experience with advanced computers, cryogenic rockets and earlier with nuclear technology point to this. The history of the Uruguay Round of GATT negotiations reveal the real intentions of G7–to retain monopoly over technology while talking of free trade to obtain access to other markets.

Among the most harmful effects of the new regime of intellectual property rights on the Third World would be the set-back to their R & D. This would prevent them from catching up with the advanced nations and make them permanently dependent. As it is, investment in advanced technology is lumpy and so high that most Third World Nations cannot go it alone and even if they make a limited effort, the only object can be that as these technologies mature, they can position themselves to exploit them.

For instance, even though India is way behind the front runners in rocketry or nuclear or aerospace or electronics or plasma fusion or generalised software or bio-technology, it is

[9]In the case of Maruti, a prime cause of the dispute between the government and Suzuki was the over pricing of capital goods to be imported from Suzuki for purposes of expansion. This was also a ploy by Suzuki to take over the company by forcing a large expansion of the equity base.

capable of posing challenges (not catching up) by investing in R & D. Even this may become a thing of the past under the new Intellectual Property Rights regime. Different processes cannot be used to arrive at a given product or concept. Laggards in development will have to produce some other product so it may not even worth researching–R & D will receive a setback.

3.6 International Division of Labour and Environment

One of the aspects of Globalisation is an international division of labour and specialisation based on comparative advantage. A comparison of Table 6 and 7 with Table 8 indicate that the pattern of investments is changing drastically compared to what

Table 7
Industrial Investment Proposals (Select Industries) Percentage Break Up for Aug 1991 to Nov 1996

Total Proposals	IEMs			LOIs	
Sch. No.	No.	Inv%	Empl%	Inv%	Empl%
Ind Group					
19 Chemicals	5,223	20.4	12.7	33	8.1
1 Metallurgical	4,901	17.1	19.1	0.6	1.5
23 Textiles	4,786	15.5	19.9	4.5	19.7
35 Cement & Gyp	702	7.8	3.4	0.8	0.7
24 Paper & Pulp	1,208	5.3	3.9	3.6	4.0
5 Elect Equip	1,784	4.3	5.3	0.6	3.0
6 Telecomm	964	2.4	3.0	0.8	3.0
7 Transport	459	2.5	2.8	5.3	4.8
8 Indus Mach	681	1.9	1.6	0.2	0.6
22 Drugs & Pharm	1,179	0.6	1.2	5.2	10.4
25 Sugar	326	0.3	0.3	10.0	23.5
Total (Actual)	30,802	5,40,987 (Rs Cr)	49,92,196	90,999 (Rs Cr)	6,32,113

Source: SIA Statisties Vol. II No. 8, Dec 1996, Min of India GOI.

Table 8
Principal Characteristics by Major Industry Group (1991-92) Arranged in Descending Order of NVA

Code	Industry	Factories (%)	Inv K (%)	Employ (%)	Output% Gros	NVA	Per Employee FC(Rs)	NVA(Rs)
35-36	Mach (not tpt)	11.4	8.7	10.4	11.8	15.1	98007	97386
40	Electricity	0.2	28.1	10.4	9.2	13.3	680198	85254
30	Chemicals	6.5	11.9	7.0	13.2	12.9	299093	122744
20-21	Food Products	17.6	7.4	13.4	14.5	8.2	58808	40769
23	Basic Metals	5.43	16.3	7.3	12.0	7.5	435662	68554
37	Transport	3.3	4.1	6.0	5.3	6.7	100572	75221
32	Non-Metal Min	8.8	4.3	5.5	4.1	6.0	150483	72204
34	Metal Prod.	6.1	1.4	2.7	2.2	2.4	67435	59801
39	Repair K Goods	1.6	0.3	2.3	0.5	1.3	16303	37598
36	Other Manf	1.6	0.8	1.2	0.9	1.2	76547	71055
97	Repair Serv	1.5	0.1	0.8	0.2	0.4	19348	38354
	Total (All)	**112** (1,000)	**221234** (Rs Cr)	**8194** (1,000)	**299196** (Rs Cr)	**54827**	**185392**	**66915**

Source: Summary from Annual Survey of Industries.
Note: FC Fixed Captial, NVA: Net Value Added

existed before 1991. 65% of all investment proposals are for 5 sectors, namely, Chemicals, Metallurgical, Textiles, Cement & Gypsum and Paper and pulp. Most of these are highly polluting industries.

In the case of the Third World it has been argued that they should not be sensitive to pollution since development is more important. Further, because of its cheap and unskilled labour, it is supposed to have an advantage in agriculture and low and intermediate technology products. These assumptions imply that India should concentrate effort on agriculture, intermediate technology and for polluting industries.

Pollution imposes hidden costs on society which people have to bear. Mr Larry Summers then the Economic Adviser to the

World Bank presented this logic sharply by arguing that polluting industries should be relocated in the Third World, since it is optimal that people there die of disease than in the advanced countries (Reported in *The Economist* in February 1992). As pointed out, under the garb of technology and capital inflow, India may be becoming host for heavily polluting industries relocating from the advanced countries to India (like, chemicals and metals). India needs to guard against likely disasters in its headlong drive towards inviting foreign capital and technology.

Further, if such technologies and production relocate in the Third World and advanced technology and clean products in the advanced countries, competition amongst the Third World can be used to keep the prices of these goods low for the advanced countries while the prices of advanced products can be kept high through monopoly over technology. Terms of trade would shift against the Third World and lead to a drain from these economies (as argued in Section 3.3).

In India, even before TNCs have entered in a big way, there is a race to export at any cost. To attract foreign investment, environmental standards are being lowered (Kumar, 1994) and agricultural exports encouraged. If successful, cropping pattern of Indian agriculture would then be geared to the demands of the advanced nations and not the Indians. A decline in the nutritional standards of the poor is likely.

3.7 TNC Led Industrial Restructuring

TNCs when they enter a Third World nation try to capture markets both by eliminating competition and establishing their hold. Existing products need to be displaced to establish their products. This requires establishing their brand names, buying out existing local brands or even whole companies producing those goods. Even the biggest Indian companies are too small to match the financial and technological clout of TNCs. They are unequal in scale of production or advertising.

Kumar (1994) argues, the penetration of the Indian market is taking place through establishing of TNC brand names and control over managements of companies in which they are interested. Thus, Lehar-Pepsi has become Pepsi. Coca Cola bought out the Indian market leader's (Parle held 60% of the market) brand names. In the soap market, Godrej after initial collaboration with Proctor & Gamble is now fighting them and TOMCO has been bought out by Hindustan Levers. In joint venture companies like; DCM Daewoo, Kinetic Honda and Maruti Suzuki, the Indian partners have had to relinquish control. Pressure is building up on other companies as well.

India, historically, before independence was an open economy with low tariffs. This caused several Indian industries to be wiped out in the Nineteenth century. Only during the two World Wars when the British rulers needed Indian industries were they allowed to grow. Also, in some cases, like sugar industry, when tariffs were imposed, the industry grew rapidly. As an open economy, Indian industry and the economy stagnated under British rule during the first half of the Twentieth century. Even though times have changed, it is a hardly reassuring history and throws doubt on the model of unquestioning Globalisation.

The lowering of tariffs and removal of quantity restrictions since 1991 has led to dumping by foreign companies of goods, like, ball bearings, chemicals and drugs, DAP fertilisers and capital goods. In contrast, it is interesting that where tied aid is provided, goods are sold at higher prices. NTPC was reportedly being forced to buy at 30% higher pries from the Japanese who had offered project aid. BHEL's order book has suffered since it is unable to match the credit offered. It is a classic case of capturing the market and then raising prices.

3.8 TNCs and Privatization

Privatization consists of two activities–disinvestment of PSU equity and private provision of public services. The first is a policy issue which is based on the notion that state should retreat from economic activities to enable the markets to expand. The second consists of response of individuals to breakdown of public services like, drinking water, electricity, health and education. TNCs have interest in both.

Public sector in India is seen to be a drag on the economy. The fiscal deficit is taken to be a result of their dissaving. It is argued, disinvestment of PSU shares will promote efficiency and solve the problem of budgetary deficit. However, disinvestment has been slower than desired since a) there has been political opposition to it, b) (more importantly) the stock markets have faced repeated crisis and c) Indian capital is not large enough to absorb the huge assets involved.

TNCs have eyed the purchase of profitable PSUs. For instance, it has been reported that Siemens and ABB were interested in BHEL, one of the best run Indian companies. In fact, privatization has the potential of turning PSUs into subsidiaries of the TNCs. When the first round of privatization occurred in 1992, it was widely reported that forward trading took place on behalf of the TNCs and their agents.

In fact, if even 49% of the equity of the biggest of the Indian public sector companies, like BHEL, Indian Oil, ONGC and SAIL are sold at their replacement value, the Indian capital market would not be able to absorb it except at throw away prices. Only the TNCs have the capital to buy these companies equity at prices close to the replacement value. There was talk of a debt equity swap as attempted in Chile, Brazil and Mexico. In fact, this was due to pressure from the IMF and the World Bank even though it was clearly unnecessary.

Further, the TNCs or the Indian capitalists are unlikely to invest in the PSUs unless they get management control. This is feasible even with say, 5% of the equity as long as the government, usually the largest share holder, agrees. If management control is not available to the private sector (Indian or TNC) they are unlikely to invest large sums and privatization will not work. After all, the logic of privatization is a change of style of management, otherwise nothing would have changed. In India, businessmen do not invest only for book profits. That is why they do not even relinquish control over loss making units.

It may be argued that if a TNC purchases a public sector concern, it would run it well, bring in technology, etc. However, this does not logically follow. To maximize its global profits, it could use the firm to expand its own sales in the Indian markets. This could be through shutting down the Indian company to eliminate competition or running the plant such that it sells its own products with a minimal of value addition in India. Over a period, it could even claim that the plant needs to be shut down since it is not profitable or that Indian labour is not productive etc. In any case, it may result in an increased outflow of foreign exchange under a variety of pretext as already pointed out[10]. The indigenous technological capability would be adversely affected given that a bulk of it has been associated with the Public Sector.

Further, most of the so called sick PSUs are not necessarily sick considering their asset base. If revaluation of the assets of the public sector units is resorted to and a part of the loans from the government converted to equity, given its responsibility for creating the mess in the first place, these units will turn the corner.

Financial restructuring along with revaluation of assets should be resorted to even if privatization is thought to be desirable since then government can obtain a higher price for its assets, therefore, the budgetary support would be higher. Such a privatization will also give a fighting chance to many of the presently sick PSUs to turn the corner. With a higher asset base, they would be able to raise more funds in the market for working capital and revival. Unfortunately, the NEP has not addressed these problems. The haphazard privatization of the public sector imposes a heavy cost on the nation. Tandon (1997) analysing international experience of privatization finds that it has not been very successful since by itself it is no panacea. He believes, market conditions are critical (p. 3210).

Clearly, neither Indian capital nor the government have a clear line of thinking on the PSUs. Disinvestment is sought to be attempted while to increase demand in the economy the size of the Plan is sought to be enhanced. PSUs are beset with many

[10]The Maruti episode proves that TNC is not even happy with equal (50%) partnership and wants control. However, control is a matter of the larger partner conceding control and this is feasible in many cases as has been the case with the Indian private sector since before 1991.

problems which need to be resolved but they are the whipping boys in the existing ideological climate. Indian capital does not even realise (or is helpless) that it is axing its own feet under pressure from international capital.

3.9 Globalisation and Financial Sector

One of the corollaries of opening the economy to inflow of foreign capital is financial opening up of the economy–its closer integration into the world financial markets. Foreign capital would not like to be tied to the Indian economy since it is looking for global profit maximization; it likes to enter and exit when it suits it. It would also like Indian financial markets to be free and more closely integrated so that it could exploit opportunities as they arise. It pushes for financial deregulation–internally and externally.

For instance, if foreign capital invests in industry it may wish to raise additional funds in the stock markets and want the price of its stocks to rise. This would be facilitated by inflow of foreign capital. Investors would also want to take money out of the country when the opportunity or the need arises. In other words, flows of FDI and FII are linked up. Further, many of the TNCs are also active investors in various international financial markets to make a profit, to cover risks of fluctuations in currencies, stock prices, etc. (See Korten, 1995, 1999). Hence they prefer opening up of all the financial markets. Consequently, India introduced capital account convertibility for foreign capital even though Indian capital does not have such a facility.

However, such a situation results not only in the flows of FDI but also of hot money which have the potential for destabilising the markets, as has been seen in S E Asia since 1997 (and in India since 1995). Today, the S E Asian, the Japanese and the S Korean economies are portrayed as financially unsound due to the so called existence of 'crony capitalism'. However, this is a false argument since links between banks and industry have always existed even in Europe and the USA. Further, if the economy faces a crisis, the portfolio of non-performing assets (NPA) increases as has happened recently in Asia. The real problem is that unstable markets lend themselves to speculative activities and discourage long-term investments. They also tend to make policies ineffective and reduce governments' capacity to give direction to the economy and solve its problems. (See Kumar, 1996 and 1997).

3.10 Slow Response of Foreign Capital

In spite of the many concessions already offered to foreign capital. FDI into India is small (Table 9). The ratio of actual inflow to approvals has been small (21%) since 1991. The higher figure for 1991 reflects the pre 1991 situation. There is no doubt that a time lag problem exists but in comparison to China (the ratio is around 40%), India lags far behind. Something other than a time lag is

Table 9
Annual Foreign Collaboration

Item	1991	1992	1993	1994	1995	Total Up to Oct 96
No. Approved	950	1520	1476	1854	2,337	10077
Tech Collab	661	828	691	792	982	4607
For Inv	289	692	785	1,062	1355	5470
Amt of For Inv (Rs Cr)	530	3,890	8,860	14,190	32,070	88290
Actual Inflow FDI + NRI	351 (66.2)	675 (17.4)	1787 (20.2)	2,982 (21.0)	6,370 (19.9)	18479 (20.9)

Source: SIA Newsletter, Nov. 1996. Min. of Industries, GOI, p2 and p 10.

Note1: Figures in brackets are per cent of Actual to approvals.

Note2: Actuals/Approvals for 1996 were 21.4%, for upto Nov 1997 it was 20.9% and for the total upto Nov 1997 it was 20.1% (Economic Survey 1997-98: 87). In $ terms, approvals declined in 1996 but rose in 1997 while the actual continued to rise through the period.

important. Growth rate in approvals has slowed down since 1996, so that the ratio may temporarily rise but it does not augur well for inflow of FDI in the long run.

Foreign companies are being offered favourable terms like lower taxes, sovereign guarantees, higher debt-equity ratios and freedom from social obligations. In the case of the power sector they were offered 16% post tax rate of return in $ terms. FII is given 10% concession in income and capital gains taxation. Foreign banks have few restrictions on computerization or little obligation to set up rural branches. Table 10 shows that investment (65%) is tending to concentration the 6 advanced states. UP and Haryana probably refer to areas in the proximity of Delhi and should be read as Delhi. Regional disparities can only worsen.

Table 10

Industrial Investment Proposals (Statewise) Percentage break up for Aug. 1991 to Nov 1996

Total Proposals	IEMs			LOIs	
States	No.%	Inv%	Empl%	Inv%	Empl%
Maharashtra	17.9	18.2	17.3	12.2	16.5
Gujarat	14.8	20.2	14.5	19.9	8.5
UP	9.9	9.7	9.7	9.0	13.3
TN	9.8	6.0	8.4	9.8	14.5
AP	6.8	7.8	6.4	9.7	9.4
Haryana	6.5	3.5	6.0	4.1	6.4
Total (Actual)	**30,802**	**5,40,987**	**49,92,196**	**90,999**	**6,32,113**
		(Rs Cr)		(Rs Cr)	

Source: SIA Statistics Vol. II No 8. Dec 1996. Min. of Industries. GOI

The uncertainty in the economic scenario represented by the fluctuations in economic variables (Kumar, 1996) is being compounded by the prevailing social and political uncertainty. TNCs react to this by delaying their investments. The economy suffers because TNCs are a cause of the uncertainty and because their response to concessions is muted.

In a nutshell, indiscriminate opening up to attract FDI from TNCs is not justified either by the experience of the recent successful industrialisers of India's own historical experience or by the prevailing world circumstances of India's own stage of development. If TNCs enter India in a big way, it will pose problems but if they do not then too under NEP there would be problems (perhaps even greater).

4. Size of Market and the Middle Class

One of the inducements held out to the TNCs is the supposedly large middle class market. It has been variously estimated to be around 250 million individuals, about 27 per cent of the Indian population, and to be larger than most world economies. The argument is erroneous, since even, if it is true that the Indian middle class is numerically large, its purchasing power is not[11]. The Indian economy is about 1% of the world GDP. Even if the Indian middle classes earn the bulk of this income, they are small in absolute purchasing power (See Table 3 and Kumar, 1994).

In fact, a bulk of the Indian middle and upper middle class is below the poverty line of most of the 20 high income countries. Certainly the Indian middle class aspires to have the standard of the Western middle class but cannot purchase most of the goods that the latter takes for granted. The Indian middle class market is potentially large but that is not the reality of today.[11]

In 1995, there were around 10 million colour televisions and automated two wheelers in the country. Even if the ownership of these items is a criterion for belonging to the middle class, there

---

[11]Various market surveys show that even those who have small incomes own consumer durables. Such data are used to argue for the existence of a large Indian middle class. Typically such data are unreliable since most Indians do not correctly report their incomes. The NCAER income survey in 1976 gave a total for national income which was 45% less than that given by the National Accounts Survey. Thus people not only did not declare the black incomes they did not report the white incomes correctly. It is quite likely that those reporting small incomes and owning consumer durables are hiding a bulk of their incomes and those with genuinely small incomes will not be purchasing such goods.

would be no more than 10 million middle class families out of a total of about 180 million, that is, about 6% of the total. However, TNCs interested in selling their premium products are looking to those families which spend freely. These are the owners of personalised four wheeled vehicles.

Families owning cars and jeeps may not number more than 2 million if one nets out taxis, multiple ownership of cars and jeeps, etc. There would be some families (specially in rural areas) who could afford to keep a personalized four wheeled vehicle but do not. They would perhaps have a colour television or a two wheeler. Assume that one third of the owners of CTVs and two wheelers belong to this group, then the Indian middle class of the kind in which the TNCs are interested is no more than 5.3 million families or 3% of the population or 27 million individuals.

Even this group will have an average annual family income (inclusive of black incomes) of less than Rs 10 lakhs of $25,000. Since this class invests a major portion of its wealth in real estate, its consumption of consumer durables still does not match that of the average middle class family in the rich nations. The rest of the middle class of say 200 million may provide a big market for detergents and soaps, tooth paste, cheap audio system, processed foods, tea, plastic goods, etc., but not for premium products.

In the Eighties, the country had made the mistake of believing that there was a large market for consumer durables and this could provide the engine of growth. Mrs Gandhi first in 1982 and Rajiv Gandhi more so after 1985 tried to boost the demand for consumer durables. After an initial burst of demand, met by imports and import intensive production, the markets saturated after 1989. Growth started petering out and the country simply faced a balance of payments difficulty.

Globalisers do not distinguish between essentials and inessentials and suggest that imports be freely allowed–a clear signal to the rich to import what they wish to. There is implicit faith in the market's self corrective mechanism. It is argued that a rise in net imports would lead to a devaluation of the rupee and increase in the price of imports, and therefore, a fall in the demand for imports. Among other things this ignores the fact that demand for luxuries from the rich is inelastic since they are hardly price sensitive. The squeeze would take place on the import of essentials as their domestic prices rise[12]. But, this would make the rate of inflation go up and real wages would fall. The consumption of the rich would be at the expense of the poor[13].

Amongst the actors, fuelling the growth of the Eighties was demand created by rising fiscal deficit. The reduction in the primary fiscal deficits by the government since 1991 and little rise in aggregate private investments resulted in the industrial recession of 1991-94 and the slow down in the last two years. This effects could have been more severe but for the reduction in the current account deficit and the difficulties faced (due to pressure from TUs) in retrenching staff and closing down plants and offices.

Suppose that NEP are successful in attracting foreign capital and technology to India, it will mean the capital intensity of production will rise and aggravate unemployment. The top 20 TNCs in the Fortune 50 list produced in 1990 an output 6 times larger than India's GDP but their work force was only 7% of India (Kumar, 1994). Not that India is about to be taken over, it points to the prospect that increases in output can be achieved without generating additional employment. (See Korten [1995] for the US context and Kumar [1993a] for Indian experience.)

If high technology is to produce for the local market, it would displace local production and cause a rise in unemployment[14]. When displacement is from Indian small and medium scale, loss of employment is large and goes unreported. In the case of Indian

[12]This argument differs from that in Korten (1995). He assumes that the poor do not consume imported goods (p 168) but in India typically, edible oil, pulses, fertilisers, petro goods, etc. are imported and enter the consumption bundle of he poor.

[13]Even if markets are flexible and self correcting, history is not since time is unidirectional. Human misery takes its toll. Children who may have to suffer malnutrition or go without education or girls who have to go without medical treatment would party a price even if markets recover. This is no consolation.

[14]Korten (1995) reports that Fortune 500 industrial firms shed 4.4 million jobs between 1980 and 1993. During this period, their sales increased 1.4 times and assets by 2.3 times. The average salary of the CEOs increased 6.1 times. (p. 218).

large scale sector the displacement would be less but has been reported in many instances and resisted by the TUs[15]. In some instances, TNCs may farm out work to small and medium scale businesses but these would be mostly in high technology areas with low employment potential and not in the traditional small scale sector. Capital intensity would rise even if small and medium scale sectors expand.

Some have argued for allowing FDI into relatively low technology areas rather than in others since that would generate employment. These analysts make the wrong comparison. They forget the TNCs will displace Indian producers in the low technology areas by far more capital intensive technology and thereby make additional employment generation difficult. The issue is not to protect either high or low technology areas but both sectors need protection for different non-comparable reasons. (Kumar, 1994 discusses this in greater detail).

Under the proposed 'Exit Policy' millions from the middle and lower middle classes would lose jobs. This would reduce demand and deepen recession[16]. The government has been unable to push this policy aggressively due to political opposition. In a nutshell, if labour market component of NEP were to be implemented, recession would deepen further.

In brief, the net effect of entry of TNCs with their capital intensive technology and the pressure it puts on Indian industry to also go in for similar technology has been a decline in employment rather than an increase[17] in spite of some growth in small and medium sectors. This effect coupled with the earlier mentioned

---

[15]Firms like TOMCO and PAL which were either taken over or went for collaboration with TNCs tried to fire a large part of the work force and faced long strikes.

[16]Any impact this may have on increased investment could take time so that immediately express capacity would manifest itself and that would dissuade investments. Demand has become a problem without large scale retrenchments pointing to what could have happened.

[17]A comparison of Tables 4 and 8 indicates that while in 1991-92, Fixed capital per employee was Rs 1.85 lakh, the proposed investment is Rs. 10 lakh per worker. As Table 6 and 7 show, investment approvals are tending to be for the capital intensive sectors.

reduced market for Indian organised sector due to imports and the reduction in demand for the government sector is keeping the base of economic growth narrow.

What would happen to the 8 million who enter the work force every year? Who would give employment to those who are retrenched due to closures and exit policies? Indian industry facing loss of markets, unable to compete globally and facing an uncertain investment climate in India has increasingly turned to trading and speculative activity in the share market (as explained below). If this trend persists, there would be deindustrialisation and greater unemployment.

5. *Uncertain Industrial Climate*

5.1 Growing Uncertainty

Due to the stagflationary tendencies in the economy shown by the negligible growth in the industrial sector in the last two years and the potentially high inflation in spite of its low rate just now, it is unlikely that total investment in the economy is going to increase. With excess capacity in several sectors, inflow of foreign capital may slow down in the coming years. This is the dilemma of investment in and growth of the Indian economy.

Other than the government and the TNCs the source of investments is the Indian private sector. It has raised large amounts of capital since 1991. What has this meant for investments and is this trend likely to continue? Indeed, the market has displayed highly unstable behaviour since 1991, so that the large amount of Capital raised in the markets has not helped raise the level of real investment in the economy. Reports suggest that upto 1995, money was diverted for speculation in the secondary market itself or into the real estate market. Managements have been buying their own scripts to prevent hostile takeover bids.

NEP have introduced uncertainty for Indian businesses in four ways. First, the threat of takeover and loss of control over management. Secondly, the risk of technology since they do not have access and cannot develop the latest technology. Thirdly, threat of entry of new players and finally, inability to influence policy the way TNCs are able to. With all this, Indian capital is tending to take a short term view by moving into trading and speculation (for immediate gains).

Indian business are familiar with this since speculation and trading have been the most profitable investments due to the link with the black economy. Due to the increased uncertainty, this picture is unlikely to change in spite of concessions to capital. The Indian private sector is then unlikely to increase its levels of investment, and therefore, fail to boost the growth rate of the economy.

The expected increase in the rate of growth of the economy then depends on the actions of foreign capital–Foreign Direct Investments (FDI). The dilemma for the Indian economy is that if it comes, it creates uncertainty for Indian capital and if it does not come, given other factors, the economy will tend to stagnate.

5.2 Concessions to Investment

In a market driven reform process, policy cannot directly be used to generate demand to end recession. Only concessions to investment can be given in the hope that higher profitability will result in higher levels of investment. This is what has been attempted since 1991 but without success. The reason is that the reform process also simultaneously raises the degree of uncertainty and, therefore, the higher expected profitability is discounted by businessmen.

Take the case of incentives to exports. Since January 1991 the Rupee has devalued substantially viz-a-viz the $ and raised the profitability of exports. Inflation and withdrawal of export concessions have eroded only a part of this gain. Yet, exports have not shown a sustained surge. Leaving it to the markets has not worked. Exporters have repeatedly sought state intervention.

It is argued that investments are better than loans. In the present context, with low interest rates internationally and the high profits being earned by a majority of TNCs in India, this argument is weak. Foreign investments have to be serviced even if with a time lag (in many cases, this lag is small). This calculation ignores the costs associated with use by TNCs of transfer pricing etc. But, the biggest costs are indirect, like, budgetary concessions, increased uncertainty and stagnation in investment, loss of policy control and inability to fulfil national goals.

In sum, opening up to global influences creates uncertainty. Individual businessmen find this difficult to cope with and require help from the state. The Indian state (and businessmen) has realised this but slowly and perhaps too late. It is TNCs with their more advanced technology, brand names, marketing skills and financial clout which is ideally situated to take advantage of the concessions to investment. Indian capital has lost markets and its share of profits despite the concessions obtained by them.

5.3 Investment in R & D

Absorption and development of technology will be critical for sustained long-term growth of the Indian economy. TNCs are unlikely to develop technology in India; they will simply import it where needed. Indian capital facing growing uncertainties is unlikely to compound them by trying to develop its own technology. R & D is known to be the riskiest of all investments specially when competitors already have more advanced technology. The public sector facing a resource crunch and under attack on grounds of poor profitability is unlikely to risk more investment in R&D.

Yet, all successful industrialisers have been technologically dynamic while the trend in India seems to be in the opposite direction. The Japanese resorted to the famous 1:4 formula which stipulated that for every yen of technology imported four yen be spent on its absorption. Indian (private) industry did not even spend a fraction of the funds needed to absorb technology and resorted to repeated imports of technology. The National laboratories and CSIR have by and large not been able to perform the task they were required to because of other reasons. NEP do not correct these deficiencies and now the sword of TRIPS and TRIMS is hanging on Indian research. In brief, Globalisation will adversely affect whatever little indigenous R&D was taking place and make Indian industry even less dynamic than it has been.

6. Conclusion

NEP hit at the very root of the indigenous strengths of the Indian economy, developed since Independence. Temporary phases of good growth cannot hide the overall trends. It is not a question of 'there must be some good in NEP'. It is a package which must be viewed as a whole and not in bits and pieces. Its negative effects on the economy and specially the poor relate to its totality (See Kumar, 1991b). Here it is argued that the few positive aspects are much more than negaled by others.

Globalisation under NEP spell trouble for Indian industry. The public sector is being dismantled/gifted to the private sector. The organized private sector is unable to withstand the competition from the TNCs. Hence sickness and recession can be expected to deepen. The traditional small and the medium scale sector faces a crisis due to shrinking markets. A few success stories apart, the country may deindustrialize. Indian capital confronts increased uncertainty and may move into trading and speculation and as a junior partner of the TNCs. This fits well with the past practices based on the black economy.

Technological backwardness will grow and threaten the country's independence. There are serious social costs associated with the increased presence of TNCs and their implication for the environment, for inequity, for food security, for regional differentiation and for social strife. With opening up, the economy has become far more unstable than earlier and this will affect the already marginalised in society. (See Kumar, 1996).

Can TNCs be expected to act in India's best interest? Unlikely since they mostly originate in advanced countries whose interest they advance. Even for themselves, they look for global profit maximization and not just what they may be able to generate in India so that they may not have a long-term interest in the economy. Competition in the economy is unlikely to increase in general since the TNCs are likely to cater to the demand from the upper income groups (3% of the households) and are likely to collude with each other as they do in the international markets.

TNCs would not be interested in developing technology in

India but only in selling their intermediate and low technology at a price. WTO would help in this by strengthening control over technology. TNCs would encourage exports only of certain items (based on agriculture and polluting technology) under their own control. This would enable them to corner the profits and also keep the international prices of these goods low. In effect, income terms of trade would turn adverse for the Third World as a whole.

A nations' competitiveness or its comparative advantage are far more complex than simply a matter of entry of a few firms, be they TNCs. Since TNCs are typically interested in premium products, neither will prices decline nor will choice increase for the common man. Given the small size of Indian markets for the products of TNCs and the possibility of their further contraction due to decline in the size of the middle class with retrenchment in organized industry and the likely recession, TNCs by themselves cannot take India to a new growth path. Investments by TNCs are small compared to the total but have tremendous potential for destabilization. At least in principle, Indian industry may act in India's best interest but that cannot be expected from TNCs since that is not their interest. There can be no blanket preference for TNCs in all areas as globalisers would like. The question has to be Globalisation for what? It has to be based on the interest of the majority of Indians.

Index